# Diana

## The Last Word

# *Diana*
## The Last Word

### SIMONE SIMMONS
#### *with* INGRID SEWARD

St. Martin's Paperbacks

*To those who are close to us and are in a far better place*

DIANA: THE LAST WORD

Copyright © 2005 by Simone Simmons and Ingrid Seward.
Update copyright © 2007 by Simone Simmons and Ingrid Seward.

Cover photo © Tim Graham / Corbis.

Grateful acknowledgment is given to Rex Features for permission to reproduce the photographs of Oliver Hoare and Hasnat Khan, and to Alpha for the remainder.

ISBN: 0-312-94863-8
EAN: 9780312-94863-4

Printed in the United States of America

First published in Great Britain by Orion Books
St. Martin's Press hardcover edition / July 2005
St. Martin's Paperbacks edition / July 2007

St. Martin's Paperbacks are published by St. Martin's Press, 175 Fifth Avenue, New York, NY 10010.

10 9 8 7 6 5 4 3 2 1

# Contents

# List of Illustrations

# Author's Note

Diana was one of those people who are able to compartmentalise their lives. Sometimes they overlapped, but in her mind they always remained separate, which enabled her to switch between them without allowing one part to impinge on another. She was always a princess, but at the same time she was a mother, a lover and a tireless charity worker.

She was one of the closest friends I have ever had and we talked about everything and anything in an open, girlie way, without secrets or subterfuge.

Diana told me everything that she was thinking in the way that women do—and many men don't. She always said, 'Simone, if anything happens to me, write a book and tell it like it is.'

That is what I have done.

# 1

# JFK

Behind the shy glances, the radiant smiles and the occasional tears, the glamour and the good works that went to make up her public image, lay the passions which made Diana the extraordinary woman that she was.

She wanted to be loved, but more than anything she wanted to *give* love. To the deprived and disadvantaged; to her sons, William and Harry; to her husband, Prince Charles, if only he had allowed her to—and to men with whom she became romantically involved.

I know, because Diana told me. Sitting on the floor, perched on the edge of her bed, sitting on the sofa or in the kitchen, eating the occasional Italian takeaways and microwaved ready meals and drinking endless cups of herbal tea, we would talk for hours on end about her hopes, her cares, her interests and her love affairs. She held nothing back. She was far too open-hearted to bottle up her feelings. If a project caught her interest or a man her eye, she wanted to discuss it, right down to the frankest detail.

And, as is the way when two friends are gossiping, one topic would lead easily into another. That is how she came to tell me of the fling she had with John Kennedy Jr.

Diana and I were in her sitting room at Kensington Palace. She was wearing a pair of stylish yet comfortable beige suede ankle boots, a pair of jeans and a V-necked cashmere sweater that cost a great deal of money. We were sitting for a change on the sofa rather than on the floor when she brought up the subject of the remarkable woman she admired: Jackie Kennedy Onassis. She couldn't understand how she could have wed Aristotle Onassis, 'that Greek Frog', as she called him, especially after she had been married to Jack Kennedy.

She described the late president as 'delicious' and from there the conversation moved on to his son, John Jr.

She asked me what I thought of him and I said that I didn't really have an opinion as I didn't know him. She had a picture of him pulled from one of the newspapers she had delivered every morning, pointed at it and said, 'He's very good-looking isn't he?'

She had met him in New York in 1995 when he was trying to persuade her to give an interview to his magazine, *George*. She turned down the request for the interview but agreed to meet him in her suite at the Carlyle Hotel on the Upper East Side.

Diana was staying at one of the penthouse suites with large plateglass windows looking over Central Park and across the Manhattan skyline to the Twin Towers. The rooms, with a grand piano in one, were elegantly furnished in the manner of a private house rather than in the bland style favoured by so many hotels. The room was $3200 a night, which Diana thought expensive.

When Kennedy arrived she was bowled over by his easy American charm and the physique he worked so hard to keep in shape. She told me, 'We started talking, one thing led to another—and we ended up in bed together. It was pure chemistry.'

Diana was usually very circumspect in her courtships and approached them cautiously, insisting on getting to know the man and then examining her feelings to see if she really wanted to make an emotional commitment before she was prepared to make a sexual one.

Diana had given the Royal Family something that it was conspicuously lacking, which was sex appeal. She was the

Ginger Rogers to Charles's Fred Astaire in the way that she brought glamour and romance to a dull, dusty institution. And as she made the transformation from a shy bride into a beautiful and mature woman, she came to like the effect she had on people and the way that men started to look at her. But there was always something of the ingénue about her. She did not have real womanly confidence, and, although she could be an outrageous flirt, there was always an innocence about her. Not every woman is aware of her sexuality, and Diana really was not aware that she had any real sex appeal.

With Kennedy it was different. He made her feel desirable, wanton and very womanly. It was, she admitted, a moment of pure lust—the only time in her life that she succumbed in that way.

My mouth dropped open. I was so flabbergasted that for a few seconds I couldn't say anything. She had just started seeing Hasnat Khan and, although there had been no real physical contact, she was very much in love with him which I thought would have precluded anyone else. I cried out, 'What! You're joking, aren't you?' and I really thought she was.

She replied, 'No, I'm not. It happened. And he was an amazing lover—a ten, the tops.'

Diana was keen on that rating system. James Hewitt came in at nine, Oliver Hoare as a six. Hasnat Khan was saved the embarrassment of being rated. Prince Charles, on the other hand, barely made the chart at all.

Diana felt very pleased about her encounter with JFK Jr. She thought it was fantastic that for once she had got someone (other than Hasnat) whom she wanted, as opposed to being someone else's catch. It put a notch on her belt and she was tickled pink that it was JFK, one of the best-looking and most sought-after men in America, with a real body beautiful that came from endless workouts in the gym. He was a year older than her and three inches taller, which counted for a lot because Diana didn't like short men.

What gave their brief liaison an extra dimension was that she admired him and the way he had dealt with the pressures which came with being the son of America's best-loved president. Looking to her eldest son and the responsibilities he was born to inherit, she said, 'I'm hoping that William grows to be as smart as John Kennedy Jr. I want William to be able to handle things as well as John does.'

Being Diana, she naturally wanted to take the relationship further. She started fantasising about what a powerful team they would make, and how, if everything went right, she could have become part of America's 'royal family'. On a trip to Washington she had been taken on a tour of the White House and told me afterwards, 'I would have loved it there,' and thought that, were Kennedy to follow his father into politics as everyone expected him to do, she might eventually become the First Lady of the United States.

Looking back, I wish I had asked her more, but the conversation then moved on to Grace Kelly and Diana's conviction, based, it must be said, on no evidence, that the former film star had been murdered when she let slip that she was planning to divorce her husband, Prince Rainier of Monaco. She identified with Kelly, a comparatively ordinary girl who had become a princess, just as Diana had.

She felt much the same about Jackie Kennedy, who had married a serial adulterer, yet succeeded in becoming an international symbol of grace and good taste. She thought Jackie O had been the perfect statesman's wife, a role that she imagined that she too might be able to perform with style and dignity as the consort of her son.

When she got back to England she had John's astrological chart prepared and discovered that because he was a Sagittarius and she had Sagittarius rising, they were compatible in a number of respects, but not enough to sustain the relationship.

Kennedy always spoke highly of the Princess and described her to friends as 'fascinating, stimulating and beautiful'. For a short while afterwards they stayed in touch: she telephoned and they had long-chats across the Atlantic. But it is always difficult to maintain a long distance relationship and there was never an encore. She had more love to give than any man could take, and when it came down to it, I think he found her too needy. I told her, 'You want him 24/7 but let's face it, unless you live in the United States you're not going to get him 24/7—and probably not even then.'

She accepted that reality and, instead of dwelling on what might have been, accepted her short liaison with Kennedy Jr for what it was—an exhilarating fling. The following year he married Carolyn Bassette and Diana wrote to wish him well. She hoped that his marriage would work out better than hers had. By then, of course, she had become deeply involved with Hasnat Khan, although he refused to consummate their relationship until her divorce came through.

I cannot help but wonder, though, what would have happened if Kennedy had been able to give her what she wanted, and she could have taken the stresses of being the consort of a Kennedy. They might both still be alive today.

It was not to be. Diana had her own life to live, with all that that entailed.

# 2

# Meeting Diana

Diana was one of the most insecure people I had ever met. That inner pain drove her to seek relief and comfort in some very odd ways, and there was hardly a therapy that, at some time or other, she hadn't tried.

Some were of undoubted benefit. Others were pure quackery. A few were downright harmful.

On the surface, of course, she appeared to have everything going for her. But, like a number of other well-known and successful women who find themselves in the harsh glare of the public limelight, that wasn't enough.

It was to try and fill that inner void that she kept rushing from one treatment to the next, never quite satisfied with what she found, searching for the elusive answer to her problems. She felt that she was missing something vital within herself, that somehow she wasn't complete as a person. She put herself through all those therapies to try and rid herself of the torment she had endured since she was a child, sustained by the idea that they would eventually act like a magic wand and make all the pain disappear.

That quest brought her to the Hale Clinic on the edge of London's Regent's Park where I was working as a self-employed therapist. I had been recommended to the Princess by another therapist there, and she had just undergone a colon cleanse the morning we were introduced.

The formal introductions were made, after which she laughed and said, 'Just call me Diana.' I said, 'In that case just call me Simone.'

I was very open-minded about the Princess. She was the most photographed woman in the world—glamorous, beautiful and with the sheen that only comes from expert and expensive grooming—but I thought, OK, no matter what she is supposed to be, she is still a person. I never seem to be in awe of anybody. I saw her as just another one of my patients and that is how I treated her—both then and afterwards. I judge people on who they are, as opposed to who they are supposed to be or what they look like.

We went upstairs to the treatment room I used on the top floor of the building. It was small and plain, like a doctor's surgery, with only room for a table, a treatment desk, a couple of chairs and a soft side light.

I asked if she would mind if I took off the new pair of Russell and Bromley shoes my mother had just bought me which were hurting my feet.

She said, 'Not at all,' and kicked off her own shoes, explaining that she felt more comfortable when she wasn't wearing any, and she much preferred to walk around barefooted whenever the opportunity allowed.

Without further preamble, she took off her blue pin-stripe jacket, laid it neatly on the chair and then lay down on the treatment table. I dimmed the lights and explained that when I worked it would be better if we both kept quiet, although that, as I soon discovered, was not something that came easily to Diana. She was vulnerable—like a little bird that has been hurt when it fell out of the nest—and that inner ache expressed itself in nervous energy.

On that first occasion, however, we managed to get through without too much commotion. At the end of the half hour she sat up, said she was a little dizzy, but added that she felt as though a heavy weight had been lifted from her body.

'What did you discover?' she enquired. I told her that I had felt the little bumps in her aura which indicated her stress points. She nodded, said how helpful I had been and how much better she felt. She made an appointment to come and see me again in a couple of days' time and then declared, 'When you are working you have the most amazing other-worldly eyes.' I said that was a compliment, coming from her.

On the second visit it was clear that Diana wanted to talk, but, because we had only just met, she was reluctant to open up; and I, for the same reason, felt it wiser not to say much. She explained that, after our first session, she had felt movement inside her body, but that she didn't want to tell me for fear of taking up too much time. She was very polite and apologetic, and initially she even managed to stop jiggling about.

However, when I told her that I could sense things in her aura, her reticence disappeared and she started asking endless questions. That was destined to become the pattern of our sessions.

There is nothing magical or mystical about what I do, which is tapping into the electromagnetic energy that everyone has, and then trying to balance it, to even out the 'bumps'. It does not require an act of faith for it to be effective: it works just as well on those who do not believe in it. I have treated a number of athletes, including a premiership footballer who came to me for treatment for a damaged knee on the recommendation of one of England's top coaches. He was sceptical, but after six sessions he had to admit that his knee was better and that he was able to resume training.

Diana was more attuned, but that did not make her an easy patient. Ideally, we should have worked in silence so that I could concentrate, with my eyes closed, as I moved my hands about a foot above her body, trying to sense where the problem areas were. During the first few meetings our relationship was formal and everything went well. She kept her eyes closed and once actually fell asleep. That was as it should have been.

But then, as we got to know each other better, she started talking and that made it extremely difficult to treat her. Diana was such a fidget that I usually only managed to keep her quiet for the first ten minutes, after which she would start to talk, asking numerous questions, never still for more than a few moments.

When I told her to stop talking, she would explain that she had to tell me something while it was still on her mind and that she found it impossible to relax until she had. Then, as soon as she had said whatever it was she was thinking about, some other thought would occur, she would sit up and I would keep having to physically push her back down again.

On one occasion her mobile telephone started ringing. It was on a short cut-off and I ignored it and carried on. But the call had disturbed her and she started talking, and when she wouldn't stop I gave up and told her to sit up, have a glass of water and said that we would have to resume another day. She had a large and very expensive Chanel bag with her. Inside was a thick Filofax address book and diary, and, as she rummaged around to find it so that she could write in our next appointment, four mobile phones fell out.

Another time I had brought a tin of Grether's blackcurrant pastilles for my throat and I gave her one to try and calm her down and give her mouth something to do instead of talking. By the end of the session the tin was empty.

Despite the interruptions, Diana started reaping the benefits. When she did manage to keep her eyes closed she could feel exactly where my hands were, even though I wasn't touching her. Afterwards she felt energised and her vision had intense clarity.

More than anything, though, Diana needed someone to lean on, someone who was understanding, someone who would listen to her—and I've always been a good listener. It wasn't a role I could have foreseen for myself, but after a while she started treating me as a mother figure whom she could confide in. I had something which few of her other friends had, which was patience, plus a lot of time. Also, I told her exactly what I thought, even if it wasn't what she wanted to hear. She didn't always like it, but most of the time she appreciated my honesty.

We met three times a week and Diana was soon asking

me a lot of questions about the spiritual side of healing and
about herbal medicine. Then there were days when she
would say after a healing session, 'Can we actually sit and
talk?' She would ask me, 'If this thing or that thing happened, what would you do?' These were usually hypothetical
questions.

Sometimes, though, she was being deliberately mischie-
vous, using the words other therapists had used, or asking
me about men in such a way that I knew she was talking
about someone she was involved with or was interested in. I
would warn her that there were certain people that she had to
be careful of. By the way she talked about people I could
sense what the situation was between them.

That led her to wonder how I seemed to have what she
saw as an uncanny ability to 'see' certain people in her life. I
obviously did not know who they were, as they were not
people in the public eye. But *she* knew who they were and
would put names to them. She didn't always like what I said
about them, and that led to our first argument.

I had told her something that she didn't like—that her relationship with a man she was keen on was not going to end
in marriage and that everything wasn't going to be hunky-
dory. The next day her secretary called and cancelled all our
appointments. I was angry and cornered her in a side room
when she next came to the Hale Clinic and said, 'I want a
word with you.' I then told her in a straightforward way, 'If
you have a problem with me, tell me to my face.'

She went very quiet and her face flushed. No one had
spoken to her like that for a long time, and I thought to myself, that's it, she's never going to speak to me again. But,
frankly, I didn't care. It was important for me to have my say
because if Diana wasn't prepared to listen to what I had to
say I wasn't prepared to heal her. Healing incorporates the
truth, and, if someone can't face the truth and wants to carry
on living in their own little fantasy world, they are not ready
to be healed.

What I said struck home. We sat down and Diana started
to open up. She explained that she wasn't used to anyone be-

ing so direct with her—that, after so long cocooned behind palace walls, she had almost forgotten what it was like to hear people say what they actually meant. 'The courtiers all speak in riddles,' she said. 'They never say what they mean and they never get to the point, but leave it to you to figure out for yourself what they meant.'

That isn't my way. I don't know how to speak in circles. With me you don't have to read anything into my words. It's all there in plain English. Being such a straight talker isn't always an advantage, of course, and it cost me my first job. I went to work in a dress shop, and on my first day a woman came in. One of the other sales assistants urged her to try on a certain dress and when she came out of the changing room she looked at me, said, 'You're new here, aren't you? What do you think this looks like?' I replied, 'You look like a sack tied up in the middle.' She was very upset and I was fired on the spot.

In Diana's case, it worked the other way. Although shocked at first, she then liked the way I came straight out and said what I thought. I found that I was able to unburden myself with Diana, who was also a good listener, and, because of her own problems, had a ready understanding of other people's difficulties. She brought me down to earth with my romantic dreams. For instance, when my boyfriend went off with my best friend, Diana was really able to relate to that because of the Camilla situation. We talked it over and over, for hours on end.

That is the way women are. There is no woman I know that can go for more than a week without sharing things with a friend. It is completely different to male friendships. We share our thoughts; men share a drink. Very few men will talk about their emotional experiences. Most women do. Men don't talk on the phone and women do. Men can get the whole conversation done in about five minutes, while we women like to go over and over things and discuss it until we are completely satisfied.

We both had our say that day in the Hale Clinic, and it was from that point onwards that our friendship started to

develop. Diana came to appreciate that if she wanted a
straightforward answer, I would give her one. She did not
have to go looking for clues or hints, as if she was playing a
mystery board game. It was there—upfront and in the open.
And I came to value her companionship and the insights she
gave me into my own life. She became my best friend.

It was our differences that gave zest and colour to our relationship. She loved to know about people and their lives,
and wanted to hear all the gossip about people who worked
and came to the Hale Clinic. It wasn't so much that she was
nosy, it was more innocent curiosity. And she really wanted
to know what was going on in the world 'down on the
ground in Tesco's', as she put it.

I happened to be living above a Tesco supermarket in
Hendon in North London at the time and she was fascinated
by my description of life out on the streets. It was nothing
out of the ordinary, little different in fact from the way millions of other people go about their daily routine.

To Diana, however, who had spent most of her life either
in a grand house or a palace, it sounded extraordinarily interesting. So did my work, and she wanted to know how I
had started healing. I explained that it was something I had
been doing since I was a little girl, that as a child I used to
see auras around people and could sense if there was something physically wrong with them. It used to upset me, but
then I realised I had this ability, this gift to make people feel
better.

What had really brought it into focus was the terrible injury my sister Rachel suffered when she was involved in a
crash in 1981. The car spun, she was thrown out and landed
on the back of her neck on the pavement, causing brain stem
damage. I was abroad at the time, but came straight home,
rushed to the hospital and found her in a coma with a tube in
her mouth. She remained like that for months. I went to see
her every day and gave her all the healing I could. It definitely helped. She was on a life-support machine that moni-
tored her heart. It remained constant until I started to heal.
When I held my hands over her the nurse noticed that her

heartbeat changed. She said, 'Rachel can hear you.' Slowly but surely over the next nine months my sister's condition began to improve.

It turned out that Diana had met my sister when she visited the hospital in Northamptonshire, where Rachel later went on the long road to her recovery that is not yet at an end. Diana was intrigued by the uncanny coincidence—or was it predestination?—that had brought us closer. It was a slow evolution, mind you. I was not the sort of person who automatically fitted into either her life or her background.

She was an aristocrat. I came from a respectable, middle-class background. She was the daughter of an earl who had once worked for the Queen. My father, Harold, was a great big pillar of a man who had owned a small factory in Old Street in the City of London manufacturing clothes for the larger women. He took great pride in the fact that he and some friends, including Ronnie Scott, had started a jazz band together in the East End. Ronnie later opened his famous jazz club in Soho, and my father remained a friend of his for the rest of his life.

Diana had been parted from her mother, Frances, when she was a little girl. My mother, who by yet another coincidence was also called Frances, was a housewife and also a talented artist. I grew up in a warm, open, friendly house in Hendon. It was large and comfortable but it certainly wasn't Kensington Palace.

Our early adult life had also been very different. I was interested in art and managed to get a job as a fashion sketcher (I had inherited that talent from my mother), but had broken a tendon in my finger at a rather boisterous party a couple of days before I was due to start. It required an operation and three months of physiotherapy, so I took a convenient job in a hospital. By the time my finger had healed, the job was gone and I became a medical secretary instead. In 1990 I fractured the base of my spine and was unable to work, so the following year, to earn a little extra money, I began healing professionally. Two years later I took the room at the Hale Clinic where I first treated Diana, and where we discovered how at ease we were in each other's company.

She began telephoning me on a daily basis and we chatted about everything and anything including the issues of the day, which she was always much more interested in than people gave her credit for. She also talked about what the newspapers were writing about her. And she was very open about her family. About the father she loved who had died in 1992; the brother with whom she had such a volatile relationship; the husband who, despite all the upset and heartbreak, remained so central to her life—and about the mother she hated.

She took the damage they had caused her everywhere she went, and a few months into our sessions she asked me if I healed buildings. I said I did and she asked me if I would like to heal Kensington Palace, which I said I would. A few days later, I drove to KP, as Diana always called her London home. I arrived at six in the evening and was let in by the butler, Harold Brown, and shown up to the drawing room. By that time, in 1995, Diana's marriage was at its end and Charles had moved out, yet the apartment still bore his heavy imprint. His Prince of Wales feathers motif was everywhere—on the wallpaper in the hallways in the main common parts, even on the carpets.

Everything was spotless. Diana had two Filipinos who came in every day, and they removed all the knick-knacks and books off the shelves and tables before they started dusting and polishing. But I didn't like the atmosphere and nor did she. She found it oppressive. I did too.

Healing a house is no easy business, however. You have to feel for the pockets of unbalanced energy and then try to balance them. I used myself as a 'transmitter' and pushed the energies around using my hands, which I held palm up and open before me. It requires a lot of my energy. What made it even more exhausting was that Diana wanted me to do everywhere at once and her apartment at KP was very large.

I tried to explain to her that it wasn't easy to cleanse a

house of bad energies, and that it is very difficult to do it all at once. I said, 'You can't be serious—you don't really expect me to do the whole apartment in one evening, do you?' She replied in her little girl voice, 'Yes.'

We were in the big salon where eight years before broadcaster Sir Alastair Burnet had interviewed the Prince and Princess for the TV programme about their lives. I asked her where she wanted to start and she said, 'Why not here?' She asked me if I wanted a cup of tea. I asked for a mug as the cups at Kensington Palace were so small they would only hold a couple of sips. We drank the tea and then I got started. I did the salon, her little sitting room, and then worked my way to her bedroom.

That wasn't fine at all. It had once been the marital bedroom and there was a lot of negativity in there which gave it a heavy, oppressive atmosphere. It took me all of forty minutes just to do that one room. She later had it completely redecorated and added a new, very attractive padded and buttoned headboard to the double bed.

After the bedroom, I felt very tired, but Diana insisted that I did Charles's old study and William's and Harry's bedrooms and their little kitchen on the floor above. The boys' rooms were easy to work on compared to hers, but when I had finished I had to call a halt. I simply didn't have the strength to do the rest of the apartment. I was worn out.

Diana, on the other hand, was on a high. She said that, despite the hurry, she could already feel a change in the atmosphere. She wanted to capture more of that mood change and she said she wanted me to do some healing on her. I agreed. After the strain of working on the building it was a bit like the warming-down sessions athletes do after a race. Had anyone been looking through the window they would have been astonished. There was the Princess of Wales, wearing a mini skirt, a pair of tights, a cardigan with a T-shirt underneath, her shoes off, lying on the coffee table in the big salon with me holding my hands over her.

By then, though, I really had had enough. I went straight

home to my flat above the supermarket in Hendon, got into bed and telephoned my parents. I told Mum where I had just been and what I had been doing—she was very taken aback.

In the beginning my mother had been sceptical about my healing work. Occasionally, when I was a teenager, she would get mad with me and scream at my father, 'Harold, your daughter is a witch!' She was a bit like that the first evening I visited Kensington Palace. When I told her that I had been doing some healing on the Princess of Wales, she didn't believe me. I said, 'Mum, it's true.' She replied, 'Come on, Simone, you're our daughter—what have you got to do with people like that?' I felt like a six-year-old again.

The following day I told Diana what had happened. She found it amusing and pointed out that, even in the closest families, relations between a mother and a daughter are not always easy. They certainly weren't in this instance. My mother just couldn't accept that I knew someone like the Princess of Wales. The leap from Hendon to Kensington Palace was too great for her to comprehend. To her way of thinking, royalty were the great untouchables who didn't mix with ordinary people. Diana telephoned her once to tell her that she really did know her daughter, but even that didn't convince my mother. On another occasion, Mum called me on my mobile phone when I was at KP. When I put the Princess on the line, she said, 'How do I know that you are who you say you are?' A couple of days after that call, Diana invited her to Kensington Palace. Only then did she finally realise that I really had been telling the truth.

My mother's incredulity didn't affect my relationship with Diana. She continued to seek my help and, because she found it more convenient for me to go to her rather than for her to come to the clinic, I became an increasingly frequent visitor to the Palace.

At first we did the healing in her bedroom, just in front of the chaise longue covered with embroidered cushions and her cuddly toys which stood at the foot of her bed. She brought in a foldaway treatment table which she kept propped against a wall in the adjoining room. Soon we were healing in any room we happened to be in, and Diana was even strong enough to carry the heavy treatment table into the first-floor dining room.

Harry, who was nine when I first met Diana, was sometimes there. He never actually sat in on our session, but he was occasionally there on a Sunday afternoon or school holidays, when I popped by to have a chat and a cup of tea with his mother.

One day I did some healing on Harry, who was feeling unwell and looking very run-down and waif-like in a T-shirt and socks without shoes. We went into the small sitting room and after first sitting on Diana's lap, with his head snuggled into her shoulder, he settled down between us on the sofa.

Diana explained to him that it wouldn't hurt, that he would soon feel better, but he wasn't worried. I sat with my palms turned towards him and let the energy flow forth. It wasn't a proper session but he enjoyed the attention—he always liked snuggling up next to his mother. She liked giving him and William as much attention as possible, which was one reason why she asked me if I could teach her how to heal so that she could care for them if they were unwell or unhappy.

I told her that I could, because anyone can do it if they put their mind to it. There is no mystique about healing. There has to be the right motivation, though, and it isn't money. It has to stem from a genuine love of humanity, of really wanting to help. Then it comes down to being able to get the right energies flowing in the right direction. To do that you have to be able to concentrate, to direct your attention to the matter in hand.

Diana found that hard to do. She was forever calling me and saying that she couldn't do it, that her mind kept wandering off. It took a long while before she got the hang of it, and the other treatments she was submitting herself to certainly didn't help. She thought that if she had a load of therapies all at once, it would help her even more.

She once had five different therapies in a single day. That

was absurd. I told her, 'You're having acupuncture then you're having acupressure, shiatsu, colonic irrigation, aromatherapy massages and a few other things as well. What a waste of money. One will negate the other. You are stark staring mad, spending so much. You're not made of money!'

Acupressure is when somebody uses their fingers to stimulate the pressure points. Shiatsu is a Japanese form of deep massage also on the pressure points. Both are based on the theory of yin and yang, of striking a balance between the passive feminine and the active masculine sides of nature. They can be very effective, but Diana was having them one after the other and all they were doing was counteracting each other. I told her: 'You may as well not have anything— and save your money.'

But Diana never really understood about money and carried on regardless. The therapies were important to her, because she thought they would provide the answers she was looking for, and they became her way of dealing with her problems. Underneath all that public glamour and glitz she was very unsure of herself. She commanded the attention of the world but she did not have much sense of self-worth. That is what drove her to seek comfort and reassurance in the strangest of places and ways. She was desperate to understand herself and thereby release what she called her 'real self'.

From 1993 to 1997 she was attended by Susie Orbach, the psychotherapist. During those five years, Diana was constantly being taken back to her childhood and encouraged to analyse what happened in an attempt to make her realise that she wasn't responsible for the break-up of her parents' marriage.

In the short term Susie did a lot of good, but I don't think anyone ever needs five years of therapy. It is not necessary to keep going over the same ground again and again. If you have recognised the problem, and then hopefully come to accept that what happened is over and done with, the therapy should stop. Diana, however, had a very hard time coming to terms with things that happened in her childhood. She kept relating everything back to her childhood and her feeling of unworthiness.

For a short while she visited Vasso Kortesis, a peculiar woman who sat under plastic pyramids. She was introduced to Vasso by Fergie, who thought she was wonderful. Diana also went to see Jack Temple to try and rebalance her energies. He had built up an impressive client list because, in that peculiar world, when one person finds someone who seems to offer an answer, the others all rush to see him or her. What they should be doing instead is to stop thinking about themselves and get into the world and help others, instead of following each other like so many sheep to see him. The Prime Minister's wife, Cherie Blair, was a fan of Jack Temple and went to see him regularly. Jerry Hall consulted him after her divorce from Mick Jagger. The Duchess of York was also a great believer and wrote the foreword to his book, thanking him for clearing her 'energy blockages'.

Once again it was Fergie who made the recommendation, and for a time Diana was taken in by what he offered. She told him that when she was a little girl she had pierced her right cheek with a lead pencil and that the point had broken off in her face. Using what he claimed was his 'special lead extracting process', he claimed to have pulled the poison out of her. He also told her that she had been poisoned in the womb by a lead crystal decanter, which had caused her bulimia. To help her deal with her difficulties he gave her an amethyst crystal.

Temple, who died in 2004, called himself a 'homeopathic dowser healer'. To put it bluntly, I thought he was a genuine crackpot. He claimed he could take you out of the twentieth century and back through time by using fossils. Not rare fossils, but those interesting but really rather ordinary shells and stones excited children can pick up on the beach.

He taped some of those fossils onto her body. I saw her one morning when she had just returned from seeing Temple in his bungalow in West Byfleet in Surrey, where he had built a miniature Stonehenge in his back yard. When I looked at her I couldn't stop laughing. The sticky tape had left white

stripes running across her legs. I asked, 'Are you doing a ze-
bra impression?' She looked ridiculous but couldn't stop
herself from laughing at the idea.

Diana tried to explain to me that Temple had told her that
before mankind came along there was purity and innocence
in the world. I pointed out that there was also savagery and
chaos, which made Temple's theories complete rubbish. She
was paying £150 for each visit to Temple. I told her that she
was being abused—that she was paying an awful lot of
money to supposedly go back in time instead of getting on
with life and going forward. We are here to evolve—not to
try and regress back into the Stone Age.

I said, 'The guy has charged you a fortune. And that is
what he has done? Seriously, what benefit do you feel from
it?' She admitted that she had felt no benefit at all. She was
very embarrassed. She followed my advice and gradually
called a halt to many of her therapies. She also took to heart
what I said about Temple and stopped visiting him.

It wasn't easy to wean her off these questionable treatments. The problem was that Diana was looking for some
miracle combination that would get rid of all the pain she
was feeling. But all she was really doing was trying to get
away from KP and the pressures of being who she was. She
even went to see people when she was happy. It was a form
of escape which became a bit of an addiction.

Although she did eventually start to ease off, it was not
before she had been badly injured. Temple was harmless
nonsense. Some of the other therapies, however, were actually dangerous. She insisted on seeing an osteopath at least
once a week. It was far too much and she started to get bad
back aches and headaches. Her X-rays showed that the ver-
tebrae had been worn down by over-manipulation.

By the autumn of 1996 she wanted treatment for the pain
caused by the over-manipulation of her neck, and, although
she had cut down her sleeping pills, she wanted to stop using
them altogether. So I took the matter in hand.

A few years before, I had fractured my spine slipping on
some spilt milk in a supermarket. I was told by the doctors

that I had permanent nerve damage in my left leg and was unlikely ever to be able to walk properly again. I wasn't prepared to accept that and took myself off to see Dr Lily, a Chinese woman who at the time spoke little English but is the most remarkable acupuncturist I have met. She cured me, and on my recommendation Diana agreed to see her.

To her it was another new treatment and that always excited her. This time, though, I knew she was going to be treated by someone who knew what they were doing and, in a safe and practical way, could be of real help—at the very reasonable cost of £25 a session.

We arranged to meet at AcuMedic in London's Camden Town where Dr Lily works. Diana arrived in a chauffeur-driven car, dressed very elegantly in a skirt and blouse. Everyone recognised her when she walked in but that didn't bother her. She was too intent on getting on with treatment.

She brought her X-rays with her that showed the damage to the cartilage in her neck caused by the over-manipulation. Dr Lily looked at them briefly, took her pulse, and examined her tongue, to which the Princess exclaimed, 'No one has ever asked me to stick my tongue out at them before,' and then allowed her to watch me having some needles stuck into me.

The Chinese believe the body is interconnected with certain pressure points that act like junction boxes in an electrical circuit. For instance, there is a point between the thumb and forefinger which connects to the digestive system, while the ones around the feet regulate your waterworks and your hormones. The needles go everywhere: the legs, wrists, hands, stomach and sometimes at the top of the scalp. And once they were in place, Dr Lily would give them an occasional twiddle.

I was worried that this would put Diana off, because, although it didn't hurt very much, I am sensitive to acupuncture and kept saying 'Ouch' every time a needle was inserted. She didn't seem to mind, though. In fact, she found it rather funny.

When it came to her turn she lay down on a treatment

table. She was much braver than me and without a murmur and only an occasional sharp intake of breath allowed Dr Lily to put the tiny needles into her legs and hands and on the top of her head.

That first session lasted forty minutes. It was the beginning of a course of treatment that was to last until the end of Diana's life, and only a couple of days before she died she telephoned Dr Lily and told her that she was desperately tense and stressed and couldn't wait to get back to London for another session. To Diana a visit to that little room in Camden Town was something to look forward to. It was almost a treat because Dr Lily rationed the number of times she was allowed to visit. She wouldn't let Diana do what she usually did when she became engrossed in a new therapy, which was turn up whenever she wanted, sometimes as often as every day.

She was quite strict in other areas too. She was horrified when Diana told her how often she went for colonic irrigation, and told her how unnatural it was to have jets of water flushing through you, pushing toxins back into the intestines, and how damaging that was to the sphincter muscles. Diana looked rather sheepish and promised to cut back, which was just as well, because whereas most people confine themselves to one treatment every six months, she was having as many as three a week.

Diana was never one to keep control of her enthusiasm. She wanted to know everything about the treatment and kept asking questions. Why does this needle go here? What is this pulse for? What is this a sign of?

Dr Lily's youthful appearance also intrigued her. She was in her fifties but could have passed for thirty-five. There wasn't a line on her face and Diana, who was approaching her mid-thirties and, like all women of that age, was starting to worry about growing older, was always asking her how she managed to stay looking so young.

In the effort to find answers to her queries, she started buying books on Chinese medicine and remedies and the energies that traverse the body. She said to me, 'Chinese medicine is five and a half thousand years old and ours has only been developing for the last hundred and fifty years, so they have a head start on us.'

She bought so many books she could have started a library. She became expert in the subject—or thought she was. She started calling me up and saying, 'According to the book I have here, so and so is suffering from this or that.' She became quite convinced that she could diagnose people's disorders just by looking at their photographs.

She would show Dr Lily pictures of Prince Charles and ask why he was going bald so quickly. She also brought in photographs of Princess Margaret, Prince Philip and even the Queen. Dr Lily was very light-hearted about it. She felt that it was helping her to understand how acupuncture worked. Diana, however, was being deadly earnest. And a little bit of knowledge can be, if not dangerous, then misguided, to say the least.

She decided that Nelson Mandela had something wrong with his spleen and his kidneys and told him so during her visit to South Africa in 1997, when he had a swollen elbow. Mandela was very fond of Diana, but goodness knows what he thought of her diagnosis.

She also told John Major, the British Prime Minister at the time, that his kidneys and heart needed attention. He just laughed it off. There wasn't much else he could do. He wouldn't take it seriously, even if she did.

There is no doubt, however, that Diana derived some practical benefits from acupuncture, which cured the cause rather than merely the symptoms of her ailments. She had felt lousy at first, but she soon started to sleep better and, gradually, with the aid of the herbal capsules Dr Lily gave her, she was able to break her dependency on sleeping pills. We had found a practical solution to at least some of her problems.

What she never lost, however, was the desire that sometimes bordered on the obsessive to know what was going to happen next in her life. She wanted a week by week, even a day by day rundown of what was going to take place, so she could be ready for any pitfalls.

That accounted for her curious passion for astrology and fortune-telling. For some people they are innocuous amusements, but Diana really believed that they could give her an insight into the future. She had been keen on Penny Thornton, only to fall out when Penny started getting publicity as Diana's astrologer. She then turned to Debbie Frank to study the stars and chart the movement of the planets on her behalf, and her love life in particular.

But she wasn't only interested in herself. She would ask about what the future held for Princes William and Harry, and about Charles's health, which always caused her great concern.

And she was always asking if good things were going to happen to Fergie. She really cared about her and said that they were real 'soulmates'. But friendships depend on trust, and when the butler Paul Burrell got close to the Princess their relationship took a battering.

He would tell her that friends had telephoned him from America and told him of things Fergie had supposedly been saying about her on television. When Diana asked him on which show Fergie had been making these remarks, he would say that he couldn't remember, so there was no way of confirming or disproving what he told her. Diana did phone other friends in America to verify Paul's account. The trouble was that she believed him which caused a great deal of friction between her and Fergie, while at the same time giving Burrell something of a hold over Diana by appearing to know more than she did.

He dealt with other people in the same way, myself included. After his mother died, Paul claimed that he had acquired the ability to see into the future and Diana started calling him, not 'my rock', but 'Psychic Paul'. When he answered the telephone he would ask, 'Can I take a message?' He would then tell Diana that someone had called, adding, 'And I think I know what it is they want to talk about.' Of course, he already knew exactly what it was they were calling about, because they had just told him.

Diana eventually sussed out what he was doing, but that

did not undermine her belief that it really is possible to foretell the future.

She had a collection of rune stones with symbols inscribed on them which she kept in a small cloth bag. She would sit on the floor, ask me to relax and to think of what was all around me. Then she would pick out the rune stones herself, spread them out on the carpet (which she insisted on doing herself), tell me to close my eyes and concentrate, and then she would do a reading. She was very pleased when her predictions came true, which I have to confess, they always did. She would say, 'See, I told you so.'

She also subscribed to the notion that certain stones had magical properties which could affect your luck. A couple of years into our friendship, she asked if there was a way of healing precious stones and crystals. I told her, 'You just stick them in a bowl of salt water, leave them for a month, and take them out at the next full moon!'

She replied, 'I've bought a couple of crystal books and they said you can bury them in the earth.' And that is exactly what she did with several precious stones, including a spectacular sapphire.

One day, we were having a lunch of pasta and salad served to us on a round walnut table by Burrell in the dining room with walls the colour of burnt orange. I had taken two forkfuls of spaghetti when she suddenly produced this enormous gem out of her pocket and said, 'Feel this.'

As I took it in my hand she explained that, although she loved the stone, it didn't feel good. It always brought her bad luck, she said, because it must have some very bad memories attached to it.

I told her to immerse it in salt water and put it on the window ledge. She replied, 'I couldn't do that. The staff would see and laugh at me. They'd think I'd lost my marbles.'

I joked that I still had the marbles left over from my school days and that none of them looked like this. It was a large oval sapphire which had been part of a necklace given to her by the Saudi Royal Family which she had had dismantled. She took it out of my hand, put it down on the table, served me some more salad, and declared, 'I'm going to bury it later on in the walled garden.'

She could just see the garden from the dining room window. The trouble was, so could the Austrian-born (Australian raised) Princess Michael of Kent who lived in the neighbouring apartment. The two women were at daggers drawn. Diana used to spy on her through her little opera glasses. She was convinced that 'the Führer', as she sometimes called her, was likewise spying on her.

I left Kensington Palace at 3.30 p.m. that afternoon when she went off to St James's Palace to sign some papers. That night she telephoned me, and said she had buried the sapphire. She then put it out of her mind until the month was up.

When she went back later for it, however, it was nowhere to be found. She telephoned me and said, 'It's gone!', thinking it had magically disappeared.

She never did find out what had happened to it, and, to be honest, I don't think she really cared. If it had been one of the stones the Queen Mother had given her, there would have been an enormous fuss. And if it had been a picture of her boyfriend, or something to do with the children, Diana would have been beside herself. But no one else seemed to have noticed that one priceless sapphire had gone missing, while as far as Diana was concerned it was just another stone. She liked having them and wearing them, but she never placed great store by them. She was much more interested in what they might tell her than what they were worth. To her, they were a means to an end, like mediums and astrologers.

The medium she placed great trust in was Rita Rogers. Diana initially went to see her to try and make contact with the father she adored, and had been astounded by how much Rita seemed to know about their relationship. She reminded her of incidents from her childhood that Diana had all but forgotten about, and initially was able to give her messages from the Earl who had died in 1992.

There was only so far along this road you can go, however, and ultimately Rita fell from favour, although Diana still kept in touch with her. I kept pointing out to Diana that, no matter how much faith you have, there is only so much a medium or a clairvoyant can achieve. It isn't a tap you can turn on and off when the fancy takes you. They might be able to outline a basic trend, but they can't fill in all the details. Go and see a medium every year or two, by all means—but not every week or two, which is what Diana was doing. She was allowing it to affect her life. She was becoming a psychic junkie.

I tried to explain that she should never allow herself to become reliant on what a medium or a physic or an astrologer told her, that she had to take responsibility for her own life, but she didn't like that. By doing it her way, when things went wrong as they sometimes do, she could blame the medium instead of reproaching herself. It was her way of apportioning blame, which Diana was very good at.

And, of course, they did get things wrong. None of the astrologers or psychics predicted the divorce. They all said she would get back together with Prince Charles. They were telling her what she wanted to hear. I was the only one who said, 'You have to face reality here.' I recognised that the marriage was well and truly over, that it was too late for reconciliation.

I pushed home that point after the *Panorama* interview. I told her that while truth might hurt, half truths and lies leave you not only with the pain but also with a deep sense of disillusionment.

That didn't stop her looking. But no matter how many treatments she tried, she never quite managed to still the anguish that nagged away at her—or shed the disenchantment that caused her to suffer. Yet, ironically, it was through her devotion to alternative therapies that Diana met the man who turned out to be the love of her life, Hasnat Khan.

# 3

# Charles

Marriages often go wrong in the bedroom. Diana's never went right.

We talked about it for hours, over endless cups of tea drunk sitting on the floor of her little sitting room, while she was lying on my treatment table, at lunch and supper, on the telephone.

It took a while before she opened up, but eventually her desire to tell her side of the story proved irresistible. She wanted to unburden herself and there was nothing unnatural about that. It was a womanly thing to do. By being open and honest, she was seeking to relieve herself of the guilt and confusion about the failure of her relationship which had been preying on her mind for years.

It was a sad tale she told me and in the details are to be found the seeds of dissatisfaction and frustration that eventually destroyed her marriage to the Prince of Wales. The kernel of the problem was contained in the remark she made to me one day while we were having yet another cup of camomile tea. Charles, she said, 'had no clue as to a woman's geography'.

She added that, had she been older and more experienced, she might have known how to deal with that. But she was a twenty-year-old virgin when she wed Charles, and by the time she realised what was missing, their relationship was so disaffected that reconciliation was impossible. He had found in his mistress the succour he was too artless to provide for his wife, while she had turned elsewhere for the physical comfort she needed and believed she was entitled to.

I told her that it was a common enough story, that millions of other couples had confronted the same problem, and that all she had to do was look at the divorce statistics for the proof of what I was saying.

That didn't make it any easier for her to accept. She had entered into marriage full of hope and anticipation. 'Do you know how I used to feel when I was with Charles?' she asked. 'I used to get butterflies all the time—you know, that butterfly teenage feeling.'

He had been a kind and attentive suitor, she recalled, and she had been swept along by the romance of it all. 'He really was my Prince Charming,' she said.

In those early days they wrote love letters to each other and she really opened her heart out to him. She was very passionate, and told him how her spirits lifted when they were together, how head over heels in love with him she was, and how she was looking forward to spending the rest of her life with him.

As the wedding approached, however, she started to have misgivings. She found out very early on about Camilla Parker Bowles and became fixated about her. I told her, 'Look, I am a little bit older and I can see that Charles was in love with Camilla when he was in his early twenties, and love like that doesn't die. You always have a soft spot for someone who filled a big chunk of your early life, and it stays with you forever because it's carefree and fun.' I likened it to the butterflies she felt when she and Charles were first together.

She found that hard to accept, even all those years later. She found it impossible at the time. She had convinced herself that, because of Camilla, Charles's heart wasn't really in the marriage. She shared her fears with the Queen Mother, whom she stayed with at Clarence House for a short while after the engagement was announced, and also her grandmother, Ruth Lady Fermoy and with her mother, Frances Shand Kydd. They told her that she was suffering from pre-wedding stress and that she had no need to worry because she would soon get over it. They were more concerned about the historical significance of the service than with her doubts about Charles. They kept saying, 'Don't be paranoid—it's all in your imagination.'

She tried talking to her eldest sister Sarah, but she wouldn't listen. She had once dated Charles and according to Diana, 'she was jealous of me'.

Only her father, Earl Spencer, treated her with consideration. He told her, 'We are going ahead with it and if things do go wrong I will always be there for you.'

It was reassurance of a kind, but even the supportive hand of her father could not calm the nerves she suffered on the day of the wedding. Her doubts had brought on the onset of bulimia and the dress kept having to be taken in to accommodate her wasting figure. The designers, David and Elizabeth Emmanuel, were still making final adjustments on the morning. 'I loved the dress,' she recalled, although she hadn't realised quite how long and heavy the train was until she started walking up the aisle of St Paul's Cathedral and almost tripped over. She had looked wonderful that day but underneath it all, she said, 'I was shaking like a leaf. I didn't want to go through with it. The night before I lay in bed thinking, "You've got to call it off."'

As she walked towards the altar she spotted Camilla in the congregation. She had been invited by Charles. 'I was furious,' Diana recalled. 'I wanted to turn round and run.' If she had had the courage, she said, she would have done what the girl played by Katherine Ross in the film *The Graduate* did, which was hitch up her dress and bolt out of the church. The idea of becoming tangled up in that long train as she attempted to make a run for it always made her laugh. There were several moments during the ceremony itself when she struggled to stop herself from giggling—at the sight of the 'ridiculous' hats the women were wearing, and when she blurted out Charles's names in the wrong order.

'I had to see the funny side of it, otherwise I would have burst into tears,' she said. 'I felt like a sacrificial lamb.'

That feeling was compounded on the honeymoon. She was convinced that Charles had spent the night before the wedding with Camilla. She told me she had the evidence. She never revealed what it was, but when they were aboard the Royal Yacht *Britannia*, and she saw him wearing the cufflinks with intertwined 'C's that Camilla had given him, she believed that her suspicions had been confirmed. She told Charles, 'You're married to me now—why do you want to wear those?'

It was an inauspicious start to a marriage that was running into problems even before it had properly begun. Charles wasn't communicative. Always active, she wanted to go off and do things, but he was singularly lacking in joie de vivre. 'I wanted to sing and dance and do exciting things, but all he wanted to do was take it easy, read and sunbathe.' To Diana's way of thinking, he seemed more intent on impressing the dignitaries, like Egypt's president Anwar Sadat, who were invited to dine aboard ship, than he was in paying court to his wife.

'I was bored,' she said. 'It was like being stuck with an eighty-year-old man.'

Fed up and lonely, she started chatting to the crew. That was something he never did, and he disapproved of his young wife's breach of royal protocol. When she came back and told him the gossip she had picked up he would ask, 'What on earth are you doing? You shouldn't be talking to the staff like that.' She replied, 'If you are not going to talk to me, what do you expect me to do?'

It was at night, however, that the real difficulties manifested themselves. It was before sex education became a compulsory part of the school curriculum, but Diana had taken the trouble to read the appropriate books. She had stayed at Buckingham Palace throughout most of the engagement and had once climbed into Charles's bed during a massive thunderstorm. Apart from a few kisses, however, nothing had taken place. It was with expectation, therefore, that she first entered the marital bed.

'I had read all that stuff about being swept away and the

earth moving, but it wasn't like that at all,' she recounted. 'It
was all over in a moment. I just lay there thinking to myself,
"Is that it? Is this really the big deal everybody makes it out
to be?"'

The fact that she found the experience painful only served
to exacerbate her disappointment. She felt uncomfortable and
let down. Henceforth, sex with Charles was not something she
looked forward to. All he wanted to do, she said, was 'jump
my bones'. Her description of Charles's amorous technique
was blunt, crude, but graphic: 'Roll on, roll off, go to sleep'.

On a scale of one to ten, she later awarded her husband a
lowly one.

Matters only got worse when they came off the Royal
Yacht and went up to Balmoral Castle. The Queen, the
Queen Mother, Prince Philip, Princess Margaret and her
children, David and Sarah, were there. So were Prince Andrew and Prince Edward. What was supposed to be a honeymoon had turned into a family outing. Diana was somebody
who should have been in a five-star hotel rather than in the
middle of nowhere with a lot of stuffy people with whom
she had little in common. The routine was formal and old-
fashioned and she loathed the long walks in the drizzle and
rain. The Royal Family never put the heating on, even when
the weather turned cold, which it frequently does in Scotland. Everyone dressed for dinner, but all she wanted to do
was pull on an extra sweater and sit in front of a fire. 'And
the minute you went out of a room there was always somebody switching off a light behind you,' she said.

The Prince was in his element, shooting and fishing and
walking across the moors, but Diana hated every moment
and was often in floods of tears. Charles didn't know how to
handle her. She wanted him to put his arms around her but he
never did. Instead he called in a psychiatrist. The doctor recommended that, for the good of his wife's peace of mind,
Charles should take her back to London. He refused to, and
told her to invite a girlfriend from London up to Balmoral.

Carolyn Pride, with whom Diana was sharing a flat when
she first became involved with the Prince, duly came to stay

for a few days, but that didn't make the situation any better. She knew for certain then that her intuition had been 'one hundred per cent correct' and that she should never have gone ahead with the marriage.

Diana's obvious unhappiness had not dampened Charles's marital demands, however, and by September, only two months into a marriage that was already in crisis, Diana was pregnant. To add to her bulimia, she now started suffering from morning sickness. 'I was a terrible mess,' she said.

It was while she was carrying her first child that Diana threw herself down the North End staircase at Sandringham where the Royal Family, with its new and utterly miserable member in tow, had moved en masse for the New Year holiday. She did not feel guilty even though she might have damaged the unborn baby—she really wanted the baby—but as a means, she admitted, 'to get attention. I wanted Charles to put his arms around me and say he loved me but all he ever did was give me a pat on the back.'

She put what she called his 'emotional retentiveness' down to his childhood. She liked analysing Charles's upbringing in her search for the clues that would explain his attitude towards her. Diana reckoned that if Charles had been brought up in the normal fashion, he would have been better able to handle his—and her—emotions. Instead, his feelings seemed to have been suffocated at birth. He never had any hands-on love from his parents. His nannies showed him affection but that, as Diana explained it, was not the same as being kissed and cuddled by your parents, which Charles never was. When he met his parents they didn't embrace: they shook hands. Because of his upbringing he couldn't be tactile with his own wife. She said, 'The only thing he learned about love was shaking hands.'

In olden days that might not have mattered, but it wasn't an endearing way to approach a modern woman. Diana had read the books and the magazines and she wanted a lot more. She didn't want to be patted or have her hand shaken. She wanted to be loved, absolutely and totally, by a man who would devote himself to her.

She was asking for a lot, and I warned her that it was probably more than any man would ever be able to give her. Listening to her, she did sometimes sound very childlike, but at the time Diana was still very much a child herself. Charles had been her first boyfriend, and when it didn't turn out as she expected, she simply didn't know how to handle the situation. As she always pointed out, however, he could have tried a lot harder than he did. Instead, all she got was either indifference or a blast of his temper.

The Windsor men are notorious for their short fuses and Charles was no exception. When he was angry with her he would shout and scream, and didn't seem able to control himself. She put it down to the way he had been so thoroughly spoilt as a little boy. The Queen Mother had always indulged him, the staff at the various royal palaces had fawned over him, and as he grew older he had surrounded himself with a lot of 'yes' men. The result was that when anyone disagreed with him he would fly off the handle and start throwing things. He rarely caused any damage because he tended to grab the nearest thing to hand and if that happened to be a newspaper it would flutter harmlessly to the floor, which would amuse Diana no end.

Occasionally, however, his tantrums scared her. Her defence was to walk away without saying anything, which annoyed him even more and sent him off into another rant. He would always apologise afterwards, but these outbursts put yet more pressure on Diana. 'I thought I was going to explode,' she said.

The feeling was so overwhelming that she started self-mutilating herself with knives and forks and any other sharp object she could find. She explained that the hurt it caused physically was a lot less than the hurt she was feeling inside. She compared slashing herself to a volcano erupting and said that she could feel the lava spurting out of her body.

It wasn't molten rock she saw. It was her own blood, along with the intense emotional pain and frustration that was being released.

She said that Charles couldn't understand the emotional

relief she felt when she hurt herself in that awful way. I told her that there was no one who could understand that, other than someone who had done a similar thing to themselves. It was beyond an ordinary person's comprehension and it was certainly way beyond anything Charles had ever encountered. In his overly sheltered life, a kiss had been regarded as an unbecoming extravagance and he recoiled from the sight of his wife's self-inflicted stab wounds. If this had happened later, after Charles had learned more about the ailment, I am sure he would have reacted differently, but then he saw it as another pathetic cry for attention rather than a sign of the deep depression he had been at least partly responsible for.

The birth of William might have led to an improvement in Diana's mental health. Motherhood invokes the deep-rooted human instinct to nurture and care for something beyond our own well-being, even at risk to ourselves, and Diana was absolutely delighted by what she referred to as the 'miracle of life'. Charles had been quite attentive during the labour. He wasn't in attendance throughout, as was widely reported: not knowing what to do, he kept looking in and then dashing out again. But at least he had been in the Lindo Wing at St Mary's Hospital in Paddington and she was grateful for that.

Once the couple and their first-born got back to Highgrove, however, the old troubles soon reasserted themselves.

In the beginning, she had liked the grand house near Tetbury in Gloucestershire where the Waleses made their country seat, and she had been keen to fulfil her duties as a wife and hostess. But, as she soon discovered, this was *his* house. He had little interest in, or time for, the few friends she had managed to make before she was swallowed up by the Royal Family, and Diana, so unsure of herself in her new role, stopped inviting them. It was *his* friends she had to entertain and she disliked most of them. She thought them old and dull, regarded them as the most terrible of snobs, and despised the way they agreed with everything Charles, their future King, had to say, even if it happened to be utter nonsense. If she objected to what he was saying (on the matter of shooting pheasants, for instance, which she had an aversion to), the 'killers', as she called them, always took his side, which made her feel small and foolish and out of place in what, after all, was supposed to be *her* home, too.

When they ventured outside Highgrove's 410 acres, other tensions manifested themselves. As heir to the throne, Charles had always been the centre of attention. Now it was Diana everyone wanted to see. And it was Diana's picture that appeared in the newspapers and magazines, not his. As she rightly insisted, it was hardly her fault but it bothered her husband. 'He was jealous,' she said.

The breakdown of a relationship is inclined to wipe the good memories from the slate, but Diana was honest enough to admit that there were moments when they had been happy together. They both had a well-developed, if childlike, sense of humour, and she said that the one thing he could do if he put his mind to it was make her laugh. She enjoyed his imitation of the Goons, from a popular radio programme in the 1950s starring Peter Sellers and Spike Milligan. And she was amused by his lavatorial jokes involving bottoms and their function. As Diana was keen on colonic irrigation, she took bottoms a lot more seriously than he did, but she did see the funny side of what he was saying.

No amount of merriment could paper over the fundamental disagreements that were affecting their marriage, however. Prime amongst them was how they were going to care for their son. Charles wanted to bring back his old nanny, Mabel Anderson, who had given him the only real affection he had known as a child. Diana didn't want a nanny at all. She had nothing but bad memories of the women who had been put in charge of her after her mother walked out. One had beaten her over the head with a wooden spoon. Another had banged her and her brother Charles's heads together. William, she told her husband, was her baby and she wanted to give him all the love and attention she had been denied when she was little.

She made her case forcefully. Charles said that this was the royal way. She countered by pointing out that the Queen hadn't made a very good job of motherhood, if he was the example of the end product—and neither had the Queen Mother, who had turned her back on her maternal obligations and left her daughters' upbringing almost entirely in the care of the hired help. No matter how well-trained and competent they might have been, in Diana's view they could never give their charges a mother's affection.

Diana lost the argument. Over her protests Charles went ahead and employed, first a nanny, then a relief nanny. Even when it came to the care of her own children, Diana's views were being brushed aside like so much chaff and she sank back into her melancholy. That is why she spent so much time with William, whom she saw as the only light in that dark emotional place in which she had become entrenched.

The birth of Harry produced a further decline. On top of everything else, she suffered from postnatal depression, which made everything seem even worse than it was. She disliked the nannies who she believed were coming between her and her sons whom she doted on. All her energies were focused on William and Harry. When we talked about it later, she said that perhaps she should have given her husband more attention.

She had tried to bring her marriage back into focus, and when she and Charles were alone she danced in a sexy way in an effort to excite his interest. But her endeavours to entertain his important guests foundered on the seriousness of their conversation which all too often went over her head, while her bid at seduction only seemed to embarrass her husband.

'By the time Harry was born the marriage was over,' she said, with a heavy sigh.

Before William was born, the Royal Family, who are not welcoming to outsiders, had at least taken a bit of interest in her. The Queen, especially, had made the effort to listen to what she had to say, and offered her words of encouragement. But once she had produced the 'heir and a spare' that secured the dynasty, she imagined they became indifferent to her problems.

The recommended course of treatment was a lot harsher than it had been when she was at Balmoral and Charles had been advised to take her to London. Now it was suggested that she should be treated as an in-patient in a clinic. The Spencers, including her brother, sisters and mother, joined the chorus calling for her to be helped.

Diana was terrified at the prospect of being sent to a 'loony bin'. Two of the Queen Mother's relations had been taken to an asylum when they were young, and were never allowed out again in case they embarrassed the family. Diana was totally convinced that they intended the same fate for her. She couldn't confide her fears to Charles for the very good reason that she believed he was in favour of her having treatment. Charles was the one, after all, who had told his family and hers that she was 'mad'.

The only person who took her side was her father. He told her that if she didn't want to become an in-patient, then she should refuse and make do with the therapy she was receiving at home. So she put her foot down and said, 'No,' and 'No,' again.

Her refusal meant that the only option open to the Royal Family was to have her 'sectioned' under the Mental Health Act. That was a step they were not prepared to take. The monarchy depends on public approval and there was already mounting criticism of the offhand way in which Diana had been treated after marrying into 'the firm', as she called it. The outcry that would have erupted at the news that the Princess had been driven so close to insanity by their indifference, that she had to be locked away in an institution, was simply too appalling to contemplate.

Diana was right to stand her ground. We talked at length about that dreadful, traumatic period in her life, and she admitted to having moments when her despair made her irrational. But the causes were plain to see if anyone had dared to look. Postnatal depression was one. The overnight transformation from private citizen to the most famous woman in the world was another. The core of the problem, however, was her husband's inability to understand her or respond to her needs.

As with most women, sex for Diana was a mental thing. If she felt loved she was physically fulfilled and happy. But if she felt cheated she found it difficult even to pretend there was any enjoyment. Mistrust and suspicion undermined the foundations of their relationship.

She never felt she had Charles to herself. There was always a bit he kept from her, a part of him she couldn't reach. She never felt totally secure, completely loved or able to let her guard down. It was as if there was some kind of invisible chasm between them. She would snuggle up to him only to feel the physical chill of his body. The nearer they were, the further apart from him she felt, and even when he put his arms around her she didn't feel confident he meant it. If they had had a row, and the release of emotion was such that she was exhausted and therefore relaxed, it was better—but only until the next row when their bodies might as well have been in separate rooms.

Eventually they were. Charles had failed to live up to her expectations in just about every way imaginable. She had entered into marriage with a man she believed would cherish and support her. Instead she found herself lumbered with an unsatisfactory lover and a husband who sided against her when things became difficult, who didn't appear to notice when she made an effort to look good, who didn't even seem to care when, in desperation, she began flirting with other men. She started to ask herself if the man she had married was really the man she wanted to be with, and that caused her more upset.

Yet despite the rows and the tears and what had become the complete lack of physical contact, she continued to love him. He was the first man she had loved and that counted for a great deal. And she believed that in his way, whatever that might have been, he loved her.

What she found impossible to forgive was his betrayal.

Camilla had been a lurking presence throughout her marriage. After the discovery that he really had resumed his affair with Camilla, the pain she felt 'was like being punched in the stomach'. Her legs felt weak and she went into semi-shock. That was followed by tears and rage.

She tried to put Camilla out of her mind, but she always

kept cropping up. Early in their marriage Charles made the extraordinary suggestion that, because Diana had no one to talk to, she should try and make Camilla her friend. And because she was still at the stage where she was willing to listen to anything her husband suggested, she agreed. It was a short-lived relationship because Diana quickly realised that everything she said was being relayed back to Charles. When Charles asked her why she had stopped calling Camilla, Diana explained angrily that she had no intention of being friendly with his mistress—and that if he loved his wife he would stop calling his mistress too. Any woman would have done the same.

He took no notice, as she discovered when she picked up one of the phone extensions at Highgrove and heard him chatting with Camilla. It was shortly after Harry was born, and the discovery drove her absolutely crazy. It made a mockery of the attempts she had made to save their marriage. Was that why he turned away when she put on a sexy dance for him? She felt completely humiliated.

She started calling Camilla 'the Rottweiler'. She explained why: 'Because she looks like a dog—and because once she has got her teeth into someone she won't let go.'

She tackled Charles about the relationship but never got a proper answer. He didn't deny being with Camilla and he didn't lie. Instead, he became tongue-tied and refused to reply to her questions. It was a childish way of dealing with the situation, but then neither Charles nor Diana was being very grown up about things. He sought refuge in silence. She started making the first of those anonymous calls that were to get her into so much trouble later, telephoning Camilla in the middle of the night and then hanging up as soon as she answered. She became verbally dismissive of Charles and 'his lady', pretended she didn't care what they got up to, turned to other men for comfort, and tried to bury her emotions so that she would never feel that kind of pain again. He had hurt her deep in her heart's core. She kept asking herself, 'How could I be such a fool? How could I have been so deluded for so long?'

She became very disturbed. She was on medication (including antidepressants like Prozac which became available in 1988), battling with her husband over the upbringing of their sons, having to go out and smile at official functions and all the while wondering, 'Is my husband having an affair?' Overwrought, she ended up cancelling a number of engagements, but the fact that she managed to attend any is a wonder. A lot of other women would have stayed at home and sobbed. What helped her pull through were the visits she paid to groups caring for abused women.

Charles was never physically violent, but ill-treatment can also be psychological, and by speaking to other women Diana was able to get an insight into what was happening to her. She got to understand that she wasn't the only one in her situation, and by learning to appreciate their problems, she was better able to understand her own.

Most of the women she met had left their husbands. Diana, ensnared in the royal trap she had so reluctantly walked into, stayed put in the marital home and continued to suffer. Her solution to her plight was to take a lover, and, in 1986, two years after the birth of Harry, she embarked on an affair with James Hewitt, a red-headed officer in the Life Guards. From then on, Charles and Diana lived what in effect were separate private lives. He spent as much time as possible with Camilla, while Diana devoted herself to their sons, and, on occasions, slipped away for clandestine meetings with Hewitt. It was an arrangement that Charles, for the sake of royal appearances, would have continued with indefinitely.

This duplicitous existence was not what Diana wanted from life, however. She still longed to be loved by one man 'and one man only'. She wanted to share the rest of her life with that man. She didn't want to share that man with anyone else.

The trip to India at the beginning of 1992 was the final straw. She was at her lowest ebb and feeling very alone. She recalled, 'I felt my life was coming to an end.' It was a melodramatic way of putting it, but that was how she felt. When Charles tried to kiss her at a polo match, she deliberately moved her head away because she felt the gesture was a sham.

'That was him playing to the cameras,' she said and it made her livid.

She decided if Charles could put on a show in order to make a statement, then so could she. And she did. The photograph of her in front of the Taj Mahal was her response. She wanted to show the world how utterly alone she felt. She was using that monument to one man's devotion to his wife to illustrate that she was a woman without love.

It didn't end there. Diana had secretly been loading another and even more powerful weapon. It was deployed in June the day Andrew Morton published *Diana: Her True Story*, which gave a shattering account of her troubles and the heartless way her husband had treated her. The book was based on interviews Diana had given him through an intermediary, and it gave a first-person description of what it was like on the frontline of what the press had dubbed 'the War of the Waleses'. She had done the final edit herself and insisted that no further changes were made.

She was very excited when the book was published. She explained to me that she had wanted to get her version of events out into the open to counter the bad things that were being said about her by Charles's friends. But she was also terrified of the Royal Family's reaction. She was right to be apprehensive. Charles was incapacitated by shock, but Diana knew that the Queen, who was made of sterner stuff than her eldest son, was bound to be furious.

That is why she tried to deny any involvement. To distance herself from the project, she cut dead the friends whom she had urged to corroborate her account. None of that was going to wash. The descriptions were too precise, too detailed for Diana to escape responsibility, and it drove a deep wedge between her and her mother-in-law who was the one member of the Royal Family who had always shown her kindness and consideration.

Once again, Diana had let her emotions run away with her. She hadn't thought things through properly, and instead allowed herself to act on impulse and lash out at the husband who had caused her so much distress.

Looking back, she remained in two minds about what she had done. She insisted that she was right to tell her story. On the one hand, she deeply regretted the unintentional hurt it had caused to people who hitherto had been her closest allies. She had *permanently* lost some very good friends, and she regretted it. And she lost the good will of the Queen, the one person who could have intervened on her behalf when her royal denouement finally came. On balance, she admitted that it was probably a silly thing to have done. It left her alone and isolated, a feeling magnified by the death three months earlier of her father.

Earl Spencer had always been portrayed as gruff and insensitive, and, since his stroke, as someone whose mental faculties were impaired. That was certainly not how Diana saw him. He was the one person she had always been able to confide in, and he was the only one who knew about and sympathised with the problems that came with her royal status. He had once been equerry to the Queen, so he knew from experience how difficult and inhospitable her in-laws could be. When she ran into difficulties with them, he would remind her that the Spencers could trace their lineage back to the reign of Henry VIII in the sixteenth century, and that they were a lot more English than the Royal Family. In a sense she liked that bit of one-upmanship and found it highly amusing. It was the one thing she felt she had over them.

It was her father's subtle way of giving her his support, and she loved him more than any man she had known. He reciprocated the affection. It was a tough love and he wasn't nice to her all the time. But she was his favourite, and more than anything he wanted her to be happy. And when the going got rough, as it increasingly did, she knew that she could depend on his advice. He was the one man who had never let her down; the one man, as she put it, 'who never betrayed me'. She said that he was her 'safety net' from the painful realities of the emotional doldrums that plagued her life with the royals.

When her marriage collapsed, everyone else advised her to knuckle down, turn a blind eye to her husband's infidelity, keep up appearances and put her own feelings to one side for the good of her family. Such a pragmatic, antiquated, unfeeling approach was exactly the one Lord Spencer had taken when he tried to persuade Diana's mother to remain his wife. Yet when his own daughter was faced with the same dilemma, he abandoned the old aristocratic line. He didn't exactly tell her to pack up and leave. Rather, he told her that she should do whatever she felt would be best in the long run, for her sons but also for herself.

Diana was on an unhappy skiing holiday in the Austrian resort of Lech when she was informed of his death. She was stunned. Her first reaction was to fly back to England by herself, but she was talked out of that by the Palace guard who insisted that, for the sake of good form, Charles had to accompany her. But she made it quite clear that she was not going to allow the Palace to turn her father's funeral into an orchestrated show of togetherness, and insisted on arriving and leaving by herself. She wanted to grieve by herself, and no one, and certainly not the husband who had always bullied her to tow the royal line, was going to persuade her otherwise.

Afterwards, not a day passed when she didn't think about her father. She talked about him constantly and went to mediums to try and contact his spirit. She was bereft without him. She called him 'my rock'. It was a word that the media later attributed to Paul Burrell, but as far as Diana was concerned there was only ever one 'rock'. It was her father, and without him she had lost her mooring.

Her marriage had entered its final phase. She would make a desperate last bid to hold it together, but the problems—of outlook and attitude and, above all, those to do with sex—were too deep-seated to allow for any reconciliation. Diana's emotional needs were beyond her comprehension and Charles hadn't a clue as to how to deal with them. The marriage was coming apart, and Diana had to deal with the fall-out without her father to lean on.

# 4

# Fatal Attraction

Diana made a habit out of picking weak men, and weak men were attracted to her. They could be quite domineering and emotionally manipulative in their relationships with her. In many ways she was like a child, using whatever wiles it took to get their attention. There was no premeditated malice involved. That was simply the way she was— headstrong and impulsive, but also naturally affectionate and desperate to find someone who would reciprocate her feelings.

She was therefore susceptible to a certain kind of man who, in the effort to counteract and cover up his own limitations, is drawn to vulnerable women.

It was to cause her no end of problems in the years ahead.

I am not a psychiatrist but from what Diana told me—and she talked openly about it and at great length—there was a part of her that was forever the lonely six-year-old girl, waiting on the doorstep for a mother who never returned, anxious to win the approval of an emotionally remote father. No matter how hard she tried, or how many therapies she underwent, she never quite managed to shed that feeling of abandonment. It led her to seek comfort with men she would have been wiser to have avoided.

Her dealings with the opposite sex were not helped by her brother Charles's advice that men were only attracted to skinny women. Diana was two years older than him and when they were little she used to dress him up in dolls' clothes and, once, in a teddy bear's outfit. He was like a cuddly toy to her. He brought out the maternal instinct in her. When he reached the age of twelve, he wanted to play a different sort of game with his sister.

It came up in conversation when Diana and I were talking about early experiences. When she told me what had happened, I was speechless—and it takes a lot to shut me up. All I could do was listen as Diana told me how uncomfortable she had felt about it.

Diana did not start having her periods until she was sixteen. She recounted how, even as a youngster, she would binge on chocolates and then deliberately make herself sick afterwards. I had once suffered from bulimia myself, and we spent a lot of time talking about the effect it has on a woman's body. In Diana's case, it severely disrupted her menstrual cycle. Combined with her experiences with her brother—and the fact that Charles Althorp liked skinny women—it made for a fraught adolescence and a poor foundation to the challenges that are part and parcel of womanhood.

With that embedded in their background, many women might have shied away from men altogether, and it is true that in the beginning she found sex profoundly disappointing. Yet, despite that handicap, Diana liked men and much preferred them to women. She felt that she could learn more from men, especially the intelligent and powerful ones she met through her position as Princess of Wales. She was also of the opinion that they were more straightforward and psychologically stable, and that they complemented her more as a person than women ever could. Men might let her down, and they often did, but she was more willing to tolerate it from them than she was from women.

Diana's mother, who had walked out on her, left her daughter with a deep mistrust of her own kind, which is why Diana could be offhand with her women friends. She had a habit of suddenly cutting them out of her life, in the same way as her mother had turned her back on her.

Another important factor was that, notwithstanding anything that had happened in the past, she found men physically attractive. When she met one she liked, she would deliberately start to flirt, and that was something she became very adept at. She knew she was exercising her sexual power and enjoyed doing so.

Indeed, she could be utterly outrageous when the mood took her, and once went so far as to do a Sharon Stone on a well-known Fleet Street journalist.

It happened when she was getting ready for one of her acupuncture sessions. She was wearing a lime-green knitted mini skirt and a pair of tights with knickers attached. She had to take her tights off for the acupuncture, and as she did so she uncrossed her legs in the way the Stone character did in *Basic Instinct*.

She was not really interested in playing the raunchy minx, but in finding herself a mate. Her marriage to the Prince of Wales was her first grasp at the steadfastness she needed. When that didn't work as she had dreamed it would, it is not surprising that she went looking for it elsewhere. It proved to be a search littered with pitfalls and anguish.

The first man she became emotionally attached to after her marriage to Charles started breaking down was Barry Mannakee, the detective from the Royal Protection Squad who was assigned to guard her. He did more than that. By the nature of his job he was always close to hand, and he became her closest confidant in the royal circle. Together they would sift through the photographs of Diana that appeared in the newspapers and decide which were the best. 'He was always so complimentary,' she told me. He was also the one she turned to when she was feeling lonely or depressed. And it was Mannakee, not her husband, who took her in his arms and comforted her when her despair got the better of her and she started crying. On more than one occasion he had to go and change his shirt which was streaked with mascara from her tears.

Mannakee was tubby with thinning hair and married—not everyone's idea of a lover. But palaces are like small villages, and it wasn't long before the gossip that something untoward was going on between the Princess and her body-guard started doing the rounds in the corridors. It inevitably came to the attention of Colin Trimming, the Prince of Wales's Personal Protection Officer, who took a very stern, hands-off approach to his job. Diana found him intimidating and overbearing, and she heartily disliked him. He noted everything that she did, much to the chagrin of Diana who told me, 'It was like living in a police state.'

One day he walked into a room and saw Mannakee hug-ging Diana who was having one of her tearful fits. Deciding that his subordinate in the police force had transgressed the mark of decorum, he reported his suspicions to Prince Charles.

This was not the first time a member of Diana's staff had got into hot water for being 'over familiar'. Shortly after her engagement, Diana had moved into Buckingham Palace where she was assigned a handsome young footman called Mark Simpson. Returning from the opera one evening, Charles called by Diana's room to bid her good night and found Simpson sitting chatting with her on the bed. The Prince was affronted by what he regarded as a servant's im-pudence (or worse), and not long afterwards Simpson left Buckingham Palace and went to work for Princess Anne. Simpson, who died in 2000, was gay, yet the unfounded ru-mour persists amongst older members of the royal house-hold that he was having an affair with Diana.

In Mannakee's case the evidence appeared more substan-tial. She called him 'my fella', and said she used to flirt out-rageously with him, running her hands over her skin-tight evening gowns, lowering her eyes and asking provocatively, 'Do I look all right?' He would often answer, 'I could quite fancy you myself,' to which she would respond, in the man-ner of a screen siren, 'But you do already, don't you?'

They were exchanges of a kind that have kept tongues wagging, and were given fresh impetus by the broadcast of the video tapes recorded by her speech therapist Peter Sette-len in which she said, 'I was only happy when he was around . . . I was quite happy to give it all up . . . just to go off and live with him. Can you believe it? And he kept saying he thought it was a good idea.' In fact, I think she was making a subtle reference to James Hewitt, who was spending a lot of time in Diana's vicinity during that period.

That was very much in character. Diana enjoyed saying outrageous things, just to see the reaction she could provoke, though in this instance she obviously over-reached herself. But loving someone and being *in* love are two different things and she was quite emphatic that her relationship with Mannakee was never a sexual one. She was so honest when it came to discussing the details of her real love affairs, she had no reason to deny this one.

It did not mean that she did not care for him. Diana made no secret of her affection for her detective. She often told me, 'I loved him.' She explained, 'He was my best friend, someone I could talk to with no holds barred. He was a wonderful man. He was like a father-cum-older brother to me. But he was not my lover.'

I believed her. In the closed world of royalty, however, appearances count for a great deal, and when it became obvious to everyone at the palace that Mannakee had become overly close to the Princess, he was removed from his post. A year later, in 1987, he was killed when the Suzuki motorcycle on which he was riding pillion skidded into a Ford Fiesta that had just emerged from a side street in South Woodford, Essex.

It has been widely reported that Charles was 'shocked' by the supposed liaison between his wife and the policeman, and that it was the spur that drove him back into the arms of Camilla Parker Bowles. Diana told me a different story. Mistrustful by nature, she regularly used to search through Charles's pockets and briefcase and had discovered clues which left no room for doubt in her mind that there was more to his friendship with Camilla than she was prepared to tolerate. He used to sneak away, often on Sunday nights, to see her, with a detective in attendance. When she raised the matter with her husband, he dismissed the subject out of hand, which only aggravated an already difficult situation.

She said that Charles believed that, while it was all right for him to carry on outside their marriage, he was far too jealous ever to allow his wife the same freedom—and when he discovered how attached Mannakee was to the Princess, Diana imagined that someone had arranged to have him 'bumped off', as she put it.

I told her, 'Don't be silly,' but Diana refused to be swayed. She said, 'There was nothing going on between us but I had confided in him about everything, absolutely everything. All the gossip I heard about politics, about the Royal Family and all the goings on involving Charles. He knew too much.'

She never got over Mannakee's death, and years later was still making secret visits to the London crematorium where his remains were scattered. And she continued to blame the British secret services for the fatality. I asked if she had proof. She said she did, but if that was so, she never showed it to me.

There is no question, however, that Mannakee's tragic accident left her scarred, frightened and vulnerable. It was the opportunity James Hewitt seized upon.

They first met in early in 1986 and she was immediately attracted to him. Mannakee was still around at the time, and he warned her against pursuing a relationship with the young cavalry officer who he suspected, rightly as it turned out, was up to no good. Diana dismissed his concerns, and in fact became quite annoyed with him for interfering in an area of her life which she believed was her own to do as she saw fit. And in the beginning, at least, Hewitt was very kind to her.

'He was wonderful,' she recalled. He taught her to ride, lavished her with attention, appeared to be fascinated by everything she had to say and, that old standby, he made her laugh. She found him extremely desirable. I don't think she had ever been alone before with a man who exerted such a blatant sexual attraction.

When it came to the seduction, he was worldly enough to take it very slowly, and it started with a lot of fumbles. Diana told me, 'He brought me to orgasm a month or so before we had proper sex, so I wasn't scared as I knew what to expect.'

It was the first orgasm she had ever experienced and she fell in lust with him. Their affair was exceptionally passionate and he persuaded her to engage in oral sex for the first time in her life.

Their relationship continued in that vein, even when they were apart, and it was at Hewitt's instigation that they started having telephone sex. When he first started talking dirty to her down the line, she hadn't got a clue how to respond because up until then her experience of men was restricted to her husband. Prince Charles wasn't adverse to a little smutty chat, as was revealed in those bizarre 'Camilla-gate' tapes, when he said he wanted to be a tampon, but he was always decorous when he spoke to his wife.

It was very different with Hewitt, and from what Diana told me it sounded as if the pair of them were reading from a pornographic magazine. She went along with it. 'He treated me like a sex slave,' Diana recalled.

He didn't go so far as to make her dress up, but she admitted that there was a time when she was quite prepared to do everything and anything that was asked of her. She was under his sexual spell which is why, she explained, she wrote the sexy letters to him when he was serving in the Middle East in the first Gulf War. They were very explicit. She told me they were 'red hot'. She was writing straight from the heart because she was really missing the excitement of being in bed with him. She would have other and better lovers later, but he was the first man to make her feel that way, and in that initial flush of excitement she discarded all discretion. She had never experienced anything like that before, and when he was sent away to war she felt compelled to commit her desires to paper.

At the time she was absolutely convinced that she was in love with him. She bought him clothes, diamond tie pins, expensive alarm clocks from Asprey's and gave him a Harvey Nichols store card so that he could go and buy his socks and underwear. She told me how she used to fantasise about leaving Charles and setting up home with him. She was just a young woman having her first taste of something she hadn't believed was really possible. She said, 'I didn't know this thing could happen.'

It is tempting to be censorious of Diana's behaviour, and she had her share of critics, particularly amongst her husband's set. Charles had made her a Princess, she was the mother of two fine sons, and their view was that she should have knuckled down, played the dutiful wife and been grateful for what she had been given.

The majority of people, however, believed that Diana had the right to develop and discover herself in a way that is surely every woman's entitlement and I agree with them. She may have been a Princess, but first and foremost she was a woman with her own feelings, her own desires and her own needs. Most women—bearing in mind that she was a sexually unfulfilled 25-year-old when this happened—empathised with her.

Her mistake was choosing James Hewitt. It was an indication of just how naive she was, but because he was handsome and debonair she completely underestimated his sleaziness.

The problem, which it took her a while to recognise, was that outside the bedroom they had no intellectual relationship worth talking about. She tried to share everything with him, but he didn't understand what she was on about. Eventually she was forced to realise that 'his head was inside his trousers', as she put it, and after a while that simply wasn't enough. She would say later that, apart from the physical side, 'He was about as interesting as a knitting pattern.'

That didn't equate to love, not of the kind she was searching for. She was looking for commitment. He never gave it. He never even tried.

Diana's suspicious nature at times led her to become downright nosy. It was not an attractive characteristic, but once again her intuition proved to be correct. She started going through his pockets where she discovered the telephone number of another woman. When she confronted him about his infidelity he denied it, but she knew it to be true. She had

had him followed by the same people whom she had employed to sweep her apartment for electronic bugs. 'They gave me a full report—including photographs,' she confided.

She became upset whenever we talked about him. Her face would flush, she would bite her bottom lip and her eyes would start watering. I told her that he wasn't worth crying over. I pointed out, 'He saw your love as a meal ticket. You gave him an expense account. He charged everything to you, started living a lifestyle he couldn't afford, and never spent a penny on you apart from the occasional bunch of flowers. And all the while he was dating other women.'

I was very outspoken and stern. I told her, 'I don't believe he ever really loved you. How can he love you? He used you. Put this down as a learning curve—as a mistake you won't make again.'

What riled her most was the way he had taken such advantage of her. She felt betrayed when she learned that other women had also been buying him presents. That made her feel cheap. She complained, 'He was bloody expensive to keep.'

Just how expensive soon became terribly clear. It was Hewitt who had encouraged her to write those sexually explicit letters. When Diana ended their affair she asked for them back. She was reduced to pleading with him for their return. Each time he refused. Hewitt is a weak man who wanted to manipulate Diana to satisfy his own ego. The letters were his way of exerting control over her.

They were also an irresistible meal ticket for a man I regarded as a gigolo. The letters were Diana's copyright. But they remained in Hewitt's possession, and he drew on them in 1994 when he cooperated with Anna Pasternak, a relation of the Nobel prizewinning author of *Doctor Zhivago*, on her book *Princess in Love,* in return for a reputed six-figure sum.

Diana was appalled. She regarded the book as a work of treachery. She came to see me at 9 a.m. on the morning it was published and her face was red from crying. She was mad with him for going public, for betraying her and for not telling the truth. She was crying that she wanted everything back that she had ever given him. She kept asking me, 'How could he do such a thing? What we had was private, between us, not for public consumption. He's sold me out. Men aren't supposed to do that to women.'

She shouted, 'I hope his cock shrivels up!'

I gave her some healing and a cup of camomile tea. When she had calmed down a little she said, 'I never want to hear his name again.'

By then she was seeing Oliver Hoare, so the sexual hold he had once had over her had been broken. Hewitt had no intention of going quietly out of her life, however. He had conquered the world's most famous woman and he had no intention of letting her go. He was constantly telephoning her and she felt she had to take his calls. She was frightened not to. He still had those highly embarrassing letters and he used them like a chain to keep her in his thrall.

In desperation, Diana came to the conclusion that the only way she was going to get them back from the man she now thoroughly detested was to buy them. She had become convinced that the only reason he had asked her to write to him in such a sexually explicit way was for the intent purpose of selling them—and I believe she was right.

Faced with that dismal probability, she decided that, if they were going to be sold, she was the one who would have to purchase them, because the contents were simply too explosive for her to permit them to fall into the hands of anyone else. She was in the final negotiations for her divorce from Charles, and she was terrified that she could yet lose custody of William and Harry if the contents of those missives had been made public.

After a number of fractious telephone calls and the assistance of an intermediary, Diana agreed to meet Hewitt and buy back the letters.

Hewitt set the terms. He stipulated that the handover should take place in Spain. And he demanded that the money be paid in cash.

She discussed the matter with me at length. I told her there was a very ugly word to describe what he was doing.

Diana agreed. She was absolutely livid—with herself, for being so foolish as to get herself into this dreadful situation, but most of all with Hewitt for what she and I agreed was a grotesque act of betrayal. I warned her to be careful, that Hewitt was not to be trusted, that she was embarking on a hair-brained scheme riddled with dangers. And what made it even more extraordinary was the amount of money Diana had agreed to hand over to Hewitt.

'He wants two hundred and fifty thousand pounds—and that's what I am going to give him,' she told me.

I was absolutely flabbergasted. I asked her, 'Are you crazy? If you're going to pay that kind of money, why don't you do it legally?'

I could not dissuade her, however. She was in a very emotional state and wasn't listening to reason. She insisted that she had to fly to Spain and pay the money, because it was her only hope of getting rid of him for good.

She was accompanied on the trip by Susie Kassem, the wife of a rich Arab investment banker who had become one of her closest friends. She carried the money, she told me later, in a holdall.

To avoid being spotted by the photographers who lurk around airports on the lookout for celebrities, Diana flew to Spain wearing a wig as a disguise. The ruse didn't work. She was spotted on the flight and when she got to Benidorm she found the hotel Hewitt had selected besieged by photographers.

When she called me from the hotel that night she was in a furious mood. She told me that she had spoken to Hewitt on the telephone, but that he had told her that he could not meet her because of the paparazzi—photographers she was convinced had been tipped off that she was there by Hewitt himself in return for a few handfuls of loose change.

I told her to calm down and get out of there as quickly as possible before the situation deteriorated even further. On my suggestion, she called the manager who was very helpful. He arranged for a taxi to meet her at the back door of the hotel the following morning, and to drive her straight to the airport. She was back in London eighteen hours later, with the money, but without having seen Hewitt.

Diana never actually showed me the bank notes, but I don't doubt that she flew to Spain with a huge amount of cash. She was the only person I have met who was impulsive enough to do something as rash as that. And besides, she never really grasped the meaning of money or how much it meant to other people.

Nor did she tell me where she had got the funds from. Her father had left her an inheritance, but you don't go to a bank and walk out with quarter of a million pounds, even if you are the Princess of Wales. She certainly didn't get it from Charles, who was being very stingy with her allowance at the time. I can only assume that she borrowed it from one of her rich friends on the understanding that she would pay it back when the £17 million divorce settlement she was negotiating came through.

It wasn't the financial details of the aborted transaction that were preying on her mind when she got back to London. It was Hewitt. She telephoned me the day she returned and asked me to come round to Kensington Palace. I went and we stayed up talking until late into the night. She was spitting with rage.

'I want to cut his balls off,' she declared. It wasn't a joke. She was deadly serious, and in her fury began to formulate plans to have him kidnapped and brought to KP where she would tie him down and castrate him. It was just so much wild talk, but if her tormentor had suddenly walked in that evening I suspect she would have carried out her threat with a relish.

The despicable thing was that Hewitt seemed to be completely unfazed by Diana's anger and contempt. He continued to telephone her, promising another meeting. But each time he called the price went up. By the end he was demanding more than £500,000, at which point Diana had no alternative but to accept that he was merely playing cruel games with her, and had no intention of ever letting her have the letters back. She stopped taking his calls and left him to sink into what she described as his 'pathetic life', while she set about the altogether more positive business of rebuilding hers.

Yet however hard she tried, she could never break completely free from James Hewitt. He would go on to claim that she had told him that she had indeed had an affair with Mannakee. It was a contemptible, ungentlemanly thing to say, as Diana angrily observed, when it was a lie.

What really upset her, however, were the whispers about the paternity of her youngest son.

It fell to me to impart that unpleasant piece of news to the Princess. She was forever asking me what people were saying about her, and one day I took a deep breath and told her that the rumour doing the rounds was that Hewitt was the father of Prince Harry.

She wanted to know why no one else had told her. I told her, as I so often had in the past, 'Because most people you know only tell you what you want to hear.'

She certainly didn't want to hear this and took it very seriously. 'If people worked the dates out properly they would see that it's nothing to do with Hewitt,' she said. She took it as a gross insult that anyone could even think she was so stupid as to allow something as catastrophic as that to happen. 'It's pretty obvious that he's a Windsor,' she said. 'In colouring he is a Spencer, but he has Charles's eyes.' Diana was told in no uncertain terms that her sons should have a blood test, and, of course, everything was as it should have been. And Hewitt himself has always denied paternity.

The gossip had also reached Prince Philip and further undermined an already tense relationship with her father-in-law. Diana called him a 'bully' and the way he treated her in those final years certainly bears out her description. He used to write to her regularly and some of his letters were very nasty indeed.

She showed them to me on one of those long evenings when we were lounging around in her sitting room on the first floor of Kensington Palace. Diana was spraying coloured streaks into her hair and trying out different coloured nail varnish, including blue. And all the while we were going through her mail. She was very interested in graphology, the art of analysing handwriting to discover clues to a person's character and personality. She had a book on the subject and we kept comparing the writing in the letters to the examples it illustrated.

Diana was a great hoarder of keepsakes and correspondence. She kept the love letters she received, and those notorious tapes she made, hidden in different parts of her apartment. Some were in a beside cabinet. Others were under clothes in a chest of drawers. She also had a little hidey-hole in the wall in her bedroom. The ones we were examining were kept neatly in plastic folders inside an ornate leather box file.

If Paul Burrell ever happened to come in with tea when we were looking at letters, she would close the boxes because she didn't want him to see what was inside. The moment he left the room she would open them again.

Many of the letters were from Charles and we had an uproarious time trying to work out what his handwriting meant. That proved to be impossible; there was nothing in the book that matched his dreadful, spidery squiggle. We gave up. She then produced another folder.

That was where she kept the letters Prince Philip had written to her. They were usually typed and then signed by him. There was one that had a particularly unpleasant handwritten postscript. Diana asked, 'What do you think of this?'

It began with a brusque 'Diana', and proceeded to criticise her in no uncertain terms. The gist of it was that she was a trollop. All she had ever wanted to be was a wife and mother, and that is what she had been. It was only after her sons were born that she went elsewhere for the succour she could not find in her marriage. To imply otherwise, as Philip had done, was appalling.

What really astounded me, though, was his suggestion in another of his letters that Diana was an unfit mother. I couldn't believe that he could write such a thing to the mother of his own grandchildren. It was so cruel.

Prince Philip has claimed that he always wrote sympathetically to his daughter-in-law. That is not true. I read his letters. They were curt and very formal, and some of the things he said in them were nothing short of heartless. After I had finished reading it, Diana asked, 'What do you think of that?'

I didn't know what to say. I think I was more shocked than she was that evening. She had had the letter for a while and time had allowed the anger and hurt to subside a little. But it was new to me and I felt as if I had just smashed straight into a brick wall.

I do not know what happened to those letters. Perhaps they were put through the shredder by her mother, Frances Shand Kydd, who destroyed a number of Diana's papers after her death in an attempt to protect her memory. They may be somewhere in the Royal Archives.

What I am certain of is what those letters said—because I read them.

# 5

# Oliver Hoare

Diana's reputation as a man-eater stemmed from her affair with Oliver Hoare.

He was cultured, well-read and very good-looking but once again she had made an unwise choice.

Hewitt was a contemptuous man who took her for a ride. But Hoare was married and that immutable fact was damaging to Diana's reputation.

I asked her whether she thought it was wrong to be having an affair with a married man. She said, yes, it was. But then she tried to justify herself by saying that he didn't love his wife, that he had promised to leave her, and that they would run away and start a new life together in Italy. And she was naive enough to believe him.

I said, 'Oh, come on, Diana—that's what every married man says to his mistress. It's the classic line of a serial philanderer.'

But she was totally convinced that he was going to marry her. I kept telling her to be realistic, to accept that he was ensconced with a very rich woman, that they had three children together and that married guys in his position give the same old stories about leaving the wife and kids but almost never do.

We had a big disagreement about that. Diana, as usual, wanted to be told what she wanted to hear and what she wanted, or at least what she thought she wanted, was to become the second Mrs Hoare. She kept visiting her astrologers and soothsayers and mediums and asking them if they were going to get married and was thrilled when they said they might.

She told me what they had said. I replied that whatever they said, he was just feeding her empty promises. She said, 'No, no, no.' I replied, 'Yes, yes, yes.'

She kept insisting, 'He's going to marry me.' I told her, in my usually untactful way, 'Yes, and pigs might fly.' She went red and gritted her teeth. She didn't like that at all. We had a heated row and she cancelled all our appointments.

A day or so later I bumped into her at the clinic and I told her to come into one of the empty rooms because I wanted a word with her. I told her that if she had a problem with me, she should tell me to my face. I told her very firmly that I was not prepared to tell fibs to feed her fantasies. I said, 'I'm not going to lie to you. I would rather tell you the truth because I don't want you to be under any illusions—this man has beguiled you.'

And so he had. He had seduced her and she would never have gone along with the affair if it hadn't been for his lies. There is no question that she found him very attractive, with brown eyes and a shock of dark hair. He was also blessed with a captivating manner. As Diana said, 'He could charm the knickers off anyone.'

Hoare had been on the edge of Charles's set for some years before he directed his attention to Diana. He had first made his mark on London society as the 'protégé' of a rich Iranian lady called Hamoush Azodi-Bowler who lived in considerable splendour in Augustus John, the painter's, old studio in Chelsea. She had taken him with her to Teheran where he became interested in Islamic art and Sufism, a mystic branch of that faith. Once back in London, he became head of the Islamic department of Christie's auction house. In 1976 he married Diane de Waldner, the heiress to a French oil fortune, and started up as a dealer in Oriental art with his own shop in Belgravia.

It was through his wife, whose mother was a friend of the Queen Mother, that he first met Charles and Diana at a party at Windsor Castle and, because of their shared interest in Islamic art and Eastern mysticism, he and Charles became friends. Diana could be very dismissive about her husband's esoteric interests and often complained about how old and boring his friends were.

Hoare was sixteen years her senior, and an expert in obscure subjects which she knew absolutely nothing about and had never expressed the slightest interest in, but that didn't matter. He was intelligent, something she admired in a man. His father, a civil servant, had scraped together enough money to send him to Eton which had given him a suave cosmopolitan gloss. He was also very sexy. When her marriage came off the rails at the end of the 1980s, and with her affair with Hewitt at its end, Diana started seeing more and more of Oliver Hoare. He taught her a lot about Islamic art, gave her an introduction to Sufism, and, unlike Hewitt, who had taken her for everything he could get and then more, didn't want her money or her gifts.

With Hoare it was the other way round. He was the one who gave her the presents, including a couple of antique bracelets and a Persian rug, and she found that very flattering.

Diana was by no means his first extramarital affair. For several years he had been the illicit lover of Ayesha Nadir, the beautiful Turkish-born wife of the former owner of the Polly Peck chain of clothing stores. To my way of thinking the Princess of Wales was just another sexual notch on his bedpost.

The difference was that whereas Mrs Nadir was quite content to have Hoare as an occasional bedroom visitor, Diana wanted him all to herself. She didn't want to use that old standby of getting pregnant, which women have used since time immemorial, and always took her birth control pills, but in every other way she was demanding. It wasn't long before Hoare found himself swept along in a situation that had rushed out of his control.

In the beginning Diana would joke about the fact that she

and Hoare's wife shared almost the same name. She said, 'At least if he talks in his sleep and calls out *my* name, his wife will think it's her.'

However, Diana was extremely possessive by nature, and soon she couldn't bear the thought of her lover sharing a bed with another woman. In law she was the wife of a future king. Yet she was now in the curious role of mistress to a married man, and like inamoratas throughout history, she was unhappy with her position.

It made for a dramatic, emotional relationship. One day she turned up at the Hale Clinic with scratches from a fork on her legs and arms. She first started cutting herself in 1982 and continued to perform these terrible acts of self-mutilation when she felt unable to cope with the pressures of her life. I gave her the best advice I could think of, which was that instead of harming herself, she should visualise her pain and then write it down, paint it, or beat it out on the piano and try and get it out of her system that way. She tried that until she discovered stepping up her gym regime was the most effective way for her to release the pressure building up inside her. And it worked because she stopped wounding herself. The marks on her body, however, were the incontrovertible evidence of just how much anguish her affair with Hoare had been causing her.

She let me listen in to some of their telephone calls and I would hear him making excuses, pleading with her, promising that he would be leaving his wife any day now. Diana would start shouting and crying and pleading and the conversations would go round in another circle.

Hoare was also getting a battering at home. It hadn't taken his wife long to discover that he was having an affair with the Princess, and he told Diana that the arguments were often heated.

When that happened he wouldn't feel able to see or call the Princess for several days, which only made her more agitated. When they next met the tears would flow as she kept demanding to know why he was still with his wife instead of being with her.

He was getting it in the neck from both directions and if he hadn't been such an idiot as to get involved in the first place, you might almost have felt sorry for him. But he had no excuses. He had brought this upon himself and when things got out of hand he simply didn't know how to deal with it. Like so many of the other men in her life, he was weak.

Like Charles, he couldn't handle his own wife's emotions, and he couldn't handle Diana's emotional demands either. He became unreliable. She would make an arrangement to meet him and he wouldn't turn up. She would then rush around, trying to find out where he was, upsetting herself with the thought that he might be with someone else— his wife, in particular. When they did meet and she started haranguing him about leaving his wife, he would get up and leave.

Eventually, he couldn't take any more and stopped seeing them both. At the end of 1993 he moved out of the marital home in Kensington and into a friend's flat near his shop, just across the road from London's Victoria Station. He only stayed there for two months. Mrs Hoare held the financial purse strings and he went home.

The reconciliation did mark the end of his affair with the Princess, however. He was the kind of man who wanted women as trophies—and as she was the ultimate trophy he was reluctant to let her go.

Amidst all this emotion, caution got waylaid and the press got wind of what was going on, which only exacerbated an already complicated situation. At the start of the affair they met quite openly for lunch at restaurants like San Lorenzo in Beauchamp Place in Knightsbridge. It is owned by a lady called Mara, who had a flat close by where they would slip away after they had eaten. In the evenings she would smuggle him into Kensington Palace through the courtyard of Princess Margaret's apartment next door. The police officers assigned to protect her didn't like him. They regarded him as arrogant and too full of himself, but they weren't going to say anything. It wasn't their job to interfere with the Princess's private life.

The newspapers were not bound by those rules of discretion, however, and it became a game of cat and mouse, with Diana desperately trying to avoid their camera lenses and the photographers equally determined to get a picture of the Princess and her married paramour. Hoare started sneaking into KP with his head under a blanket. It was degrading; it was also ridiculous. And the rows that up until then had been raging behind the walls of Kensington Palace, and in the Hoares' family home a couple of miles away, became public fodder.

I do not know for sure how Diane Hoare discovered what her husband was up to, but by that stage she could hardly have been ignorant of her husband's shenanigans. What had been whispered gossip was now emblazoned in the newspapers. In some ways I felt sorry for his wife. It was all very degrading for her. On the other hand, she had the money, and could have issued him an ultimatum, and, if that didn't work, left him and filed for a divorce. That would have brought matters to a head, one way or the other. But that didn't happen. Instead, she let the matter drift and to my way of thinking that made her complicit in her husband's misbehaviour.

The whole saga of Diana initiating nuisance calls started when both her mobile and land-line started ringing in the middle of the night, but when she answered there was no one there. She would say, 'Hello, who's that?' but the line would go dead. She was so rattled that I advised her to report that she was the victim of nuisance calls.

She refused and instead asked me if there was any way she could find out who had been calling her. I suggested that she call 1471. She did that and discovered who had been making the calls.

Diana was outraged. The anonymous calls only lasted for a couple of days, but maybe that gave her the idea of making her own nuisance calls. She started telephoning the Hoares' number at all times of the day and night, sometimes from her own phones, but mostly from the public call boxes around the corner from KP.

Diana insisted she only made a few nuisance calls, but in

her misery she obviously lost count. She also wasn't very aware of new technology. We had long conversations about telephones but it wasn't until I bought a new mobile for myself that I realised it was possible to withhold your own number when you called someone. I rushed over to KP and showed Diana how to do it, but it was too late. By then she had become obsessed with Hoare. She would drive round in her car to sit and wait for him outside his shop in Belgravia. At night she parked outside his house, looking up at his bedroom window until the lights went out before returning in tears to KP where she would make those calls, hanging up when Oliver or his wife answered, then hitting the redial button and ringing back only to hang up again. The Hoares received so many that Oliver's wife ordered him to report the matter to the police who were able to trace the calls back to Diana's mobile, to lines in Kensington Palace, or to nearby phone boxes, and she found herself under threat of prosecution.

By showing her how to use the facilities on her telephone I had been an accomplice, albeit an unwitting one, in what had become a very unpleasant situation indeed but I didn't feel guilt about that. Oliver Hoare had been damaging my friend. He had told her he was getting divorced and it is so wrong to do that. He was playing with her emotions and being dishonest. I don't like men lying to women. It's an unforgivable sin for a man to lie to a woman, especially when they are in an intimate relationship, and what Diana did to him was nothing compared to what he did to her. But clearly it couldn't go on like this. She was at a juncture when she really needed to settle down.

Instead, she was making a public fool of herself, which played right into the hands of the Charles camp. Some people even started questioning her sanity. That was unfair. She was a woman who believed herself to be in love. I thought she was overstating her feelings, but there was no doubt that she was utterly smitten by him. She wasn't the first woman to get carried away by her emotions and do silly things, without stopping to think through what the repercussions might be.

Even the strongest infatuations eventually run out of steam, however. After Hoare went back to his wife, Diana started noticing a change in him. He became less and less reliable and there were moments when she worried whether he was on medication of a kind that made him erratic and hyperactive. But what finally did for the affair was Diana's suspicion that he had found someone else to amuse himself with.

Always prone to jealousy, she followed him one day from his shop and discovered that he was not going where he had told her he was. She confronted him on the telephone and accused him of seeing another woman. He denied any wrongdoing. She didn't believe him and called him a liar. His promise that he was going to leave his wife, she said, was worthless. And so it had proved.

I said to her, 'Thank goodness you've finally seen sense. You shouldn't have an affair with someone like that.'

Affairs of the heart were something Diana and I frequently discussed and we were always very open with each other. When my boyfriend let me down, for instance, she told me straightaway that he wasn't right for me, that I was better off without him, and that we wouldn't get back together again, no matter how hard I dreamed. And when my emotions settled down again, I realised that was absolutely right.

Now it was my turn to offer, not so much advice as the comfort and insight another person can bring to such an intensely personal and emotionally confusing situation. Having someone who has your best interests at heart is always helpful and she accepted that I was telling the truth, however unpalatable, in order to protect her fragile emotional state. And once she came round to my way of thinking there was no going back. Hoare didn't want to let her go, and kept telephoning her, but the moment she heard his voice she slammed the receiver down and later changed the private number he had used to call her on. 'Once it's dead, it's dead,' she said.

The affair had nonetheless left a damaging mark against her good name. The break-up of her marriage had produced a great groundswell of sympathy which had helped sustain

Diana through the worst of it. She had been deeply unhappy throughout most of her marriage and her dejection had been witnessed by the millions around the world. Andrew Morton's book, *Diana: Her True Story*, had given a stark and disturbing account of the difficulties she had encountered and the prestige and popularity of the Royal Family had suffered as a result.

The Princess had a much more rounded personality than many people gave her credit for, however. What they overlooked or chose not to recognise was that she was a woman like any other, with her own desires and needs, and that didn't always fit in well with the image of an innocent victim driven to the depths of despair by the heartlessness of her in-laws.

She had got a taste of how the public mood can change following the publication in 1992 of the so-called 'Squidgygate' tape recordings of a private conversation she had had on New Year's Eve three years earlier with James Gilbey.

The son of a wine merchant and the great-nephew of the Roman Catholic Monsignor Alfred Gilbey, the only priest in Britain sanctioned by the Pope to say Mass in Latin, he had provided a male shoulder to lean on when her affair with Hewitt went the way of all flesh. He had encouraged her when she decided to make her woes public in the Morton book and she had been a frequent visitor to his flat in West London. The Squidgygate tapes hinted at a relationship that went beyond the bounds of ordinary friendship. They were full of adolescent innuendos.

When I asked Diana about it she insisted that there was nothing in it. It sounded a bit like President Bill Clinton's defence when he was asked about Monica Lewinsky. Clinton's difficulties fascinated her. She didn't find him in the least bit sexy, but did wonder, 'What do you think his willy looks like?'

As far as Gilbey was concerned, however, she was most insistent that they never had what she called 'proper sex. It was all very innocent.'

What did worry her was how the Squidgygate tapes had

come to be recorded in the first place. She said she was convinced that people 'out there' wanted to undermine her credibility. She was referring to Charles's friends and the Buckingham Palace advisers who were becoming ever more hostile towards her. Her relationship with Hoare and the nuisance telephone calls in particular had moved the criticism up to another level. Then along came Will Carling.

She met the captain of the England rugby team at the Harbour Club gym in Chelsea. He was another person she could cry on—and he made her feel better about her shape. Her shoulders were scrawny and bony and that worried her because she was so insecure about her body. He put her on a programme of weights and it wasn't long before she was able to dispense with the padding and let her own muscles fill her jacket shoulders.

William and Harry were quite impressed by Carling, as they were bound to be—they were young and he was one of Britain's great sporting heroes—and Diana enjoyed his company. Most importantly, she found him easy to talk to.

For once, though, it was Diana who was doing the using, rather than being taken advantage of. She wanted to improve her body shape and she decided that Carling was the best person to advise her. He did a remarkable job because he made her feel good about her body for the first time in her adult life. In turn, I think that Carling was rather thrilled to be able to say that he was the Princess of Wales's personal trainer.

But, like Hoare, he was married and that soon set tongues wagging. At the beginning she denied that there was anything untoward about their friendship. So did Carling. When the stories of an affair persisted, she decided to let it go, explaining that anything she said would only fuel the rumours. She found it all quite amusing.

His wife Julia did not. In September 1995, it was announced that the Carlings were to separate and Julia made it quite plain that she held Diana responsible. She talked about saving her marriage, 'however much someone is trying to destroy what you have', and, in a remark deliberately intended to resurrect the memory of the recent scandal involving Oliver Hoare, said, 'This has happened before and you hope she won't do these things again.'

When the marriage finally imploded the press took Julia Carling's side. The *Sun*, which that year had already labelled Diana a 'man-eater', now called her a 'home-wrecker'. Another newspaper asked, 'Is Will Carling merely another trophy for a bored, manipulative and selfish Princess?'

Diana remained remarkably unperturbed by the criticism. She didn't have a twinge of guilt about the wife. She said that if the wife chose to be that paranoid, it was her problem. She also told me that she didn't regard being friends with someone as adultery. Carling had given her confidence in her body shape, but that was the extent of it. Carling hadn't been very important to her as a person, no matter what his wife might have thought.

However, the Hoare affair and Julia Carling's remarks had made a dent in people's perception of Diana. It was in an attempt to repair the damage and bring public opinion back on side that she agreed to give that notorious interview to *Panorama*. She wanted to remind people of the good work she was doing, and, when Martin Bashir first approached her to do the programme, that was exactly what he promised to do. He said it would focus on her charities.

The introduction had been made by her brother, Charles, who had worked as a correspondent for NBC television in the United States and had persuaded her that it would be a good idea to agree to do the programme.

I happened to be at Kensington Palace, when Bashir was in Diana's sitting room talking over the finer details of what was supposed to be a 'wonderful' programme about her humanitarian work, and she was very excited when she came out of the meeting. She told me how delighted she was that she was not going to be portrayed as a blonde bimbo, but as someone who was sincere about what she was doing. She saw it as something that would make all the hard work she had done for her charities worthwhile because of the exposure it would bring them. She said, 'At long last someone is taking my charity work seriously,' and we spent a long time discussing which ones she should concentrate on.

Shortly afterwards we had one of our occasional disagreements and I lost contact with her for a couple of weeks. This row was over an appointment. She called me one morning, sounding terribly upset and demanding to see me. I explained that I was booked to see a sick patient who was in a wheelchair. It had been arranged a while ago and I had organised someone to help put her on the treatment table. My patient had booked a mini cab to transport the wheelchair, and I'd rented a special room with a hydraulic table.

I felt guilty but there was nothing I could do. I had to stick to my schedule. Diana was so fraught she wouldn't listen. She refused to see it from my point of view. She had grown too accustomed to getting her own way but that didn't bother me unduly. I am not judgemental. She was a friend and I accepted her as she was. Even so, we didn't speak again until after the *Panorama* interview was broadcast on 20 November 1995.

I had watched it at home and I thought, 'This is the biggest mistake anybody could have made.' The make-up was lousy and the whole programme was pathetic.

Diana called me the following morning. When we had had a row she never apologised. Instead she picked up where she had left off as if nothing had happened. She said, 'Good morning,' asked if I was busy, and then launched straight into what she wanted to talk about. She asked me if I had seen the programme and when I said I had, she asked me what my opinion was.

I replied, 'Do you want my honest opinion or do you want me to flower it up for you?' She said, 'I want your honest opinion.' So I told her, 'You made a real prat of yourself.'

I went on, 'You looked like Myra Hindley with the whites of your eyes showing like that. That's what stuck out more than anything—the bad make-up and you feeling very sorry for yourself. It was completely unprofessional.'

It was a tough thing to say, but by then our friendship was based on telling each other what we really thought, not what the other person wanted to hear. She accepted it. She asked me if I minded going out to get the newspapers and then said to let her know the mood on the streets. I went to the supermarket downstairs and as soon as I got back I telephoned her at Kensington Palace. Half the country had watched the interview and I told her that the reaction wasn't very positive. I said, 'Did you know your popularity has gone down about fifty per cent?'

She could take that from me because she knew I was very direct. To encourage her, I added, 'But what's done can't be undone and what you have to do now is really think about where you're going from here—and who you are going to take advice from in future.'

I was furious with Bashir. Diana was in a vulnerable state in 1995 and, as she explained, 'I was very upset about things that were going on and Martin was here and I told him everything.' I believed that he had taken full advantage of her. When I told her a week later what was so obvious to me, she agreed. I asked, 'So where was all that talk about your charity work?' She looked at me and blushed. Then, ten minutes later, when the conversation had moved on to something else, she turned to me and said, 'You're right.'

Later, she explained that she had been talking informally with Bashir and he had said, 'Why don't you say all of this on camera?' If I had been there I would have advised against it and told her to stick to the charities, as originally agreed. But because of our silly argument I was not around to lend a voice of caution. Diana unfortunately got carried away, and agreed to give a full and frank interview in which she admitted to committing adultery with Hewitt and cast doubts on Charles's ability to become King.

Many people watching her deliver what looked like carefully scripted comments on television that night were convinced that it was a premeditated attack on the Royal Family. Diana eventually regretted the whole episode. It put her personal life under a microscope just when she was trying to put the past behind her and build a different kind of future for herself.

# 6

# 'My Darling Boys'

Diana took her duties as a mother extremely seriously.

I saw her comfort William and Harry when they were ill or unhappy and she was the one who drummed into them how important it is to care for those less fortunate than themselves.

And it was Diana, not Charles, who first talked to William and Harry about sex.

That does not mean to say that she did not have her problems with them as they were growing up. As any parent will testify, looking after two boisterous boys is never easy and there were times when tempers flared.

Indeed, on one occasion William was so angry with his mother that he actually pushed her. The difficulties of being the son of such a famous mother had finally got the better of him.

But that, of course, went with the territory. Diana was always telling me how determined she was that William and Harry should enjoy a 'normal childhood. I don't want them to suffer what their father went through,' she told me. 'Look what it did to him!'

That presented an enormous dilemma, for however hard she tried the boys were never going to be treated 'normally' when they were in the company of the royal courtiers. They were rich, privileged and titled—and William was born to be

King. That made them different from every other child in Britain.

I sometimes wonder if Prince Charles may not have had a valid point when he tried to persuade her to raise their sons according to royal tradition, with the emphasis on decorum rather than on having a good time. On reflection, I think Diana did the right thing. Harry's pitfalls, in particular, have been painful, but at least he will have been taught some valuable lessons. It is only through experience we learn right from wrong, how to avoid hurting people, and most importantly, to take responsibility for our own actions. That was something Diana and I discussed at length and agreed that it is part of our personal growth.

But Diana was a young woman with her own ideas about how best to bring up children. She was emphatic that 'my boys', as she called them, should be spared the ruthless, unremitting regulation and discipline their father had to endure when he was young—and which she believed had rendered him incapable of being emotionally open and honest. She wanted them to get out and enjoy themselves in the way other kids of their age do.

In some ways, it was a no-win situation, but Diana stuck admirably to her guns and allowed the boys to live a life relatively free of royal constraints. The ivory tower where Charles wanted to confine them (backed, of course, by the Queen Mother, who liked to pretend that everything was as it was during her Edwardian childhood) would have been a poor training ground for the task of dealing with the modern world.

When Harry experimented with drugs, as many teenagers do, it made front-page news. Then there was the furore that erupted when he went to a party wearing a Nazi armband. They were stupid and tasteless things to do but if he hadn't been a prince no one would have paid it any attention. All boys behave foolishly at some time or other. But he is a prince and, of course, that puts him in the spotlight.

I am positive he intended no harm when he dressed up as an officer in Field Marshal Rommel's old Afrika Korps for a friend's birthday bash. Harry, like William, is too much his mother's son ever to set out deliberately to cause offence. There was so much goodness in Diana, so much consideration for the feelings of others and she passed that on to her sons who I thought were charming and delightful young men.

She also did her best to prepare them for the criticism that she knew would one day come their way. She told me, 'I explained to both of them that it didn't matter what people say about them, as long as they know they are loved and wanted. And they are!'

The first time I met Harry was when he had to come home to Kensington Palace from his preparatory school, Ludgrove, because he was feeling unwell. He was ten at the time and he was sitting on Diana's lap with his arms round her neck, his head snuggled into her shoulder and sucking his thumb.

The introductions were made and when we started chatting he told me that he really liked being there by himself so he didn't have to share Mummy with William. But although he was a bit under the weather, he made the effort to talk to me and ask me what I was doing—very like his mother was good at doing, in fact.

When I got home Diana rang to tell how me how observant he was because, without being told, he had guessed that I like cats, candles and crystals, which I do. She was very pleased at his perception, though I suspect she gave him a few clues. He really was an adorable boy who was brave and excelled at sport. But he suffered from dyslexia and, until he received specialist help, found it hard to read and write. He was very embarrassed about that, which obviously concerned Diana who went out of her way to boost his confidence at every opportunity.

She had no such worries about William, who was smart enough to get a place at Eton. The famous public school has high academic standards, so she was very proud when he did so well in his entrance exam. 'He's really got it,' Diana told me, bursting with maternal delight.

William teased his mother when she became enthusiastic

like that. So did Harry. They both loved to pull her leg—and anyone else who came within target range of their good sense of humour. What really amused William, who is an excellent mimic, is to call people up on the telephone and pretend to be his father, which is what he did to me once.

When he was at home one day he called my number and demanded, 'How do you know my wife?' in that familiar clipped accent that comedians have so much fun with.

By that time he knew me quite well, so knew what to ask about my work and what I was up to, I became completely flustered. I guessed that it had to be the husband of one of my clients and when he said, 'This is Charles,' I was completely taken aback. I thought, 'Oh my goodness, why is he calling me?'

At that point William burst out laughing and I could hear Diana giggling in the background. It really was a very good imitation and if you close your eyes you can picture Charles's mouth and chin tightening up as he speaks. It was slightly lost on me at the beginning, however, because I was probably the only person in Britain who didn't know exactly what Charles sounds like, which is why it took me a few moments before it clicked.

Others (and there were quite a few) were fooled immediately because William is a great practical joker. He is also something of a phone addict, a habit he must have learned from his mother who always seemed to have a mobile stuck to her ear. I'm sure he would have liked to have stayed on the line all day, and it was on the phone that we had our first conversation.

When I called up one day he happened to answer and asked, 'Who's that?' I said, 'Who are you?' He replied, 'It's William, do you want to speak to Mummy?' I said yes, and he said, 'She's not around.' That might have been the end of it, but William did not want to end it there. He asked me who I was, and when I told him he said that he had heard about me and started bombarding me with questions: how had I met his mother, where did I live, how much I earned, why I had cats and not dogs, did I have children, was I married, why wasn't I, what had gone wrong, what my parents were like and were they still married?

He then asked whether I was psychic and enquired, 'Are you one of the spooks?' I said that I would call myself a healer, not a spook, but that I do see things in people. He got very excited about that and wanted to know about himself. I told him that at his age he really didn't need to worry about the future or what it holds. 'You're too young,' I said. 'No, I'm not,' he replied.

We talked for about forty minutes and it really was strange to be hit with such a barrage of questions from such a young person. And despite my warnings, he really did want to know about the future.

Diana thought William would make a fantastic King, although at the time he wasn't interested in the job. It had rather started to intimidate him. He is a Gemini, and Geminis have mercurial and enquiring minds, but when they are young you have to make sure they learn how to focus and concentrate, and try not to let them get bored. Diana had done his chart and said that he was born under a king's star which meant that he had planets at a particular degree in Leo and was destined for great things. I don't believe children should have their futures told and Diana agreed. She was amused at first and then became annoyed when she discovered that William had been calling her medium, Rita Rogers, to ask for a reading, but she was hardly in a position to object, because that was another habit he had acquired from her.

On other matters, however, William was so sensible that he put the rest of us to shame. He was never an ordinary teenager and always sounded much older than his years. Diana used to describe him as 'my little wise old man'. That was due in no small part to the way she was so forthright with him. 'I don't keep secrets from my boys,' she told me, and that gave them wisdom beyond their years.

She had made it her business to involve them in her charity work. She took them to hospices and to meet patients with Aids to prove to them that you cannot catch the disease merely by being in the company of sufferers. She believed it was very important to show them the other side of life, which is why she took them to see the homeless and helped to clothe and feed them which gave William and Harry a real sense of purpose.

When she explained that some of these unfortunate people were there out of 'choice', as they wanted to escape their normal lives, William was quite shocked. How bad could life be, he wanted to know, to drive men and women onto the streets? The thought had a profound effect on him and when BBC television held a debate in 1997 on the future of the Royal Family, it was William who said that it would be a good idea to sell off the royal palaces and use the money to build homes for the homeless, or, even better, turn the palaces themselves into shelters for the dispossessed. He became quite animated and said to his mother, who was phoning the premium lines at that moment, 'Do you realise that instead of wasting all that money on the phone calls, you could give it to me and I could do something useful with it?'

The calls Diana made that night were to vote against the very institution her son had been born to inherit. She kept pressing the redial button on her land-line to add to the numbers calling for the abolition of the monarchy. It was an odd thing to do in the circumstances, especially with the future King sitting beside her, but Diana had a rebellious streak of her own. We talked a lot about William's future, but when I suggested that because he was so creative he should do something in the arts, she said, no, he won't make any money doing that, what he should do is business studies. And making money, she said, was important, without seeming to take into account that William is destined to be one of the richest men in the world.

The weight of what lies ahead sometimes caused friction between the brothers. They were always competitive, but that was encouraged by the Queen Mother who lavished her attention on the first-born William while all but ignoring his younger sibling. That certainly didn't do much for Harry's self-confidence, which was another reason Diana directed so much affection his way.

In turn, both boys truly adored her, and they were very pleased when their friends told them that they wished they had her for a mother. Some of the other mums were pretty dowdy, while Diana was glamorous and fun and always took a lot of interest in their lives. She even asked William if he had kissed any girls and what it was like, which used to embarrass him no end, but she wanted to know everything he got up to, especially when it came to his dealings with the opposite sex.

When they were very young all their affections were focused on their mother and Diana told me of the time when William said that if he had his own way he would marry Mummy. Harry pitched in and said, no, *he* would. An argument started which ended with William declaring that only one of them could and as he was the oldest it had to be him—and besides, he was going to be King so he could do what he wanted.

When he was older, William would always ask her about the movie stars she had met, ask if they were as beautiful in real life as they were on the screen, and beg her to get their autographs. He had a big thing about the model Cindy Crawford and had a poster of her pinned to the wall behind his bed at KP. Seeing her son's interest, Diana arranged for her to come to tea, but he was so shy that he turned bright red and could hardly get a word out.

He was even more embarrassed when Diana found some girlie magazines hidden under his bed. She pretended to be angry and she told him it wasn't a very clever place to hide them, but secretly she was delighted. She said to me, 'Thank God, he's a normal red-blooded boy—unlike so many in the royal household.'

Trying to explain about the ins and outs of sex to them did cause her a lot of concern, however. She asked me what the best approach was and I said I didn't know, as I learnt from my school friends, which maybe they hadn't. I was surprised they should be so naive, but it was an indication that, for all Diana's efforts, they really did live in a somewhat different world. In the end she decided that since

Charles didn't want to get involved, it was better that they heard about it from her.

She was very straight with them and said, 'I'm going to explain to you where babies come from.' William was quite cool and asked a lot of questions. Harry, on the other hand, was horrified.

Diana made sure they appreciated the importance of love. She explained that when a man and woman meet each other and fall in love, this can be followed by having a child. She added that sometimes people were not in love which can lead to the problem of unwanted children and, if things turned out really badly, that could turn the mother onto drink and drugs because of the psychological pressures of having had a baby too young. Diana had read books about child psychology, and putting a lot of emphasis on the moral obligations was a clever way of getting across the message that sex is not purely about enjoyment but also involves responsibility.

It was all a bit tricky, as it was bound to be, but she got through it all in the end. As she said, 'It really comes down to common sense.' What really worried her was that the difficulties she had had with their father might sully their ideas about marriage. She was very matter of fact about it and did her best to explain that she still loved Charles and that he loved her but that he occasionally found it hard to show his love.

There were times when William found that difficult to accept. His first few months at Eton had been disrupted by the press reports about her friendship with the rugby player Will Carling. Then shortly afterwards came the *Panorama* interview.

William's reaction devastated her. He wouldn't speak to her afterwards and when he came home all hell broke loose. He was furious that she hadn't told him that she was going to do it, furious that she had spoken badly of his father, furious that she had mentioned Hewitt. He hated the idea of everything being on television and he knew his friends would poke fun at him, which they did. He felt she had made a fool of herself—and of him.

He was so angry with her. He started shouting and crying

and, when she tried to put her arms around him, he shoved her away.

The following morning he came to her bedroom and presented her with a bunch of flowers. She was still somehow convinced, however, that he would hate her for the rest of her life, and when I saw her later there was a look of hopelessness on her face. She kept asking me, 'What have I done to my children?'

She cared more about them than anything in the world, and made a promise that in future she would always tell him what was happening and what she was doing. The anger eventually subsided and the kisses and cuddles she lavished on them helped to repair the emotional rift.

What she couldn't do, however, was give William and Harry what they really wanted, which was a happy, united family. In 1995 she asked them what they wanted for Christmas and they both said, 'For Mummy and Daddy to get back together.'

Diana burst into tears, because that was what she wanted too.

# 7
# Divorce

In her heart Diana never really wanted to separate from Charles, and she certainly didn't want to see her relationship with the Prince end in the finality of divorce.

She was stunned when, on 18 December 1995, she received a hand-delivered letter from the Queen telling her that, in 'the best interests of the country . . . an early divorce is desirable'.

Diana interpreted it as a command and took it very badly indeed. Her agony was almost physical. When she rang me on the morning that the letter arrived, she was in floods of tears and kept saying, 'No one has the right to order someone to do something like that. That has to be left to the couple in question.'

I went straight round to Kensington Palace. She was supposed to be doing a couple of engagements that day, but she wasn't up to it. She was too agitated. We made a cup of herbal tea and then went into her little sitting room to talk.

She could not understand why what she called 'this disaster' should suddenly befall her, because for months she had been asking her psychics what the future held, and they had all assured her, over and over again, that the marriage was going to survive and she had convinced herself that they knew what they were talking about. She kept saying, 'This can't be happening. They told me I would get back with Charles.'

I had been telling her all along not to put her trust in 'fortune-tellers', that it was up to her to take responsibility for what happened in her own life. Whenever she had asked me about Charles, I had told her that the rift was too wide and the damage done too great for either of them to disregard, but she still found that all but impossible to accept. She had become what I call a psychic junkie. She had convinced herself that what they were telling her was absolutely true, and as a consequence she had allowed the soothsayers to dictate her actions. She was very taken aback when their predictions proved wide of the mark.

With the future she had been told to expect abruptly taken away from her, she went into denial. Even with the Queen's letter in her hand, she was still trying to insist that it wasn't happening, that there was still a chance that there would be a last-minute reprieve.

If she had stood back and looked at her situation sensibly, and with a clear eye, she would have seen that things had gone too far—and that nothing the psychics told her was going to change that. She had been officially separated from Charles for three years and three days. Diana went so far as to count it in hours and minutes. But nothing had happened since to suggest that reconciliation was possible. If anything, the couple had grown even further apart and their differences had become entrenched.

One explosive row was over Tiggy Legge-Bourke, the daughter of one of Princess Anne's former ladies-in-waiting whom Charles had employed after the separation to help him look after William and Harry. Tiggy was a boisterous, jolly hockey-sticks sort of girl, with an earthy sense of humour who quickly established a good relationship with the boys. When they came back for weekends with Diana after spending time with their father, they would tell her how close Charles was to Tiggy, and how they had seen her popping in and out of his bedroom. There was an innocent enough explanation—once the Princess had left, the Prince became less uptight and ran a more relaxed household at Highgrove—but Diana took that as evidence that she was

having an affair with her husband. More poison was added
to an already venomous atmosphere.

'I know what they're doing,' she told me. As proof she
pointed to a photograph of Tiggy she had seen in the newspaper that morning wearing a brooch, with the Prince of
Wales's feathers made up in diamonds. I said, 'So what—
what does that prove?'

She was getting ready to go out and was smartly dressed
in a navy blue pin-stripe suit. But there was nothing elegant
about her mood. She was literally jumping up and down in
fury, and her face was getting redder and redder. 'Charles
isn't that generous,' she said. 'You know that, Simone. He
has only ever given those diamond brooches to his lovers.
And he always needs two women in tow.'

I did not know Tiggy, and I had very little idea what she
was like, so all I could do was listen as Diana talked. I stayed
with her from early morning until three o'clock in the afternoon, listening to her going on about Tiggy, trying vainly to
calm her down. At one point she was so desperate she got
out her rune stones, scattered them on the carpet and asked
them, 'Is Charles having an affair with Tiggy?' The stones
gave an inscrutable answer.

What really infuriated her, however, was Tiggy's relationship with the little Princes. She was beside herself with rage
when she read in the newspapers that Tiggy had described
them as 'my babies'. She was full of vitriol. She was almost
at fever pitch when she said to me, 'They are *my* children.
They are not Tiggy's children. She has no right to call them
her babies.'

She already loathed Tiggy for encroaching on Charles.
She really loathed her now for usurping her position in the
lives of her sons. A confrontation was brewing and it took
place at the Christmas party that the Waleses, despite their
separation, continued to hold every year for their staff. This
one took place at the Lanesborough Hotel at London's Hyde
Park Corner on 14 December, four days before she received
the letter from the Queen.

I knew what was coming because Diana had summoned

me to KP a few days earlier to tell me what she had discovered. She rang at 9 o'clock in the morning, which is not my best time and said, 'Please get over here. I need to talk to you.'

I told her, 'Don't be silly, I've got to get up, have a cup of tea and a bath.' She said, 'I can give you all the tea you can drink here.' I asked, 'What about the bath? She replied, 'You can have one here.'

I declined. Diana was very uninhibited and often invited me into her bathroom for a chat when she was soaking in the tub. Sometimes, if we were having a really good gossip, she would insist that I followed her when she went to the lavatory so as not to break the conversation. But if that was all right for Diana, it wasn't all right for me. I really didn't want to talk while I was in the bath.

An hour later, when I got to KP, Diana was even more tense than she had been on the telephone. She plied me with tea, sat down on the floor of her sitting room, where we propped ourselves against the giant cuddly toy hippopotamus.

She said, 'I have got to tell you about Tiggy. She's destroying my life and trying to take the boys away from me.' I tried to reason with her and said, 'Even if she was having an affair with Charles, what does that matter? They are Charles's children too, but they are nothing to do with Tiggy.'

She was not to be placated. She talked of warning Camilla that her royal lover was now having an affair with someone else—not as a womanly favour, but as a way of wounding Mrs Parker Bowles. I cautioned her against doing anything so rash and told her it was pointless saying anything until she had got her facts straight. Then she told me that she 'knew' that Tiggy had been pregnant with Charles's child. She had already told a lot of people and delighted in the mischief she was making, in the belief that she was hurting Tiggy as much as Tiggy was hurting her. I knew there was more ahead and it came at the Christmas party where she went up to Tiggy and said, 'So sorry to hear about your baby.'

She was implying that Tiggy had had Charles's baby aborted.

Tiggy was very upset and understandably so. She got her

lawyers to write to demand a formal apology. It was passed to
Robert Fellowes, the Queen's private secretary and Diana's
brother-in-law, who in turn wrote to the Princess. His letter
arrived on the same day as the Queen's. Diana ignored it. She
was feeling very triumphant about what she had done. All she
would say was, 'Believe me, I know what I'm talking about.'

Diana was a good detective who was always painstaking
in her quest to find out what her husband was up to. In this
case, however, she had clearly overstepped the mark, and in
doing so had created even more trouble for herself. But, as
she had done many times before, she allowed her emotions
to dominate her reasoning and became obsessed with what
she believed to be the truth, even though I pointed out to her
that she and Charles were separated and she had taken lovers
of her own.

She wasn't having any of that. Her rationale was that her
affairs were a reaction to and a revenge for Charles's affair
with Camilla, and for the way he had ignored her emotional
needs. I knew, though, as she did herself, that she needed an
all-encompassing love, in much the way she needed food and
water, which was a lot more than Charles was able to give.

His inability to provide her with the emotional support
she required did not give her licence to seek it elsewhere.
Charles took an outdated and chauvinistic view about infidelity and believed that, while it was all right for him to go
off and do his own thing, Diana should stay at home and
play the dutiful wife. She was not prepared to do that. She
maintained, quite rightly in my opinion, that she was entitled
to the same freedom he had claimed for himself. When she
used that freedom, however, it only served to give Charles
the opportunity and the excuse to spend even more time with
Camilla.

All this really upset Diana. She had played the wrong
emotional hand and in her confusion she started blaming
herself. I had never met anyone before who was so apologetic. She kept saying that everything would have worked
out if only she had been able to control her emotions, if she
had been a little older when she married, and therefore more

able to deal with the problems that marriage throws up. She blamed her upbringing and her mother.

Above all, she kept saying that if only she had been thinner, he would still fancy her and everything would have been all right. It was a symptom of the bulimia she had suffered from nearly all her adult life and which she never escaped from until a year or so before her death. Despite all the exercise she did and the care she took over her diet, which gave her a superb figure, she continued to look at herself in the mirror and see a fat person. And to her, fat equalled ugly. I kept telling her that that simply wasn't true, but she wouldn't listen. She really thought that if she had been slimmer and therefore what she considered to be 'more desirable', Charles would never have strayed in the first place.

Despite the stones she referred to in order to try and discover what the future might hold for herself, she really had misread the runes. They could only guide her but it was through her own actions that she exacerbated an already difficult situation. She thought that by telling the world in the *Panorama* interview how badly she had been treated she would somehow lure Charles back into their marriage. She had been very badly advised. Martin Bashir had hit gold and played it for all its worth. He had cajoled Diana into saying a lot more than discretion would ever have allowed. When she declared that she wanted to be an ambassador of good will and the 'queen of people's hearts', what she meant was if she were given the opportunity to help people around the globe through her charitable works. To many, however, she appeared to be staking a claim on the constitutional territory that rightly belongs to the Queen.

The Queen had clearly run out of patience with what she saw as the Princess's erratic behaviour which she felt was doing a lot of harm to the monarchy. I could see it from the Queen's perspective, and told Diana exactly what I thought: the interview had been an unmitigated disaster. Diana, however, never quite appreciated the trouble she had made for herself. That was why she was so distraught when she received the letter from her mother-in-law telling her to get a divorce.

Her mood switched backwards and forwards between anger and despair. One minute she was shouting, 'How dare the Queen consult the government and the Church of England without first consulting me? What about my feelings? This is *my* marriage—not theirs. Never mind the Royal Family—what about *my* family and *my* sons.' Then a gush of resignation would sweep over her and she would whisper, 'That's it, then, that's ditched my last chance of saving my marriage,' and burst into tears.

She telephoned the Queen at Windsor Castle and had a long talk with her. Diana told her that, despite everything, she still wanted to get back together with Charles, for the good of William and Harry but also because she still loved her husband and that she really wanted their marriage to work. It was a desperately unhappy situation—for Diana, for the Queen who clearly had a lot of sympathy for her daughter-in-law's plight, but also, more surprisingly, for Charles, to judge by the letter he wrote to Diana shortly afterwards. It was very nice, full of expressions of regret, and he made a point of saying what a sorry state of affairs this was, and how sad he felt. The couple had reached the stage when they were hardly talking to each other, but that command from the Queen had come as a shock to both of them. She showed me the letter, which was written in Charles's spidery, almost illegible hand, and from the tone of it I got the feeling that he had been knocked for six by the divorce order, just as Diana had been, and that he was as devastated as she was by the finality of it all.

It was just about Charles's last expression of affection, because as soon as the divorce negotiations began in earnest, the rows again erupted, as they usually do when lawyers become involved. By the beginning of 1996 it was getting nasty. Diana was taking a real hammering. When she called me over on the morning a sheaf of legal documents were delivered to Kensington Palace, she was hysterical.

They had just been delivered from the office of her solicitor, Anthony Julius, and they came in two volumes, each four inches thick. She had obviously read through them by the time I got there because she knew which pages to turn to. She would point things out and say, 'Look at that!'

I put my arm around her to comfort her and I could feel her shaking. Julius had told her it was normal in divorce cases; that where the couples are fighting you start off by taking a hard line and then end up thrashing out a compromise. I told her, 'These won't be the final terms, it's all quite normal in a divorce case—these are just part of the negotiations.'

She snatched her hand away and shouted, 'No!' I shouted back, 'Yes!' Diana really did feel as if the end of the world had come. She was shaking so much we had to make her a cup of a camomile drink to try and calm her down, but it didn't do much good. She sat with her elbows on the stainless steel kitchen surface with her head in her hands, grinding her teeth together in anger and frustration.

The terms of the divorce as laid out in those documents were severe indeed. They stated that if she wanted to leave the country on anything that could be described as official business, she had to get special permission. I told her that there was no benefit to be gained from losing her temper, that shouting wasn't going to help, because sooner or later she was going to have to accept that she wasn't going to be allowed to do as she pleased and set herself up as a rival court to Prince Charles—and certainly not to the Queen. I said, 'You are going to have to give up some things. You won't be allowed to take an ordinary job to earn money. You won't be allowed to become an ambassador of good will. And your movements will be restricted.'

She replied, 'They want to keep me under their thumb.'

I said, 'Of course they do—you are a loose cannon as far as they are concerned.' She agreed with that and found the idea quite amusing.

What truly terrified her, however, was the possibility that her sons would be taken away from her. It was a stark warning of just how determined the Royal Family can be when they feel their interests are being placed in jeopardy. Marriage had made Diana famous and given her a role. Now she found herself being pushed to the sidelines and without any

proper mission into which she could direct her energies.
Even her rights as a mother were being questioned.

Without really thinking about it, Diana had assumed that
she would be the one who would have a decisive say in her
children's upbringing. But William was the heir to the throne
(Harry was the spare), and that fact put the whole matter on
a completely different footing. They were not going to allow
her to have the final say. Neither of the children she had had
with the Prince of Wales was ever going to be hers and hers
alone. That was a fact of royal life and Diana had always accepted it, but the letter went a lot further than that. Her interpretation was that her sons would be taken away from her if
she didn't agree to certain things, and that she would never
see them again.

She obviously wasn't going to allow that to happen. She
was being pushed into a corner. She felt that her life was being
stripped away from her and she was petrified. Charles's sup-
porters argued that by refusing to knuckle down and do things
the royal way she had brought this on herself, but that seemed
a simplistic and decidedly old-fashioned way of looking at
things. Britain is no longer a cap-doffing, forelock-tugging society where deference takes precedence over the rights of individuals. I told her that if the worst really came to the worst she
could always take her case to the European Court of Human
Rights. She had never heard of it before, and I had to explain to
her that it was somewhere she could go if she was denied her
rights as a mother and a woman. She thought this was a great
idea, and I am certain that she would have resorted to the court
if Charles's lawyers had tried to carry out their threat.

They must have known that too, because the demand was
later quietly dropped.

A great many other issues had to be discussed, however,
and that meant any number of long days and longer nights
when we sat huddled in her sitting room or in her kitchen,
talking over her problems and existing on a diet of home-
cooked pasta, the occasional meal cooked by her chef, or a
takeaway Italian (I went to collect the food, she did the
washing up afterwards). Every day brought a new drama.

Diana would blame it on Charles, while I kept urging her to blame his lawyer, Fiona Shackleton.

Charles certainly didn't make it easy for her, though. During the negotiations, he started cutting back on her allowance and raising endless objections to the amount of money she was spending. In 1994 his friends had leaked the story of Diana's annual expenditure to *Daily Express* columnist Ross Benson, claiming that it added up to £160,000 including £91,000 for clothes and £9500 on hairdressing. It was a clear warning that the Prince was no longer prepared to subsidise what he regarded as his wife's 'extravagance', and when the lawyers began their haggling Diana was compelled to work within a budget for the first time since her marriage.

She was lucky that she got most of her clothes for free from the designers, in return for the publicity she gave them. I could not afford that kind of largesse and she got upset and told me that she could no longer afford to pay my bills for the healing sessions which we had first held at the Hale Clinic but were now conducting at Kensington Palace. When I sent her an invoice for several months of treatments she telephoned me and complained that, even though I had given her a large discount, it was more than she could afford. I said we'd discuss it the next time we met but she insisted I went over immediately.

When I arrived she was standing at the top of the stairs, waving my bill and saying, 'This is too much. Charles has restricted my money.' It was only for £600, hardly a fortune to Diana, but a lot of money to me. I wasn't prepared to stand there quibbling. I felt that friendship meant more than a few pounds, so I took the bill out of her hands and tore it up, telling her that the friendship was more important, but with healing, there has to be an exchange of energy. Chastened, Diana offered me a large and expensive sound system, still in its boxes, as compensation.

I told her, 'I've already got a sound system. She replied, 'Well, you can listen to this in another part of your flat when you're moving from room to room.' I had to tell her that my whole flat would have fitted into her drawing room and that I really couldn't accept her offer. She then asked me if there was anything else I'd like, so I told her that I'd love one of the five-wick scented candles that came in a terracotta pot set inside a wicker basket.

The telephone company was not so amenable. They wanted full payment—and Diana's phone bills really were exorbitant. They often ran to more than £5000. One month they topped £10,000. Charles couldn't understand how she could possibly spend that much money on calls. Nor could Diana, whose grasp of money and its value was always tenuous, to say the least. I could. I had been with her on the phone for hours on end, every day, and deep into the night. The telephone was like a security blanket to her, it was her lifeline to the outside world and it was costing her an absolute fortune. The solution I suggested was that, when she called a friend, she should ask them to call her back. Unfortunately, she tried it out on me and when my bills started going through the roof I had to tell her to stay on her line or I would end up being disconnected.

Charles never got to grips with Diana's spending and in the end gave up trying. That didn't stop him from piling on the pressure, that was understandable because, as heir to the Throne he had his position to protect, but it was the way he went about it that so upset Diana. She became heavily reliant on sleeping pills again. The royal lawyers tried to browbeat her, as they had Tony Armstrong-Jones when he split up from Princess Margaret, and Captain Mark Phillips when he was divorced from Princess Anne. Both advised her to stand her ground, which she did, but she found it hard going. The Tiggy episode had left a bitter residue, and the row over the future of William and Harry caused her an immense amount of suffering. Her children were her life and she could not understand how the husband whom, despite everything, she still felt so much love for, could even think of using them as a bargaining tool. She thought it was a terribly cruel thing to do, and she couldn't understand what had possessed him.

It was a measure of how unworldly Diana was. She had gone from schoolgirl to princess, a transformation of breathtaking speed that had deprived her of the chance to learn that human relations are all about compromise. She had overly romantic, unrealistic, almost childlike expectations of love and marriage, and in her naivety she wanted Charles to be something he wasn't. She was looking for a man to devote himself to her, twenty-four hours a day, seven days a week. I told her that no one, man or woman, would ever do that, that they had their own lives to live, but she wouldn't accept that.

She was bewildered by it all and clung to the thought that Charles would miss her and the children so much that he would drop Camilla and meekly return home. Yet she was quite insistent that she didn't want her children influenced by the Royal Family, or mollycoddled by an army of nannies. She couldn't have it both ways, because if Charles had agreed to a reconciliation, William and Harry would inevitably have been drawn back into the royal circle and its way of doing things, which is precisely what she didn't want. At the time, however, she couldn't see the contradiction. Her obsession with Camilla had blinded her to the realities of the situation. Diana blamed her for everything that had gone wrong and it took a long time and a lot of talking to persuade her that it couldn't all be Camilla's fault. Eventually she came round to my way of thinking and said, 'She can't be all bad—after all, she is a Cancerian like me, so she must have some good qualities.'

The muted recognition that her rival might possibly have a few good points, if only astrological (Diana was born on 1 July, Camilla on 17 July fourteen years earlier), did little to improve the dealings between the two camps. To her credit, Diana never tried to use the boys as a weapon in the divorce negotiations. She hated it when people described her as 'manipulative', and took the view that all she was doing, by whatever means were available, was to protect her position. She would not deploy William and Harry in what came to be dubbed the 'battle of the Waleses'. She wanted them with her as much as possible, but at the same time they represented the tie that she hoped might draw the family back together again, and she never tried to stop their father from seeing them.

If she saw that as a concession, he did not. Like Diana, he was convinced that he had right on his side and the longer the bargaining went on, the more intransigent Charles became. Diana wasn't the only one who found the Prince difficult to deal with at this time. So did the Queen.

She had been the one who had decided that the Waleses' marital mess had to be sorted out, and had written the letter calling for a divorce, but she continued to provide what Diana called 'a very good ear' because the Queen was always a very good listener. For the good of the monarchy, but also because she was fond of her daughter-in-law, she felt that the best solution would have been for the couple to put their differences behind them and try again. That was what Diana wanted, and that is what she told the Queen when she went to see her, which she frequently did. She would tell the Queen how much she adored her husband, and she came back from those meetings full of optimism. The fact was, however, that they didn't offer any real solution to the problems because, as kind and considerate as the Queen might have been, she had to deal with her son as well as her daughter-in-law—and Charles was becoming ever more difficult.

From what Diana told me it was obvious that Charles was not getting on with his mother. She recalled how they would have terrible arguments in front of her. Although Charles had a problem controlling his temper, he did not sink to shouting at his mother, but according to Diana he wasn't very nice to her on occasion. In fact, he was quite rude to her. He was in his mid-forties and had reached the age where he felt that he was entitled to conduct himself as he saw fit, without having to defer constantly to his mother and her advisers. They didn't see eye to eye any more. They had split into two warring factions. It was the House of Windsor versus the House of Wales and that placed Diana in a no-win situation. She wanted Charles to be faithful, and told the Queen that she would only give the marriage another chance on the condition that Charles never saw Camilla again.

Charles refused. From the conversations I had with Diana, I gathered that Charles had concluded that he should never have married Diana but should have gone against the wishes of his mother and father and married Camilla instead. He hadn't, of course. As Diana said, 'Charles is a coward.' What he was not prepared to do was compound his past weakness by resuscitating a marriage he felt he should never have entered into. It had taken him the best part of two decades to realise that he only wanted to be with Camilla, but once he reached that decision he was not going to be shifted, no matter what his mother counselled. To be with anyone else, he insisted, would be morally wrong.

At this juncture even Diana had to accept that the marriage was well and truly over, and it suddenly hit her that perhaps the Queen had been right after all and that it was time to bring it to its conclusion. It took a few months but that was quite quick for Diana, who had a habit of thinking one thing and then changing her mind shortly afterwards. But once she decided that she had reached the end of her marriage, she set about wringing the best settlement possible out of the Royal Family.

The first sums offered were paltry, and I said to her, 'I can't see that lasting you very long.' I told her that the courts were now inclined to award the wife anything up to half her husband's assets, and since Charles had the income from the Duchy of Cornwall to draw on, that added up to a great deal of money. She asked me how much the Duchy was worth, I didn't know so we did a bit of research, came to a figure and then hatched a little conspiracy together and decided that she should go for the full fifty per cent.

She eventually settled for £17 million, plus the right to see William and Harry every five weekends. Diana didn't think it was enough. Even though she wasn't very realistic about money, she knew that £17 million was a lot but wanted it to give her security for the rest of her life.

She also had to meet the legal costs of her divorce and they were enormous. She was beside herself when she got the bill from Anthony Julius. 'This is daylight robbery!' she shouted.

As is often the way with lawyers, Diana hadn't realised

how expensive it was all going to be, and when the invoice arrived it came to vastly more than she had imagined. I said to her, 'And to think that you complained when I gave you a bill for six hundred pounds.' She laughed at that but she certainly wasn't laughing about her legal fees. 'It's a rip-off,' she declared, and swore that she would never get involved with lawyers again if she could help it.

It wasn't as if the settlement was particularly spectacular. As Diana observed, a lot of women who had been married to men a lot less wealthy than Charles had walked out of their marriages with more money than she did—without the indignity of having restrictions placed on their future actions and activities. She hadn't even retained the title HRH. As part of the settlement, Diana had to agree to surrender that honorific which stands for Her Royal Highness.

Initially she was rather miffed, and said, 'This is their way of forcing me out of everything.' Stripping her of that HRH was the Royal Family's way of letting her know that she had become an outsider. Diana, however, was unbowed and made it clear that, while she may have been pushed down the pecking order, she had no intention of curtseying to her neighbour, HRH Princess Michael of Kent, who now ranked higher in the royal hierarchy. She said, 'HRH or no HRH, I'm not showing that bitch any deference.'

But once she had got over her pique at what was intended as a public humiliation, and despite what so many people said, the loss of that royal appendage didn't really bother her. We talked about it and agreed that it was only three letters—and they didn't amount to much in the modern world. She said, 'Where is the hurt? Where is the pain? I have my kids, I have my home, and the most reassuring thing is that the boys said to me when I told them I am losing the title, "You will always be Mummy."' That meant more to her than any HRH.

On 28 August 1996 her divorce became absolute. Diana immediately had her letter headings changed to 'Diana, Princess of Wales.' She insisted that she still loved Charles but the panic—of losing him and being on her own—had subsided. I sensed that she was glad it was finally over.

# 8

# Dresses for Sale

Even when wearing jeans and a baggy T-shirt, which she usually did when we were together, Diana exuded glamour.

It wasn't just me who was impressed by her style. Women around the world took note of what she was wearing and, like the Hollywood stars of old whom she so admired, she had the power to create a fashion trend, be it for low-cut evening gowns, dungarees, casual bomber jackets or, most famously, that 'Shy Di' haircut.

When she decided, therefore, to sell off a great part of her wardrobe, she wasn't just getting rid of a few unwanted dresses. She was making a clear and public declaration of independence.

That, at least, was how many people chose to interpret the sale, held at Christie's in New York in June 1997. What they didn't appreciate was that, while Diana was deliberately shedding the accoutrements of the past, she was also using it as an opportunity to show how dramatically her relations with Charles had improved.

It was to signpost their rapprochement that Diana wrote in the catalogue that 'the inspiration for this wonderful sale comes from just one person . . . our son William'.

The emphasis was on the word *'our'*. She wrote that to tell the world that she and Charles were friends again. 'Why has nobody picked up on that?' she asked.

The answer, I told her, was that no one was looking. People were more interested in the nasty details of their divorce
negotiations than Charles and Diana's attempts to patch up
their differences, and the decision to sell off a great part of
her wardrobe appeared to provide the confirmation that they
were still getting at each other. The Royal Family occasionally gives away its old clothes to charity shops, but always
discreetly and anonymously. For what they regarded as reasons of decorum, they never before offered them for public
sale. It was William who broke that tradition. It really had
been his idea, which is why Charles let the sale go ahead
without making a fuss about it.

William came up with the plan during the Easter holidays
when Diana took him and Harry to the Caribbean island of
Barbuda for a holiday. One day on the beach, he said to her,
'Mummy, you really don't need all those clothes. Why don't
you sell them for charity?'

Diana had her phone by her side even when she was lying
sunning herself on a lounger (she brought me back a sarong
with the message 'Even paradise has a telephone' printed on
it) and immediately called me to say, 'William's come up
with this wonderful idea—and he only wants ten per cent!'

He was joking, of course, and there were still any number
of problems to solve before the clothes finally came under
the auctioneer's hammer. When William made his suggestion, his parents were indeed still locked in that bruising divorce battle which had even embroiled the Queen. In April
1996, a month after Diana and the boys came back from the
West Indies, the Queen was due to celebrate her seventieth
birthday at a dinner at the Michelin-starred Waterside Inn at
Bray in Berkshire. It would have been a rare outing for the
Queen, who had seldom eaten in a public restaurant, and she
was greatly looking forward to it. It had been arranged by
Prince Edward and it was all top secret—until Diana leaked
the news to the papers. The dinner had to be relocated to
Frogmore House in Windsor Great Park, much to the fury of
the Queen who remarked, 'Thank you, Diana, for ruining yet
another day for me.'

Diana didn't think she had done anything wrong. She told me that she hadn't meant to spoil the Queen's day, and was only having a little fun at the expense of the Royal Family who she thought took everything far too seriously. 'Guess what I've done,' she said when she told me about it.

She thought she was being funny. In fact she was behaving like a child, and if she had thought about it properly, she would have realised that what she was really doing was having a subconscious dig at the family for causing her so much distress.

The main contention had been over the futures of William and Harry. She was terrified at the thought of losing them and for a long period she was unable to bring herself to exchange a civil word with their father.

Once the issues had been settled and the divorce granted, however, the Waleses found that they had more in common than their bickering had led them to suppose. What brought them together was the death of Laurens van der Post. Charles had placed great store in the advice offered by the old sage and had made him one of William's godparents. Diana was not so enamoured. She regarded him as one of those 'old fuddy duddies' who she felt exerted far too much influence on her often impressionable husband. But she knew how close Charles had been to him, and when he passed away at the age of ninety in December 1996 she had made a special effort to offer him her sympathy.

The Prince was grateful for Diana's heartfelt concern, and responded in kind. The difficult moment had passed, and they started calling each other. He even started popping round to Kensington Palace for a cup of tea and a chat. They were rebuilding a relationship that had almost been destroyed in the turmoil of their separation. When we were talking on the phone, she would often break off and say, 'My ex is here.' Charles very soon became Diana's closest male confidant and completely usurped her other male friends, who were pushed into the background.

That wasn't enough to persuade her to accept the Queen's invitation and join the rest of her family for the annual

Christmas holiday at Sandringham. Christmas was always the worst of times for Diana, especially as, since the separation, she seldom had the boys with her, and she hated the festival anyway because it stirred up the unhappiest of memories for her.

It was at Christmas time that her mother had left home and abandoned her when she was just six years old. She was never able to shake herself free from the trauma of that recollection, and the Royal Family's Yuletide get-togethers did nothing to soothe the feeling of abandonment which welled up in her as the holiday drew near.

She was not one for playing Scrooge. Always generous, she took great pleasure in buying gifts for family and friends. She gave me a hand-painted silk scarf from Bulgari, but not being a scarf person I asked her what I should do with it. She suggested framing it. She was good-humoured about it and a few days later presented me with a hamper of exotic fruits from Fortnum and Mason with the missive, 'Anything you like you can eat or juice—as long as it's healthy.'

This was all very much in the Christmas spirit, and if she had ever been allowed to organise the day as she would have liked it, I am sure she would have enjoyed it. But that was not possible. She was never allowed to have her own Christmas. Ever since her marriage, she had been forced into the role of guest (and not always a welcome one) in her mother-in-law's house and she resented it. She didn't like the company of her royal relations, didn't care for the archaic rituals that the Queen Mother had imposed and the Queen continued to uphold, and disliked the strained formality which left her feeling out of place and lonely.

Once her divorce was finalised, Diana vowed that she would never again submit herself to the 'ordeal' of a royal Christmas.

Instead, she chose to spend her first Christmas Day as a newly single woman at the K Club in Barbuda, where she had been the previous Easter with the boys. She begged me to join her, saying how much fun we would have together and how nice it would be to be able to lie in the sun and talk to each other without either being on the telephone, or curled up on the floor of her sitting room at Kensington Palace. She never mentioned paying for me, but, although it would have been far too expensive for me, the real reason I refused was that I had already made my own arrangements. I had decided to have my mother and my sister round for Christmas dinner, and, with my mother's health failing, I felt I could not be out of the country. On reflection, I wish I had gone, and it reminded me of the old adage about grasping life with both hands as the opportunity may never arise again, which of course it didn't.

With me unavailable, Diana took her 27-year-old personal assistant Victoria Mendham, whom she had been away with before, but to judge from the telephone calls I received, this time it did not turn out to be a happy arrangement.

Diana swam and played tennis and romped with the children she met on the beach, but she told me she was having an awful time because of Victoria's eating habits. She kept calling me on the phone to say, 'I don't think Victoria is happy.' She asked me, 'How would you feel having a healthy breakfast, lunch and supper while all that the person opposite you is eating is grapefruit after grapefruit with only a glass of water to drink.'

She had already noticed that Victoria was losing weight and had asked if she was bulimic, telling her that if she was she should seek professional help. She wasn't being uncaring. After all, if anyone knew about eating disorders it was Diana, who had suffered from them for most of her adult life. In Victoria's case, however, Diana became convinced that it was more a sign of obsession than any deep-rooted medical problem. Victoria had worked for the Princess for seven years, idolised her boss and was very much a Diana 'wannabee' who just wanted to be as thin as her heroine.

Diana didn't like that and it was obvious to me that their association was fast approaching its end. A few days after they got back from the Caribbean, she made the mistake of failing to cover up for Diana when she was off meeting Hasnat Khan. Her employment was abruptly terminated.

The press had got wind of her friendship with Khan, and, in an attempt to throw them off the scent, she got me to telephone Clive Goodman at the *News of the World* to say that she was still seeing Oliver Hoare. He didn't believe me and said he was going to double-check. At the same time Diana had desperately been trying to get hold of Victoria, who for once happened to be out and had no idea what was going on. When Goodman eventually got through to her and asked, 'Is the Princess seeing Oliver Hoare?' she said, 'Of course not,' which Goodman took to mean that she was seeing Khan after all. Diana was furious when she heard what had happened. As far as she was concerned, that was it. Victoria was out. Diana even asked her to pay for her own airfares to Barbuda which was childish and unkind of her, because she knew full well that Victoria couldn't afford them out of the £25,000 a year she paid her.

If the end was brutal, it was not unexpected. Victoria had become a friend but Diana cut everyone off sooner or later. It was her safety valve. Her thinking was, 'I'm going to break away before you have a chance to really hurt me.' That was her means of self-preservation, and Victoria was just one of many who suffered because of it. She was very hurt because she really admired the Princess, to the point where, when Diana gave her clothes away to charity shops or sold them to second-hand clothes stores, Victoria would go back and buy them for herself.

She would have loved to have been able to purchase one of the dresses that came for auction but that simply wasn't possible on the salary she had been earning. The clothes were truly spectacular, which only added to the price people were prepared to pay for them. Diana didn't mind who bought them, and found the idea that some might be purchased by American transvestites very amusing. All she was concerned about was that they should go for a great deal of money, which they did—the sale raised over $3,250,000 in aid of the Aids Crisis Trust.

Diana never mentioned how much they had cost to make in the first place. That simply didn't interest her. To her they were clothes, not price tags, and there were so many of them that sorting through them took several days. I had been the first person she told about her decision to sell, and we started going through them the day after she came back from Barbuda.

They were kept in her very large, white-painted dressing room which was on the ground floor of Kensington Palace. The first thing you saw on the right-hand wall was the medicine cabinet which was stuffed full of vitamins and mineral supplements.

Further along were the wardrobes which extended in an L along the back wall. There was a big mirror on the left-hand side, and a table and chair for dressmakers when they came to do the alterations, and a little window high up as it was downstairs below the garden level. It took three hours to make a preliminary stock check.

I didn't count them but there must have been well over a hundred outfits in there, including one embroidered with real pearls. One dress was just like a Cinderella ball gown. I had never seen it before and she said, 'That's because it is so not me. I couldn't go to the ball in that—I'd have turned into a pumpkin.'

I couldn't imagine Diana in rags but the fact that she chose that particular fairytale as a comparison, even in jest, was an insight into her insecurity. Each dress was like a different skin behind which she had hidden herself as she searched for a look that illustrated the way she saw herself.

A lot of the designers misread her needs and used her as a clothes horse for their wares, instead of tailoring their clothes to her psychological requirements. John Galliano, for instance, produced a dress that had looked wonderful in sketches but in the end she thoroughly detested. He had sent her the sketches with a note saying how much he would like to make an outfit for her, and because she needed a dress for the annual gala ball at the Costume Institute of New York's Metropolitan Museum in December 1996, she agreed. She showed me the sketches, and the one she chose would have looked lovely in a stiffish silk taffeta material. But when he brought it round to Kensington Palace for a fitting, she discovered that it had been made up in thin silk. She was too embarrassed to say anything to him but she told me, 'I've made a big mistake. I hate it.' She was so disappointed. I said to her, 'He probably hates women. If this is how he sees you, you would have been better off staying at home in your nightie, because that's what the dress looks like.'

It was Galliano's first dress for Dior. It was the first and last one he made for Diana. He had failed to understand that she wanted something that expressed how she wanted to see herself. It had taken her a long time to settle on that self-image and you could chart the changes in her life in those wardrobes. There was the little girl lost look, the regal period when she was trying to dress like a conventional British princess, the Hollywood stage when she discarded the Royal Family's sartorial conventions and went for flash and glamour, and Chanel-inspired outfits she wore when she was trying to emulate the cool sophistication of Jackie Onassis and Audrey Hepburn.

Number 38 in the catalogue, for instance, was what she called 'my *Roman Holiday* dress', as she thought it would have been perfect for the film in which Audrey Hepburn played a princess who slips away from her courtiers to find love with a man of her choice. We used to watch old movies together on Saturday afternoons on her large television set in a wall unit in her sitting room. Diana liked 'weepies' and *Roman Holiday* was one of her favourites. She used to say how much she envied the princess who was able to escape and be normal for a day.

Number 79 was the one she wore on her first visit to the White House in Washington where she danced with John Travolta. She had looked full of joy in the photographs that were taken of them together, but Diana didn't like it. She explained, 'I would have had such happy memories of that night if I hadn't been having such a bad time with Charles at the time.' That didn't affect its commercial value and it fetched £133,835, the highest price of all.

Number 75 belonged to what she called 'my Hollywood period'. It was tiny and tight and very Rita Hayworth. She wore it with long, black satin gloves and a diamond bracelet to the première of *Dangerous Liaisons*, and she was thrilled to find it again. She took off the jeans she was wearing and attempted to try to pull it on, but she had filled out since she had last worn it, and no matter how hard she struggled she could no longer get into it, so that went into the sale.

Number 31 had been a mistake from the beginning. It was a long, dark green dress cut in the style of a man's smoking jacket which she wore to formal dinners at Balmoral, the castle she had come to loathe. Diana was a city girl who disliked the Highlands of Scotland. She said, 'It's great if you're the outdoors kind who likes killing animals, but there was nothing for me to do there except go for walks.' The dress looked right, but it was cut very low at the back and therefore wasn't warm enough for a part of the country where, as she put it, 'it's freezing inside as well as outside in winter and summer'. She couldn't wait to get rid of that one.

Numbers 48 and 59 were the ones she called 'the curtains', because she felt that if she had lifted her hands up to say hello to somebody, they would have drawn back and her boobs would have fallen out. When she wore Number 48 she always thought that she was in danger of falling down, and when she tried on Number 23 she started laughing so hard that she almost fell over. It looked like a child's birthday cake, with all the icing and pink rosettes and the pink ribbon around it. There were quite a few others that prompted her to wonder, 'How on earth could I have worn something like this?'

Some of them dated from the time when she was trying to please the Queen Mother, who had taken it upon herself to advise Diana as to how she should dress. In her effort to fit

into the Royal Family, she had listened to her suggestions
and bought clothes she thought they would approve of. In
this case, however, imitation was not the sincerest form of
flattery. As Diana said, 'The Queen Mother had terrible
taste, which is why I looked so awful.'

Number 28 was the colour of my old bedroom at home
which I had painted a garish blue and provoked my mother
to remark, 'All you need now are silver stars on the ceiling
and it's an Indian restaurant.' Number 43 looked like white
chocolate whirls and Number 34 was old-fashioned and very
Queen Mumish, which is why she didn't like it.

The hats, too, were greatly influenced by the old matri-
arch. Most modern women only wear hats on special occasions, but, as the wife of the heir to the throne, almost every
occasion was special and Diana was compelled to wear them
nearly all the time. That was the royal rule and it was the
Queen Mother who enforced it by example, stern looks and
barbed comment. Diana had tried to bring a touch of indi-
viduality and style to her headwear, but when we went
through the boxes and started putting them on she had to admit that some of them made her look ridiculous—and me a
lot worse.

She wanted to present me with one of her dresses and
said, 'Take any one you want.' I told her that just one of them
would take up my whole wardrobe because, like Diana, I
had hung onto a lot of clothes I knew I would never wear
again, including too many from the Seventies. And besides,
none of Diana's outfits would have fitted me. It would be like
fitting a square peg into a round hole, even if I had had them
altered. 'Then take some shoes,' she said. She loved the ones
hand-made for her by Jimmy Choo with pointed toes and
low heels, and she had enough of them to satisfy Imelda
Marcos. I tried a pair on but they didn't fit. As I pointed out,
'Your feet are bigger than mine.'

We had a lot of fun dressing up, but I noticed how carefully she handled everything, including those items that
made us laugh. She called them 'my outer layer', and looked
after them accordingly. After she had tried on a hat or a

dress, she would return it neatly back to its box or onto its hanger, making sure that it wasn't flattened or wrinkled, before going on to the next one. Some she covered in plastic bags, and she made sure that each one had enough room to 'breathe'. She was quite fanatical about her clothes and, although she would occasionally lend them out to girlfriends, she got very annoyed if they weren't returned promptly and in pristine condition.

Even Carolyn Bartholomew, whom she had shared a flat with in Earls Court in West London before her marriage, and who was probably her oldest friend, wasn't spared her displeasure. Carolyn had borrowed a particularly beautiful dress with a bolero top to wear at a wedding, and had then hung onto it for quite a while afterwards. That had irritated Diana. When she decided to sell it in the auction, she called Carolyn to demand its return—and was very angry when it came back looking as if it had been dumped in the back of a truck.

'She's obviously worn it more than once—and look at the state it's in,' she complained. Diana always had her clothes spruced by specialist dry cleaners, not by an ordinary High Street firm, as Carolyn clearly had used. She immediately sent it off to her own cleaners and then put it straight into the sale (it was on page 116 of the catalogue). She wanted nothing more to do with it (or with Carolyn whom she stopped talking to for a while).

Even so, when it came to actually parting with so much of her wardrobe she became quite upset and tearful, because every one of those dresses represented a part of her life and her development as a woman. She had become sentimentally attached to them, and I had to urge her on saying, 'OK, there were two huge cupboards full of things that we know you will never wear again. This is the time to have a clear-out and move on with your life. And besides, I'm sure that is what William wants you to do.'

She agreed, and the pile started getting larger and larger. When we were finished we turned our attention to the medicine cabinet. We went upstairs, had a cup of tea and then came back down again with some bin liners and filled one with bottles and packets of pills and capsules. We chucked away thousands of pounds worth of potions that she didn't need. I kept telling her, 'You don't need this—and you certainly don't need that. All you should be taking is a multivitamin, some vitamin C because you are always on the go, and some Evening Primrose oil to help your premenstrual tension.'

It really was time to get shot of the past. She didn't need all those remedies, which were nothing more than a prop to ease her marital unhappiness. And she didn't need all those frocks and gowns. The time for wearing them was past. She was a single woman again. At long last she was able to follow her own taste, and that had become more simple and refined than it ever had been when she was trying to dress for her role as a member of the Royal Family.

# 9
# Falling in Love Again

After the Prince and Princess of Wales were granted the decree absolute that ended their marriage, Diana was exceptionally upbeat and nothing could pull her down from that. She was happy that, after all the tribulations, she was a free woman at last. She celebrated by spending the night with Dr Hasnat Khan at Kensington Palace. It was the first time they made love together.

The final months of her marriage had been marked by wrangles over money, the row over her title, her almost paranoid conviction that the security forces were plotting against her, and her fear that she might lose custody of her sons. All those woes evaporated as soon as the divorce came through—and Hasnat at last allowed her to take him into her bed.

I was at Kensington Palace on the afternoon the annulment came through. She was waiting for Hasnat to arrive and she was charged with excitement and expectancy.

I was round at KP the next morning shortly after he left, and I found her light of spirit and wreathed in smiles.

Her eyes were as bright as diamonds.

I thought, 'Good luck to you.' It was what she had been looking forward to with such anticipation. After all, she had been waiting long enough to bring to its natural fulfilment her relationship with the man she was so utterly in love with.

She had known Khan for ten months, but he had refused to

consummate their liaison while she was still married. Once that impediment had been removed, he felt free of the moral constraints that had kept the Princess at a demure distance.

It was a relief for Diana. She made no secret of how much she adored him. She kept telling me, 'He's so nice—and his eyes are so intelligent. He really is my Mr Wonderful.'

This was no casual fling. Despite the unhappiness she had endured as the wife of the Prince of Wales, she wanted to marry Hasnat. She contemplated converting to Islam. More than anything, she wanted to have his baby, and a daughter in particular. Khan is a Pakistani but that did not concern her. She thought that the combination of ethnic backgrounds would make for a beautiful child.

And she was so taken by the prospect that she was quite prepared to give birth outside of wedlock.

I was shocked by the idea. I warned her, 'This is not *EastEnders*. You are the mother of the future King of England.'

She just looked at me in that baleful way of hers, but I was not going to be deterred. I said, 'You know I'm making sense. This is something you really can't get away with.'

At the end of 1996 her friend, Jemima, the daughter of the financier Sir James Goldsmith and wife of the Pakistani cricket legend Imran Khan (no relation of Hasnat), had given birth to a son. Diana said that if it was all right for Jemima to marry someone from the Indian subcontinent and have children, then it was all right for her.

I said, 'But Jemima is married. It might be in vogue to have illegitimate kids—but it's not the done thing for someone in your position. If you're married it's different. Then you can think about it and work it all out.'

The truth was that Diana simply hadn't thought the matter through. Hasnat was a Muslim with a very strict idea of how women should behave, but she put that out of her mind. She was being carried away by her emotions. She had been almost from the first moment she met him back in the autumn of 1995 when I was in hospital in St John's Wood having a hysterectomy. That fascinated Diana, who had developed a great interest in medicine. She sent me flowers, telephoned me, and said she was coming to visit because she wanted to know all the details of my operation.

I wasn't the only friend in need of medical care, however. One of Diana's acupuncturists was Oonagh Toffolo, and her husband Joe was suffering from a heart condition. In the same week that I was taken into the St John and St Elizabeth Hospital, he was taken into the Royal Brompton in Chelsea for a triple heart bypass. The operation was performed by the distinguished heart surgeon, Sir Magdi Yacoub.

Diana was engrossed. She had read up on the technical side and now she wanted to know what it was like to be on the receiving end of the surgeon's scalpel. Joe's condition was a lot more serious than mine, and she explained that she wanted to be at his bedside, to hold his hand, and practise the healing techniques she and I had been working on together. And when Sir Magdi came by to check on his patient, she was waiting to bombard him with queries. He was very patient and forthcoming, even though every time he gave her an answer, Diana fired off another batch of questions.

That was just her way. She wanted to give what comfort and help she could to an ill friend. And she wanted to know every last detail about the treatment he was receiving. All the while, of course, she was also looking for something within herself and when Hasnat Kahn came by she was certain that she had found it.

He was a 36-year-old doctor from near Lahore in Pakistan, who was studying for his Ph.D. in London and had assisted Sir Magdi during Joe's heart surgery. First impressions are very important and Diana was dazzled by him. He was the senior registrar at the Brompton and did calls at Harefield, the heart transplant hospital. He was someone who cared about his patients, had a fantastic bedside manner, and was genuinely dedicated to humanity—everything, in fact, that Diana admired in a man.

She told me later that when he walked in and saw Diana, he didn't know where to put himself. He recognised her but felt embarrassed, and for a moment was undecided as to whether to stay or go. After a moment's thought he elected to stay and get on with the job in hand. He checked Joe over and answered all Diana's questions, in a clear, simple way that she could understand.

The next day Diana went back to the hospital and happened to bump into him in the lift. He wouldn't look at her face initially, and instead stared down at his shoes. Diana was looking down too, because whenever she was attracted to someone she had a habit of becoming flustered and she didn't want him to see her blush.

British hospital lifts move very slowly, however, and after a couple of minutes studiously avoiding each other's eye contact, she looked up and said, 'You can't spend the whole journey looking at your shoes.'

He looked up, their eyes met and, as Diana recalled, 'Something went ping inside. His eyes were so warm and comforting.'

There was nothing on earth that would have kept Diana away from the Brompton Hospital after that. She phoned me up to apologise, explained that she wouldn't be able to visit me as planned, and said that she was sending me some flowers instead. I knew straightaway what had happened. I told her I had recently had a dream about a dark handsome man coming into her life. She just laughed and said that she wasn't going to talk about anything like that on the telephone.

I didn't see Diana for another month. I had suffered complications and when we did meet she wanted to know all the details. She kept prodding my stomach and asking how it felt and demanding to see the scar. When I showed it to her she was horrified and said she was sorry for not coming to see me, and that if she had known how unwell I was she would have come over to do the shopping for me. She was babbling on like that until I said, 'Hold on a minute—what about you, what about this man you've met?'

She was bursting to tell me. Up until then she had kept it a secret from everyone apart from Oonagh, who had been there at the inception. She replied, 'Oh Simone, he's my Mr Wonderful! He's very shy really, but he's very interesting and he gets me thinking.' 'About what?' I asked. She said,

'About our souls and about God. He asks me lots of questions about my beliefs, my spiritual beliefs.'

She was clearly smitten and in a very different manner to the way she was with Hewitt, Hoare and any of the other men she had been involved with, including Prince Charles. Joe Toffolo had left the Royal Brompton, but Diana continued her visits to the hospital. That was something she had been doing for years and it grew out of her spiritual curiosity about life and death. She felt that there were so many lonely people in hospital who needed someone to take an interest in what remained of their lives. She would go there after visiting hours to sit and talk to those patients who she believed needed comfort and reassurance, especially those who didn't have any visitors of their own.

Afterwards she would sit and talk at great length with Hasnat in the little room where he slept when he was on night duty. The hospital knew she was there and never raised any objections. After a while, however, her visits were becoming so frequent that it started attracting attention. So she decided to resort to disguises.

She was always complaining that she was unable to go out and do ordinary things without being pestered constantly by photographers and I had been urging her for ages to try and disguise herself. She had dismissed that out of hand. She was afraid of what she called 'the awful repercussions' if she were ever caught. But the more she wanted to see Hasnat, the more it played on her mind and eventually she decided, 'Why not?'

The first time she tried one out was in the August of 1996. I arrived at KP just after lunch where I was met at the door by a girl I had never seen before. In a prim and proper voice she said that she was the Princess's new secretary and would I like to have a cup of tea? She followed me up the stairs into the sitting room where she suddenly twirled around, tore off her wig, and shouted, 'It's me!'

She was wearing glasses, pumps, a blouse, a dark skirt that came to just below the knee, with a jacket to match. And to cap it all, there was that long, dark wig. It wasn't just the clothes. Always a good mimic, she spoke in a different manner and her body language had changed. She had become a different person. I would never have guessed it. She looked like the secretary she had been pretending to be.

I felt that all my blood had rushed to my feet and I must have changed colour because Diana insisted on lacing my tea with sugar, something I never normally take. She told me that she had tried it out on William and Harry and had even managed to fool them for a few minutes, and she reckoned that if she could dupe her own sons, there was a good chance she would be able to hoodwink anybody else.

We had to practise a great deal first. We decided what she needed to wear and I told her to do her make-up in a more yellowy way, the way a brunette would, to use red lipstick rather that her usual pink one, and more of a peach blusher in order to tone with a darker look.

The most important item was the wig. The first one she got was dark, long and plain, but after Sam McKnight had cut and styled it properly it looked like a real head of hair. Another was a shoulder-length bubble, cut with a fringe and looking as if the person had naturally curly hair. The third was elegant and mid-brown. She would have been recognised if she was blonde but with a dark wig and the make-up to match, her whole persona changed.

The first time she tried it out in public was when she went to Kensington High Street to buy a life-size inflatable sheep.

As part of his work for his Ph.D. Hasnat was experimenting with lambs' hearts. When one, then another of the lambs unfortunately died, Diana donned her disguise and went out to buy him a card. The one she picked had a picture of nine sheep on the front and a caption asking, 'Which sheep do you prefer?' Inside was the picture of another sheep, wearing lipstick and ribbons and the message, 'I didn't know you fancy sheep.' She also bought a blow-up sheep.

She sent the card to Hasnat and gave him the inflatable toy. Hasnat usually had a very good sense of humour but not on this occasion. He didn't think it was the least bit funny, which only made Diana laugh even more. That was a good sign, because when she was younger she would get very upset if her gifts were rejected or her humour failed to provoke the right reaction. Now, at last, she was finding the confidence to deal with these everyday rejections, even if the joke was in dubious taste.

The disguises also helped. They gave her a taste of the independence she had not enjoyed since she was nineteen years old and was first drawn into the royal spotlight. For the last fourteen years she had been a spectator at her own life, seeing herself through the warped prism of television, books and newspaper articles, deprived of the simple liberty to stroll down a street without attracting a horde of pushing, shoving, shouting cameramen. The wigs changed that. For the first time since she became a Princess, she was able to stroll through the park, ride on buses, travel on the Underground, go window-shopping and meet the man she cared so much for.

At first meeting, Hasnat did not appear to be Diana's type. Her previous paramours had been either very good-looking or well-connected and usually both. Hasnat was neither. He came from a completely different culture, a continent away, and his background was middle-class. He would be described as an 'Omar Sharif look-alike', but it required a good imagination to see the similarity.

Whereas Diana was always very careful about what she ate, he seemed to exist almost entirely on junk food. She wanted him to be healthier but he wouldn't listen. He was particularly fond of Kentucky Fried Chicken and she was forever complaining that her car stank of it. She kept spraying it with natural air freshener and when that didn't work, she insisted on travelling with the windows open.

He smoked constantly and his one-bedroom flat in Chelsea was a tip. Although he was thirty-six years old with a good job, he earned very little money and lived like a student. His room was strewn with papers and he rarely bothered to tidy up. Diana complained that there was 'so much stuff growing in the dirty cups that it looked like a laboratory'. It so offended her sense of decorum that she pulled on rubber gloves and gave the bedsit a thorough spring-clean. Hasnat didn't seem to notice and remained as untidy as ever.

She didn't care. (Whereas some women try to change their men only to become irritated and despondent when they fail, Diana didn't make that mistake.) She accepted Hasnat for what he was—as he did her.

She had been through gut-wrenching roller coaster romances with James Hewitt and Oliver Hoare. She didn't want that any more. She wanted a normal relationship with a normal person who was gallant, and who did not insist on controlling her—like Hewitt, Hoare and Charles. Hasnat wasn't like that. He didn't regard her as a trophy, and, in those early months when she was still married to the Prince of Wales, it certainly wasn't sex that kept him interested. She said, 'He's the only man who's ever treated me as a human being.'

Slowly but surely she was settling into a caring relationship where she felt comfortable and at ease with herself. She was captivated by everything he had to say, and she enjoyed the simple way he entertained her.

After she had invited him to KP for dinner a couple of times, he took her to his local fish and chip shop. They ate them straight out of the paper the assistant had wrapped them in. 'You can't believe how delicious they were,' Diana said afterwards. I could. They had been an occasional part of my diet when I was younger. That Diana should find it so novel was an indication of just how remote and pampered royal life can be.

He also took her to an inexpensive, unfashionable and affordable Italian restaurant near the Brompton Hospital. There was no one there she knew, none of the other diners appeared to recognise her in her wig, and the food, she said, 'was as good as San Lorenzo's—and a lot cheaper'. She really enjoyed it. A plate of pasta and a glass of wine with a friend is nothing extraordinary, but she was having the kind of fun she had been denied when she was younger: eating, drinking, going to Ronnie Scott's jazz club in Soho. And she liked the fact that Hasnat, despite having little money, always insisted on paying the bill.

After those unpretentious meals they would sometimes return to KP, with Khan hiding on the back seat covered in the blanket she had started keeping in the boot especially for that purpose. He became a regular visitor to the palace, sometimes staying the night in a spare room, always leaving early in the morning before Paul Burrell came on duty.

On the evenings when he was on call, she would accompany him to whichever hospital he was working at and spend the night in his little room. She always took a book with her to read when he was called away on his rounds. When his duties allowed and they were alone, they would snuggle up together on his small single bed, kissing, cuddling, talking and getting to know each other.

Then, in the hour just before dawn, she would make her surreptitious exit by climbing out through the window. One morning she got stuck. At 7.30 a.m., when she at last made it back to Kensington Palace, she telephoned me to recount how her wig had caught on the sill and that, when she did manage to free herself, it was hanging half on, half off, and mainly over her eyes. She thought the incident hilarious. Her laughter started with giggles and ended in great snorts of uncontrollable mirth. Hasnat derived as much amusement from moments like that as she did, and that drew them ever closer.

She really appreciated the way he began to involve her in his family. When he went to KP she let him use her telephone to ring his parents in Pakistan. At first, he said he had to go and buy a phone card, she said, 'Don't leave—use my telephone.' His calls always lasted a long time and Diana would get quite impatient waiting for him to finish. She tried to distract him by playing her grand piano, or pretending to do a strip tease, but he took no notice of her. On several occasions she rang me on her mobile and held it next to him as he chatted away in Urdu, unmindful of what she was doing.

She didn't mind. In fact, she found it all rather endearing.

Since the death of her father, Diana felt that she had no real family of her own to call on. Her relations with her brother were fractious, while the bitter disputes with Charles had led to a rift with her sisters Sarah and Jane, whose husband, Robert, in his role as the Queen's private secretary, had been delegated the impossible task of trying to force Diana to toe the royal line. That left only her mother, but Diana was unable to bring herself to forgive the woman she believed had deserted her.

Some people grow up, leave home and never look back. Diana was not one of them. Her own family had singularly failed to give her the security she needed when she was a child. She thought she might find it now with Hasnat's. He took her to see his uncle, Omar, who lived in Stratford-on-Avon with his English wife, Jane, and they became close.

Every time she went there and had something to eat, she insisted on pulling on the rubber gloves to do the washing up and clean the kitchen. When Jane was expecting twins, Diana bought nappies and clothes—always top of the range, from places like Harrods. She also brought a double pushchair, but one of the twins was stillborn so Diana went back to the shop and changed it herself.

What really intrigued her was the way Jane, a lawyer by profession, had managed to cross the ethnic divide and marry into a Pakistani family. Jemima Khan had done the same and Diana became quite friendly with the tycoon's daughter, who, at the age of twenty, had defied the conventions of her social class and wed a Pakistani sportsman twenty-two years her senior. She was forever asking Jemima what it was like to be married to someone from a different religion and a completely different cultural background. In February 1996, accompanied by Jemima's mother, Lady Annabel Goldsmith, and her friend, Lady Cosima Somerset, she flew to Lahore by private jet and spent a few days visiting the cancer hospital Imran had started, chatting to his sisters and immersing herself in the atmosphere of a close-knit family so unlike her own.

She would have liked to have met Hasnat's relations, but

after a long telephone conversation with his uncle, Professor Jawad Khan, an eminent heart surgeon who had treated Earl Spencer at the Brompton Hospital after he suffered a stroke in 1978, it was decided to postpone that get-together. At the time the Khans did not know of Hasnat's involvement with the Princess, and Jawad pointed out that, with the press taking inevitable interest in her trip, this was hardly the most opportune moment to drive the 120 miles from Lahore to their family home in Jhelum to introduce herself.

Denied the opportunity of a face-to-face meeting, Diana chose instead to start a correspondence with Hasnat's grandmother, Appa. In 1995 she sent her a picture of herself and her sons as a Christmas card, much to the bewilderment of the old lady. She couldn't understand why the famous Princess who, up until then, had been no more than a name in the local newspapers should have taken the trouble to send her a Christian seasonal greeting. The reason became clear in the ever-longer letters Diana started writing to her in which she revealed her admiration for her grandson. She was preparing the ground. As she kept telling me, 'I can't wait to meet the family that produced this wonderful man.'

She was obviously trying to push their relationship along, but I didn't see that as manipulative. It was just the way she was. In her childlike way, she wanted to know all about the family of the man she had fallen in love with.

Her first attempt at bringing East and West together was not an outstanding success, however. The only thing Hasnat ever asked from her was to help two friends from his home town who had come to London in the hope of doing some business. Diana was more than willing to oblige, and invited them to Kensington Palace to meet Sir Richard Branson, the entrepreneur founder of Virgin Airlines.

Because they both spoke English, Diana had imagined that they were both worldly and educated like Hasnat. It turned out to be two humble men who had never been out of Pakistan before. When Diana walked in wearing a short mini skirt, they couldn't keep their eyes off her legs. She kept crossing her legs and trying to cover them with her hands, feeling very embarrassed.

She compounded her discomfort by asking them if they wanted one of the bacon sandwiches she was making without considering that, as Muslims, they were not allowed to eat pork.

The whole thing was ridiculous, made even more so by the fact that they didn't have the faintest notion of what they wanted to do. Sir Richard spoke to them and asked what they wanted. These two men (she called them Tweedledum and Tweedledee after the characters in *Alice in Wonderland*) had come straight from the bazaar to Kensington Palace. It transpired that all they wanted was for someone to set them up in business, any kind of business, in Pakistan. Because of Diana's involvement, Branson was very polite but he wasn't prepared to give them any money. He told them, 'I think you need to learn about business first.'

I would have been furious at being put in this situation, but Diana saw the funny side. She certainly didn't blame Hasnat. At this stage in their relationship she was prepared to forgive him anything. The two men were his friends, he had been trying to do them a favour, and that was good enough for her. She was determined to ingratiate herself into his life and, when she finally met his grandmother, she felt that she had made the breakthrough that would result in marriage.

Nanny Appa had arrived in England with Hasnat's thirteen-year-old cousin Mumraiz to stay with Omar and Jane. Diana drove down to Stratford-on-Avon to meet them. It was July 1996, when the Waleses filed their decree nisi and Diana announced that she was giving up most of her charity work to a chorus of criticism. Appa cooked her a simple dinner of rice, salad and lightly curried pulses. A few days later, Diana invited the grandmother for afternoon tea at KP. Now it was Diana's turn to prepare the food and once again she made the wrong choice.

It wasn't bacon sandwiches this time—she had remembered that lesson from her meeting with Tweedledum and Tweedledee—but smoked salmon sandwiches which she

Diana said this dress made her feel lopsided and would have made a good pair of curtains. It eventually went under the hammer at Christie's in New York.

When we looked at this dress Diana said it reminded
her of some Wedgwood crockery.

Body beautiful. John F. Kennedy Jr. in New York.

LEFT Will Carling
BELOW James
Hewitt

Hasnat Kahn

Diana and Charles put on a show of togetherness for
Prince William's first day at Eton College.

The most frightening moment of her life was when she had to walk across a field with landmines.

VOGUE

OCT
£2.90

1961-1997

It was not the first time she had been on the cover of
*Vogue*, but it was to be the last. In October 1997 the fashion
magazine paid tribute to Diana.

made herself in her little kitchen. Unfortunately, that proved to be almost as bad. The old lady, who was on her first trip outside Pakistan, had never tasted smoked salmon before and was horrified by the notion of eating what she described as 'raw fish'. Instead she confined herself to nibbling suspiciously at the egg and cheese sandwiches.

Notwithstanding that gastronomic setback, the two women got on well. Appa called Diana 'my little tigress' and appeared to give her approval to the Princess's relationship with her favourite grandson, which was consummated the night her divorce became absolute.

With the friendship now an affair, Diana was keen for Hasnat to become involved with her boys. She felt that, now that she had met his family, it was only right that he should meet hers. It was a massive step forward to introduce him to William and Harry, but it was part of the reciprocity she believed would draw them closer together.

The introductions took place over dinner at KP on a weekend when the boys were home from school. She warned them beforehand that she had met someone she liked very much. It was the first time she had ever done that, and she was very nervous. So was Hasnat.

Afterwards Diana asked William and Harry what they thought of him. William said, 'He seems very nice, and if you're happy with him get on with it.'

Harry was not so enthusiastic.

In that first flush of romance Diana had convinced herself that she had found the man with whom she wanted to spend the rest of her life. He was scrupulously honest and never lied to her. She had this incredible respect for his work, and for his loyalty and closeness to his family. None of her lovers had that closeness with their extended families. She thought all families should be like that; close knit and supportive of each other. When she had just been with him, she had a sparkle in her eye that came from an inner brightness.

He was too independent to bend himself to Diana's wishes, however. She asked him to move into Kensington Palace. We discussed which room he would have and Diana

suggested Charles's old one, but Hasnat rejected the suggestion out of hand.

He wouldn't even accept her offer to buy him a mobile
telephone, and the only way she could make contact with
him when he was on duty was via his pager. That annoyed
Diana, who was addicted to mobiles and liked to speak to
people when the fancy took her, which in Hasnat's case was
very frequently. In desperation, she started telephoning the
hospital where he was working and leaving messages with
the receptionist. She would say, for instance, 'It's Dr Allegra
here. I am trying very hard to get hold of Dr Kahn. I have
just flown in from America and I am only here for a few days
to give a lecture, and I need to get hold of him before I go
back.' She would never leave a number, but he knew who it
was. He didn't mind at first, but after a while he started finding her persistence a trifle tedious.

What really upset him, though, was the publicity their affair eventually attracted. It is astonishing that it had gone unnoticed for so long, but that wasn't going to last indefinitely
and the story finally broke in November 1996.

It was Diana's effort to further her lover's career that led
to the revelation. The previous month, while in Rimini in
Italy to accept a humanitarian award, she had met Dr Christiaan Barnard, the surgeon who had performed the world's
first heart transplant and asked him to find Khan a job in
South Africa so that they could move there and set up home
together. 'There is no doubt in my mind that she was very
much in love with Khan,' Barnard said. Shortly after, she
had flown off to Sydney to be the guest of honour at a dinner
to raise money for the cardiac research institute founded in
the memory of Victor Chang, Khan's tutor when he had
studied in Australia. Chang had been kidnapped and killed in
a bungled ransom bid in 1991.

It was while she was in Australia that the *Sunday Mirror*
put two and two together and broke the story of Diana's love
for the 'shy caring heart surgeon', adding, 'and she wants to
be his wife.'

Hasnat was displeased with Diana for interfering in his

professional life and angered to find his name was plastered over the newspapers. What really upset him, however, was her response. The story was accurate but Diana, concerned by his reaction, chose to deny it. She contacted Richard Kay, the royal reporter of the *Daily Mail* with whom she had had a long and very close friendship, and told him the suggestion was so much 'bullshit'.

It was the wrong thing to have done. I told her, 'This is absolutely dreadful—you've really upset the guy.' To be found out was one thing. But to be dismissed in such a brusque and offhand way was bound to wound his pride. It was probably the most insulting thing anyone can say about anyone else. I said, 'Look, Hasnat is very sensitive about what you feel about him and you can't go and say something like that to Richard and have him quote you.'

Hasnat (clearly agreed with me because he) told her straight that he couldn't cope any more, and then refused to speak to her for several weeks afterwards. He was doing his Ph.D., he needed to concentrate, and he didn't want to watch his back all the time.

His silence sent Diana into a terrible tizzy. When I went to see her, she looked a mess. Her panda eyes were black from running mascara and swollen from crying.

We cooked the food in the microwave and went into her little sitting room to talk. She told me how she had been se riously considering changing her religion and becoming a Muslim in order to make herself acceptable to his family. She told me that she was prepared to give up everything for Hasnat, but he wouldn't do the same for her, that he just wanted an uneventful life. Then she started blaming the media for her woes. I pointed out that if she wasn't who she was, there would be no media attention—but that didn't register. She was crying because she was feeling hopeless and sorry for herself. I kept telling her not to worry and she kept saying I didn't understand. I said I did, because there is hardly a woman who hasn't been in a similar situation. I told her, 'He needs a break, of course he will contact you again, but you must leave him alone for a while.'

That wasn't an easy thing for her to do. She was feeling suffocated by distress, and, in the attempt to break loose from her anguish, started going on long, tiring runs through the park and the side streets around Kensington Palace, pausing only to fire off another call to me on her mobile. She was on the phone constantly, but that was fine by me. As I pointed out, Hasnat was an intensely private man who couldn't stand being hounded, and it was better that she pester me than call him.

That helped, but only up to a point. Convinced that she was about to be dumped, her obsessive traits reasserted themselves. She went into one of her stalking modes and started following Hasnat, just as she had followed Hewitt and Hoare, and was greatly relieved that he never went anywhere that would have upset her.

When he did eventually call, she apologised and they made up.

The row had left its indelible mark on their relationship, however, and things were never quite the same again. Hasnat became ever more wary of the publicity that his association with Diana would attract, while she became increasingly edgy at the thought that their affair wasn't going to end in the marriage she was hoping for.

She asked Imran Khan to act as an intermediary. She also involved Martin Bashir, reasoning that as an Asian himself, he would be able to understand Khan's concerns while at the same time be able to put across her point of view and smooth out the rifts. That didn't work out very well. She kept asking Bashir, 'What makes Hasnat tick? How can I understand a man that is so independent and so chauvinistic in some ways?' but the answers he gave weren't very enlightening.

It was then Burrell's turn to act as the middle man. He would meet Hasnat at the appropriately named Princess of Wales public house across the road from the Brompton Hospital to pass on her messages and convey his replies back to Kensington Palace, but that only seemed to complicate an already awkward situation. She was anxious to learn everything she could about his religion and his family in her effort to find out what had moulded him into the man he had become, but Hasnat was very self-contained and found it difficult to empathise with Diana's neediness. She kept asking him questions about himself but he either couldn't or wouldn't answer them.

That drove her to seek more guidance from Imran and Jemima, but their union was hardly the best example. Imran had told his young wife that, while she may have been a society girl in London, when she was in Pakistan she was going to have to toe the family line. She would live a simple life, without luxuries. She would live with his family and have his babies. She was not allowed out without an escort, which was very difficult for a young woman used to the freedoms of the West, and Diana became convinced that the marriage wouldn't last. She was right—the Khans eventually parted in 2004 and Jemima took up with the actor Hugh Grant.

Recognising the problems that came with marrying into a foreign culture did not deter Diana, however. She had convinced herself that it would be different with Hasnat, that somehow they could iron out the differences and make their relationship work. She was not dealing with reality. He wasn't going to change and there was no way she would have stayed locked up in a three-up two-down house, having children. We talked about that, but even when she agreed with me, she kept hanging onto her fairytale dream. She was determined to marry him and that so clouded her judgement that in May 1997, she flew to Pakistan to seek his parents' approval.

The meeting took place at the Khan compound in Model Town in Jhelum, Diana dressed demurely in ethnic attire. She spent an afternoon drinking tea and eating cakes with Hasnat's mother, Naheed, his father, Rasheed, and assorted aunts, uncles, nieces, nephews and cousins. It was all very polite but it was not a success. Naheed took a possessive mother's view of her son's involvement with the glamorous Western woman, and decided that she was unsuitable. To her Islamic way of thinking, Diana was tarnished goods.

Hasnat was furious when he learned about the visit. He

had never mentioned marriage to his parents and believed that Diana had overstepped the mark by once again going to see them behind his back. He was starting to feel trapped. Regardless of what Diana saw in him, he remained what he had always been—a humble doctor from Pakistan who was happy enough to live in London but saw no reason why he should fall in with Diana's Western ideas about love and marriage. She had collected a £17 million divorce settlement which would have allowed them to live in luxury for the rest of their lives, but Hasnat had no desire to become a kept man, and did not even like accepting presents from her. He was flattered by the attention she lavished on him but he didn't like the publicity she attracted or the way she was trying to take over his life.

On top of that, he was also what Diana and I called a 'commitmentphobe', someone who found it difficult to settle down. He had been engaged three times before—twice to women of his parents' choosing, once to a girl of his own choice—but had always broken them off, which Diana thought was odd. And so it was, for someone of his background and age. It struck me that Hasnat the heart surgeon was interested in other people's hearts—but not his own or Diana's.

Ideally, he wouldn't have entered into the relationship in the first place. It was Diana who had forced the pace. I do not doubt that he loved Diana, but only in his own way. And when the going became too hectic he simply bailed out.

The affair did not come to a dramatic end, however. In July 1997, he finally told Diana that they had to stop seeing each other. But she remained in touch with his family, and, right until the end of her life a few weeks later, she still nurtured the hope that they would get back together again.

# 10

# Faith

Like a child, Diana was constantly asking questions about life and its spiritual meaning. She often said to me, 'There has to be more to our existence than actually meets the eye.'

She wanted to know why we are here and, just as importantly, what awaits us afterwards. (They are questions we have all pondered. They first press to mind when we are very young.) William and Harry, for instance, often used to ask her: 'Where do we come from?', 'Where is heaven?', 'Who is God?'

Diana was not one of those parents who retreated behind platitudes. She was one of the most spiritually attuned people I have known and she had a profound belief in God and good and evil, not merely as words but as powerful forces that directly affect us all.

Unquestioning belief was not her way, however. She always wanted to know more, and when she realised that the Church of England she had been brought up in could not satisfy her needs, her thirst for knowledge inspired her to study other faiths.

The spiritual net she cast was wide and included Islam, Roman Catholicism, Hinduism, and the esoteric teachings of Sufism and the Kabbalah. She even showed an interest in the ancient nature cults where the divinity was feminine, and where, she observed, 'the vulva was worshipped instead of

reviled', as it has so often been in other religions, including
Christianity.

Hardly a day passed when we did not discuss some aspect
of what she had been reading about, and I was astonished by
the breadth of her knowledge. She was always looking for
divine guidance. She didn't just scratch at the surface, however, as so many do in this age when they want an instant answer to everything, but took the time and effort to really read
round the subject.

Prince Charles, whose own search for spiritual illumina-
tion has led him to embrace everything from Islam to the
Greek Orthodox rituals of the monks on Mount Athos, obviously had an influence on her, but she wasn't prepared to follow his lead without question. She wanted to understand for
herself, to reason things out and form her own opinions,
which was something she had never been allowed to do when
she was young. She told me that when she was a little girl
and the conversation turned from the mundane to the more
intellectual, she was the one who was always shouted down.

'I was always told that my brother was the clever one and
that I was the thick one in the family,' she said.

It was a terrible thing to say to any child, especially as it
was so untrue. She may have lacked the ready sparkle of
Charles, who always did well in exams and got a degree in
history from Oxford University, but she was a deep thinker
who had a truly enquiring mind, contrary to what most people
think. She was also naturally astute, and thought that her husband's dependency on those so-called 'gurus' he surrounded
himself with bordered on the cranky. She used to joke, 'His
ideas bear the imprint of the last person who spoke to him.'

The people Diana looked up to were not those who just
sat around and talked about what was right or wrong, but
those who went out and actually did things. That is why
Mother Teresa was such an inspiration, initially at least.

She had been told all about her by her acupuncturist, Oonagh Toffolo, a devout Roman Catholic and former nurse from
Sligo who had worked with Mother Teresa half a century earlier, and it was on her visit to India in 1992 with the Prince of

Wales that she saw at first hand the work this diminutive nun
was doing with the sick and needy in Calcutta. Diana's marriage was at its lowest ebb. She had become tired of the cha-
rade of keeping up appearances, and when Charles left for a
private visit to Nepal, she went by herself to the Missionaries
of Charity in the slums of Kaligat to the south of the city.

As she walked into the home, the nuns started singing in
beautiful, clear voices, a melodious contrast to the cacoph-
ony of poverty in the streets beyond and the wretchedness
that lay before her. Diana never drew back in the face of
misery, but on this occasion tears welled into her eyes and
she had to bite her lip as she looked down the dimly lit rows
of terminally ill men and women lying on shabby blue mattresses. Such was the overcrowding that some of the inmates
were reduced to lying in the kitchen or on the stone floor.
And all were dying, of tuberculosis or malnutrition or any
one of the myriad diseases that flourish in the festering
squalor of Calcutta. It brought to mind a scene from Dante's
*Inferno*. 'But at least they didn't die alone, unwanted and
unloved,' she recalled.

She passed among the moribund, gently handing out
pieces of sweetmeats she had brought with her. And when
she left her dress was stained with mud.

From there she went to see abandoned orphans and in-
fants who had been rescued by Mother Teresa and taken to a
special sanctuary. Diana stroked their faces and picked up a
deaf and dumb boy called Myso, whom she carried around
the nursery. 'I hugged him so tightly, hoping he could feel
my love and warmth,' she later wrote.

The experience, she told me, made her aware of her own
mortality and made her realise how unimportant we all are
in the great scheme of things. It really changed her outlook
on life and death.

Diana had very much wanted to meet Mother Teresa, but
the little nun was away in Rome having treatment for a heart
condition. As soon as Diana returned to London, however,
she flew to Italy and introduced herself to the person she described as 'an amazing woman who is doing God's work here

on earth'. She went with a clear objective: her visit to the mission had convinced Diana that the most worthwhile thing to do if she really wanted to help those desolate people was to go to India and devote six months of her life working there.

Mother Teresa dismissed the request out of hand. She may have been small in stature, but she had a large ego, and she did not want the most famous woman in the world turning up in Calcutta to steal some of her glory. She told Diana that she would not be ready to take on the job until she was at least sixty years old, and said, 'I couldn't do what you do—and you couldn't do what I do.'

Diana was very upset by that remark. It was nothing short of an insult and that is how she interpreted it. It wasn't for reasons of personal aggrandisement or publicity that she had offered her services. She had read the Scriptures and had drawn inspiration from Jesus saying in St Matthew's Gospel, 'I was thirsty and ye gave me drink: I was a stranger, and ye took me in: Naked, and ye clothed me: I was sick, and ye visited me.' With people being brought in from the streets of a city where the poverty-stricken and abandoned die in their thousands every day, the mission was desperately short-staffed and Diana believed that she could be of valuable assistance.

She never completely lost her admiration for the Albanian-born, Irish-trained nun whose work amongst the poor had earned her the Nobel Peace Prize in 1979, but the blunt way she had rejected the heartfelt offer of help made Diana wonder about her motives. They met several times afterwards to discuss how best to talk to the suffering and the dying, and in the year of both their deaths—Mother Teresa at the age of eighty-seven, Diana at thirty-six—they walked hand in hand through New York's Bronx. However, the unconditional trust Diana had once placed in the nun Pope John Paul II beatified in 2003 on the fast track to sainthood was no longer there.

Over the years, the nun had raised millions of dollars in donations. So why was it, Diana wanted to know, that the people for whom it was intended were reduced to living out their last days in shreds and tatters on rotting mattresses or stone floors in the Missionaries of Charity? Mother Teresa was alleged to have refused to publish any audit of her order, which prompted Diana to asked, 'What is she doing with the money—sitting on it?'

She knew that she could have helped raise millions more. 'But what would be the use if Mother Teresa doesn't use it?' she asked. And as she said, what was the point of raising yet more funds for the Roman Catholic Church, which was already the richest institution in the world?

These were observations she would never have dared make when she was younger (and her thoughts and judgements were forever being dismissed by her family as either naïve or plain silly), but a decade in the public eye had forced her to grow up. She was no longer the child she was when she married Prince Charles. There had been moments when she was overwhelmed by her position, but all the while she had grown in confidence and was no longer prepared to accept without question what she was told by those who claimed to know better. When she became fascinated by a subject she would hunt out the appropriate books and magazines and read them in bed at night, jotting down notes as she went along. She was a very light sleeper, which gave her lots of time for study, and she frequently called me up in the morning to talk over what she had just been reading. When her hectic schedule permitted, she would carry on reading in the day, and if I happened to call her when she had her nose in a book or article that particularly fascinated her, she would ask me to call back in half an hour, after she had finished the chapter. Like so many people who miss out on education at school—and Diana was always the first to admit that she had been a rotten pupil—she developed a real hunger for knowledge later in life, and the more she read, the more sure of her opinions she became.

Mother Teresa suffered under this scrutiny. So did the Church of England. The more she studied, the more she was drawn to the conclusion that the church her family had graced for generations was more concerned with the here and now, rather than the wider spiritual dimensions which increasingly concerned her. As the troubles in her marriage intensified, so she turned to religion for comfort, and that led her towards the Roman Catholic Church. It was sparked by Oonagh Toffolo, who was very pious, and Diana was also encouraged by Catholic friends like Lucia Flecha de Lima and, of course, by her first encounter with Mother Teresa. She liked its structure and its certainties. And she was taken by the idea of confession, which was like therapy to her.

She seriously considered converting to Roman Catholicism, as her mother had done. It would have been embarrassing if the ex-wife and mother of future Supreme Governors of the Established Church of England, the country's officially sanctioned faith since Henry VIII's rejection of papal authority five centuries before, had 'gone to Rome', as Diana called it. That was why, in part, she decided against it. We talked endlessly about what it would involve, and she admitted that she could not reconcile her own beliefs with the strict way the Church of Rome interpreted the Bible, which she thought was too narrow to provide her with the answers to life and death she was searching for.

She remained on the best of terms with the much-loved Cardinal Basil Hume, the senior Roman Catholic bishop in Britain, who, as President of Shelter, had opened Westminster Cathedral Hall as a night refuge for the homeless sleeping rough in the square beyond. Diana greatly admired that act of true charity, but she was discomforted by the displays of wealth which play such a central role in Roman Catholicism and found it impossible to square the two. The Church of Rome, she decided, was not for her.

It might have been different if she had been allowed to embrace some of the ideas contained in the non-canonical books and letters written by the Apostles and the early church fathers. Called the Apocrypha, they gave a much broader interpretation of the life and work of Jesus.

One idea that intrigued Diana was the concept of the duality of spirit and all things material, which declares that the soul is the creation of God, while the body belongs to Satan. How else could Satan have tempted Jesus with earthly riches when he was in the wilderness, if they were not his to give?

Diana also liked the suggestion that Jesus was a lot more human than Sunday school had ever taught. Long before Dan Brown's novel, *The Da Vinci Code*, became an international bestseller, Diana was wondering if Jesus had married Mary Magdalene, and what new light that would throw on the interpretation of the Gospels and the life of Christ. It would certainly assign a much more prominent role to women, which appealed to Diana, who knew through personal experience how damaging it could be to be forced to accept a secondary position, firstly in her own family, then in her marriage.

Both dualism and the proposition that Jesus was anything other than totally chaste are ideas that have been condemned as heresy by the traditional Christian churches, which made it impossible for her to assimilate them into a conventional belief system. That is why she became interested in Wicca.

The word has been synonymous with witchcraft since the Middle Ages when herbalists and healers often ended up being burnt at the stake, but there is nothing wicked about this Earth-centred faith that worships Nature. It preaches an equality between the masculine and the feminine very like the Chinese concept of yin and yang, which come into balance to create a more harmonious world, and draws inspiration from Gaia, the theory that the Earth is a living, breathing organism. At its core are the Celtic cults dating from the pre-Christian era, whose rites and rituals, herbal remedies and lore were codified in the middle of the twentieth century by Gerald Gardner, a retired civil servant, in his book, *Witchcraft Today*. It was published in 1954, three years after witchcraft was finally decriminalised in Britain.

There are no hard and fast rules in Wicca. 'Do what thou wilt shall be the whole of the law,' and its rejoinder, 'Love is the law, love under will,' is one tenet, 'Harm ye none' and 'Every man and every woman is a star' is a guiding principle. That appealed to Diana. Her involvement with neo-paganism was probably instigated by Charles, who is forever looking to the past in his search for a way for dealing with the present, but it was her own curiosity that spurred her to do so much research into the subject. She read a great deal about the subject, and spoke to as many people as she could find who knew something about it.

What really fascinated her was the emphasis Wicca places on 'the Goddess', the origin of all creation on Earth including life itself, which explains why the ancients worshipped the female genitalia. Diana loved that.

Her interest was then awakened in Hinduism and its many gods and goddesses, each one of whom exemplifies a different aspect of our existence. She read about the Veda, the sacred knowledge of Hinduism, and was intrigued by its prophecies, which date back several thousand years, yet, with their mention of aircraft and machines, apply today. And she was impressed by its teaching that no suffering or happiness is undeserved. But in the end the intricacies and contradictions of the religion of India were too complicated for her to take in.

Islam offered another alternative. In 1990 she held a long meeting at the Royal Anthropological Institute in London with Professor Akbar Ahmed, who had recently accepted the Iqbal Fellowship at Selwyn College, Cambridge. He had explained to her that Islam was not the misogynistic religion of intolerance and harems, as many in the West had come to believe, but was in fact based on the altogether more humane wisdom of the holy Prophet Mohammed who preached love and respect for women. When Diana went on an official visit to Pakistan in 1991, it was Professor Ahmed whom she asked to brief her. When she asked him what she should say, he advised her to quote Sir Allama Mohammad Iqbal, Pakistan's national poet. The verse he selected was, 'There are so many people who wander about in jungles in search of something, but I will become the servant of that person who has got love for humanity.'

In truth, it was Diana's love for James Hewitt that most probably inspired her to look into the teachings of Mohammed. In 1990 Saddam Hussein's Iraq invaded Kuwait and, as a serving officer in the Life Guards, Hewitt was dispatched to fight in the first Gulf War. Worried sick about his safety, Diana anxiously followed developments in the newspapers and on television as the battles unfolded. She wanted to know everything that was going on in the desert battle-fields, and that had led her to read up about the religion that the Iraqi tyrant kept using as a dishonest excuse for the suf-fering and countless deaths he caused. She acquired her own copy of the Koran and used to read chapters of it before she went to bed at night. And in 1994 she was photographed reading Professor Ahmed's book, *Discovering Islam*, while on a skiing holiday in Lech in Austria. She didn't go into the subject too deeply at this stage, but it gave her a foundation of knowledge which Oliver Hoare was able to build on.

It was through the dealer in Islamic art that she became more aware of Sufism, the mystic branch of Islam charac-terised by the concept of a union between human beings and God through the power, not only of love, but also of suffer-ing, which tied in with her own way of thinking. Its message of 'peace with all' had a powerful influence on Diana. And when she became involved with Hasnat Khan, her interest inevitably deepened.

That was part of a pattern. It was through her girlfriends that Diana had looked into Roman Catholicism, and it was because of her boyfriends that she began to study Islam. She was always looking for a religion that would answer her questions. After she had considered the other faiths, she asked me if I had any ideas. I suggested Kabbalah.

Madonna, Britney Spears and hotel heiress Paris Hilton are among the many who have recently become interested in this branch of Jewish mysticism, which dates from the twelfth century, although some of the symbology is believed to go back to the time of Moses. It evolved from the Torah and involves an elaborate study of the cosmology, of the uni-verse as a whole in all its forms, of the need to balance both the positive and negative forces and forming an understand-ing of the different planes and dimensions of existence through disciplined learning. It also consists of revelations on the nature of divinity, the creation, the role of human be-ings and the origin and fate of the soul.

The Duchess of York also became involved in this Western-ised version of Kabbalah through her friend Demi Moore, a devout disciple, and held discussions in London with a rabbi, Michael Berg, in the effort to try and learn more about it.

The involvement of such well-known names makes Kabbalah sound like the latest show business cult, which it most certainly is not. As Rabbi Shlomo Rifkin, chief rabbi of the Efrat settlement in the southern West Bank warned when he first heard of Madonna's involvement, 'Kabbalah is an added mystical tier to Judaism which comes after there is a total acceptance of a religious lifestyle and a religious value system. The traditional view is that anyone studying Kabbalah must first be a mature, practising Jew.'

I have been told that it can dangerous to study Kabbalah, because of the power it invokes, which, when put into practice, has been likened to real magic. A genuine kabbalist can tell you your past, present and future, as well as being a powerful healer.

Another restriction is that most rabbis will only instruct men. But although it is very complicated and requires a lot of will-power, it does offer an explanation about God and the angels and the different planes of existence in God's realm, which appealed to Diana. The self-discipline required did pose something of a problem, however, because if a subject became too complicated, Diana could sometimes lose her concentration.

With my encouragement, however, she did eventually start to grasp some of the fundamentals about Kabbalah, especially the parts which emphasise that what we presently do in life will affect what happens to us in the future and after we depart it. It was a message that was repeated in some of the other religions she studied, Hinduism or Sufism, which because of Hoare and Khan she devoted a lot of energy to. She was really serious about converting, and with this in mind, talked a great deal about Sufism and how it could help her in her spiritual life. A constant theme of her life was to question why things were happening and I think that her studies provided her with some of the answers.

This interest in the great faiths of the world certainly didn't hurt her. Quite the opposite: I believe it gave her more comfort than so many of the alternative therapies she resorted to. The mediums and psychics she consulted usually told her what they thought she wanted to hear, which all too often turned out to be totally inaccurate. Diana wanted life to be a fairytale in which everyone lives happily ever after. Through religion, she was able to grasp at least a little of the inner peace she craved.

Meditation played an important part. She often used to pray inwardly and silently talking to God, while closing her eyes, which is what she did when she visited the landmines areas in Angola and Bosnia. More powerful still, however, were those moments of contemplation.

It took her a long time to get the hang of that. She kept telephoning me to ask 'Why can't I do it? Why can't I concentrate?'

I would go over to Kensington Palace where I would sit beside her and gently explain to her how to meditate. I told her:

Sit down in a comfortable chair with your feet on the floor in a quiet room where you know you will not be disturbed for about twenty to forty minutes. If you want to put on some relaxing, background music, that's fine—just make sure you will find it spiritually uplifting and relaxing.

Now close your eyes and imagine the brightest ever sunshine shining right on top of your head. Visualise the sunshine as liquid light, going down through the top of your head, pouring through into your throat, then your stomach, liver, heart, lungs, spleen, pancreas, gall bladder, right through your bloodstream, pouring into your muscles, through every bone in your body and then down, into your abdomen, then even further down into your legs. Take deep breaths—on the in-breath breathe in the light, on the out-breath exhale the greyness and dross.

Imagine that your feet have outgoing valves at the bottom of them, and that beneath them part of the floor has hollowed out. See the liquid light pouring through your body, pushing the greyness of residual negativity, illness and pain all the way out through the valves in your feet and into the ground beneath them. See the flow going down about seven or eight feet into the ground.

Once you feel that your whole body is immersed in light, visualise the light flowing over you, as if in a shower. Don't fall asleep. Keep the visualisation going, and then, when you feel completely flooded with light and that there is a stream of light coming out of your feet, visualise this light becoming solid pale gold. Every cell in your body has become a pure golden energy. From your feet, see the gold taking the form of roots, going deeper and deeper into the earth until they are deeply rooted.

Finally, after this is completed, imagine yourself in a large, plastic, see-through egg about six inches thick that covers you from above your head, to below your feet. Imagine this egg as flexible as rubber, completely unbreakable and you're in it. Now, if you can (and don't do this if visualising it becomes difficult), try and imagine that only the outside of your egg has a highly polished silver coating to it, but you can still see out of it, as if it was a one-way mirror. This egg is your spiritual protection, and the polished surface will reflect any negativity away from you. If someone has a bad thought towards you, this will make it bounce right back to them.

The technique is tried and tested, and with practice and determination anyone can make it work. I have been using it twice a day, every day for twenty years and have found it extremely helpful in dealing with the day-to-day pressures of life. It really does cleanse the spirit, and you emerge refreshed and more at ease with yourself. It enables you to face the future with renewed vigour—and that was important to Diana.

Through her studies she had become engrossed with the thought that life after death might include reincarnation. It was something we frequently talked about, not in a self-conscious, overly intense way, but simply because it was a subject that intrigued us both. She used to joke that if she died she would come back to haunt me. That, I observed, was a two-way thing. She agreed and told me, 'I can just imagine you'd be telling me off when I am doing the wrong thing,' to which I replied, 'You can count on that.'

More seriously, Diana told me that she believed that the good and bad we do is reflected the next time round and that the after-life was part of the cleansing process where we must decide what we are going to be if we are reborn. But, unlike the Buddhists, she did not subscribe to the notion that we might return as a dog or a cat or an insect. Neither do I. Diana and I both agreed that if we have a previous or future existence it is as humans. She was convinced that she had been here before because there were certain people whom she had met whom she felt she had known in a previous existence.

When we were chatting about this one day, I was suddenly struck by the thought that she must have been someone like Cleopatra. It was just a spontaneous idea which Diana didn't go along with. All she said was, 'Oh really?' and dismissed it from her mind. About eighteen months later, however, she asked, 'Do you remember when you told me I might have been a princess in ancient Egypt? Well, I think you're right— they were all bumped off, weren't they?'

She was being light-hearted and she certainly didn't press the point, but then she started to get premonitions about her impending death in a car crash. The terrible thing was that I came to share them. In November 1996 we were sitting talking when I got this creepy vision of a fatal accident, not in any specific detail, but enough to scare me. Everything unfolded in my mind and I couldn't shake it away, so I thought I had better tell her.

She didn't like it one little bit. Who can blame her? She was full of life and she had so much to give that it seemed absurd to even think that tragedy might be lying in wait.

Yet strangely she really wasn't afraid of dying, and that was unusual. She had come to understand, in a way that few women of her age do, that life must inevitably end in death and that it is everyone's duty—to themselves and to whichever God they worship—to do as much good as they possibly can in the time allotted to them. That is exactly what Diana did.

# 11
# Looking Good

Diana didn't like her body. She didn't like its shape. She thought her hips were too slim, her feet too big, her nose too lumpy. She would have liked to have looked like Audrey Hepburn or, better still, to have had a curvaceous, hour-glass figure 'like Marilyn Monroe', who she thought possessed the ideal feminine silhouette.

She disliked her midriff most. She was always complaining about her middle. 'I want a flat stomach and a proper waistline,' she said.

She recounted how the singer Cher had had a rib removed to accentuate her waist, but even Diana thought this was too extreme. Instead she tried to whittle her waist into shape with exercise. She went to the gym almost every day and would do extra exercises at home.

I once made the mistake of telling her that I had had a 36-24-36 figure like hers when I was seventeen, and I showed her the photographs to prove it. She was shocked and said, 'How could you let yourself go like that.' She set herself the impossible task of trying to beat me back into shape, and when no one else was about she would make me lie down beside her on the sitting room floor at Kensington Palace and join her in the exercises she thought were best. We did endless upward crunches and side-to-side crunches, but although I lost weight and Diana's stomach got stronger, she never achieved the waistline she wanted.

Colonic irrigations didn't help. She had so many of them that her body couldn't function properly without them, which was why her stomach looked so distended in those swimsuit photographs the paparazzi took of her whenever she went on holiday.

She hated the way she looked in so many of those pictures, just as she hated the bump on her nose. She didn't mind the nose itself, and agreed that she would look rather silly with a pert, turned-up Hollywood-style snout, but she was self-conscious about the little lump in the middle. When I said I couldn't see it, she took my finger and guided it over her nose, saying, 'There it is—you must be able to feel it now.' Then she would get giggly and start imitating Peter Sellers playing Inspector Clouseau in the Pink Panther movies. In an exaggerated French accent she would ask, 'Can you fil di burmp?' I would answer, 'Which burmp?' and we would roar with laughter.

She thought her hands and feet were too large, although I said that while they might have been on the largish size, they were also thin and pretty, in balance with the rest of her body, and that if they were any smaller they would be out of proportion. She was always saying that she wanted straighter toes, but, as she acknowledged, you can never have those if you wear pointed shoes, as she did.

She had no complaint about her legs, though. They were superb—long and slim, well-toned and perfectly shaped. Her legs gave her the height that had prevented her from pursuing a career as a ballet dancer, but which worked to her advantage when she became a princess.

She took great care of them, and had the lower parts from the knee down, along with her underarms and her bikini line, regularly waxed. In the early days it was done by a Russian woman, but it proved to be too painful. She was very brave when it came to dealing with physical matters, but the Russian was rather brutal. Diana compared her to Rosa Klebb, the sadistic Smersh operative in the James Bond film, *From Russia with Love*. She would pour the wax on, then rip it off without caring how her client felt. 'I was a slab of meat,' Diana complained.

After a while she decided, quite reasonably, to find someone else and started going to an Iranian woman who worked in a salon in Kensington High Street where she went when she wanted a facial. She usually drove, but just occasionally she would walk there from her apartment at Kensington Palace. If any passer-by recognised her, she would look them straight in the eye and smile, which seemed to dissuade people from approaching her.

As a young woman she had the habit of casting her head forward, but by the time she reached her thirties she had learnt to hold it high. She had come to like being tall, and she walked with the confidence of a top model which served to emphasise the good parts of her figure.

Unlike most women, Diana actually liked her breasts. She could have gone without a bra if she had wanted. She bought her C-cup bras at Rigby & Peller opposite Harrods, and her sports bras came from Calvin Klein. She always wore some kind of support, even if she was wearing a backless dress, but she could easily have gone without a bra. She worked very hard to keep in shape.

An early riser who was nearly always up by 7 a.m., she always started the day with coffee. She sometimes had hot water and lemon when she first awoke, but it was always followed by a cup of filter coffee made from freshly ground beans, sometimes brought into her bedroom by Paul Burrell. She knew it wasn't very healthy but it gave her the kick-start to the day she felt she needed. And it was always followed by a glass of juice which she made herself in the extractor in the little kitchen on her bedroom floor. It was a mixture of organic cucumber, beetroot, celery or carrot and apple, which, according to Diana, was good for detoxing and helped to keep the liver functioning properly. She was finicky about what she drank. She liked mint or camomile infusions. In the afternoons she would have a glass of cucumber and celery juice as a diuretic. And she always drank at least eight glasses of water a day to flush out her kidneys and keep her skin clear of blemishes.

During their marriage, Prince Charles had forever been going on about the environment and the strange things that manufacturers put into food. He had found a willing acolyte in Diana. She once came out in an ugly rash when she juiced a cucumber. She was furious with the kitchen staff and demanded to see the bill to check where they had been bought. From then on all her fruit and vegetables came from Planet Organic in Notting Hill.

After she had drunk her juice, she would run around Kensington Gardens and come home for a quick shower (she didn't like feeling sweaty). She had a collection of expensive body lotions but usually preferred to use a Vaseline or Johnson and Johnson body lotion.

That would be followed by a breakfast of muesli or a slice of organic toast, or, if she was feeling naughty, a croissant which she was very fond of. Then it was off to the gym by 8 a.m. for an hour's hard workout. She had a clear idea of how she wanted to look, which was fit and healthy and as different as possible from the emaciated figure she had cut a few years earlier.

When I first met her, she was still taking sleeping pills and after a late night she could be very disorientated the following morning. To her great credit, though, she had succeeded in breaking her dependency on antidepressants. Despite being on the Pill, she continued to suffer quite badly from premenstrual tension, but instead of reaching for a prescription drug she now took starflower oil. And she had learned that a vitamin B complex pill was an effective remedy for her period pains. They fitted in with the self-image of the woman she was determined to become.

Her idea of beauty was old-fashioned elegance of the kind Audrey Hepburn and Grace Kelly radiated, but she didn't think much of the 'super models'—'too thin and unhealthy'.

She, of course, had looked like them when she was suffering from anorexia, although she never saw herself like that.

The feeling that she looked plump never quite left her, but once she had brought it under control she was able to take a more positive look at herself and concentrate on building up the best in herself. She loved the big-shouldered look of the Eighties, and decided that instead of the bony shoulders which she had when she was very thin, she would build them up and dispense with the padding. With the help of Will Carling, the former England rugby captain, she achieved this.

But she was very taken aback when photographs appeared in the newspapers purporting to show her legs covered in cellulite. I was at Kensington Palace the morning the pictures appeared. Diana asked me if I had seen the papers. I said I had. 'Do my legs really look that bad?' she moaned. 'What *is* all this cellulite?'

I told her that it wasn't nearly as bad as it looked. I asked, 'What cellulite? You don't have any. If I had legs like yours I'd be delighted. I said it was down to the way the photographs had been taken. I based my remarks on what I had seen with my own eyes. Except in the bad times when she was so painfully thin, Diana was never self-conscious about her body. She didn't mind getting undressed in front of people she knew well. She saw nothing embarrassing about a naked body. I had sat chatting to her while she lay in her bath and watched her dress and I had never seen so much as the tiniest patch of cellulite. She had firm legs and a great behind which was tight from all the running and gym work.

It was more than just her outward appearance that drove Diana to devote so much of her time to keeping herself in trim. She said she did it to get rid of her excess energy, but it was clear to me that she had an addiction to exercise because of the endorphins it releases into the brain. They produce a feel-good factor like chocolate—or morphine. The gym and the morning run was a double whammy, but even that wasn't enough. The more exercise you take, the more addictive it becomes. You keep working to get to the next high, which, in Diana's case, led her to start running in the evenings as well.

She didn't just run around the park. She used to go round Kensington and Knightsbridge by herself using the back streets. Late one night she called me on a mobile phone from Sloane Street, which is the best part of three miles away from her home. I couldn't believe it and asked her if she was safe. 'Of course I am,' she answered. 'No one expects me to be out running at this time.'

People had come to expect the Princess to be glamorous and well groomed, and, although she was always saying that she was really at her happiest when she didn't have to bother about it, she made it her business to live up to their demands. Even at her most casual she managed to look good. Yet her beauty routine was surprisingly simple.

In the morning she pushed her hair back in a hair band and washed her face with a plain glycerine soap, which, because of her allergies, was specially formulated for sensitive skins. She was lucky because her pale honey skin was flawless, without so much as a hint of an open pore, and her cheeks were pink, not peachy.

She liked it lightly tanned all year round which, thanks to the British weather, is a hard look to maintain. Her solution was the electric sunbed that was put up in what had been Charles's bedroom. It had originally belonged to Charles, who was very vain about his appearance, and she had claimed it as a small part of her settlement when he moved out of Kensington Palace. She would lie underneath it, naked except for a pair of goggles and a pair of skimpy knickers, for twenty minutes as often as three times a week. That surprised me. There had been a number of health warnings, cautioning that too much exposure of this kind can be extremely damaging to the skin and can lead to cancer. Diana must have been aware of that, but she carried on regardless. In every other respect, however, she took great care to keep her skin in good condition.

After she had scrubbed her face she applied a toning lotion, usually rosewater and glycerine, and a pre-moisturising mix of one drop of rose oil to two of geranium oil which she made herself. If she saw a spot she would dab it with witch hazel, and sometimes she would lightly steam her face with water that had just boiled and had a couple of spoons of sea salt in it.

She would then apply a very light Guerlain moisturiser, followed occasionally by some Yves St Laurent Touch Eclat concealer under her eyes if she was going out to an appointment.

When it came to her make-up itself, she was very eclectic. She loved *Vogue* magazine and used to read all their tips on make-up. She would rip out the page and then go to Harvey Nichols in Knightsbridge to have a look. She used to love trying out new products, in much the same way that teenage girls do. She didn't expect them to shut up the shop for her. Quite the contrary. She was the most famous woman in the world, yet she became just as excited when she spotted other celebrities as the ordinary shoppers were when they spied her. When she saw someone well-known whom she recognised, she would smile and wave—often to their acute embarrassment.

Those shopping trips could keep her amused for a whole morning. She usually came home with more of the same, however. She sometimes painted her own nails and loved trying out different colours, but only at home. I once persuaded her to try blue to match her eyes. She liked the result and I thought it looked fabulous, but she wouldn't go out in it except on her toes, which didn't count, because she was wearing close-toed shoes. By then she had a clear idea as to what suited her best and preferred to stay with her own look rather than follow the wackier fashions.

As with nail polish, so with make-up. While some of her friends were prepared to experiment, she stuck to a light pink Guerlain blusher and a pinkie brown lipstick worn under a natural gloss. And because she knew that her eyes were one of her best assets, she took great care when she made them up. She never curled her eyelashes, confining herself to some hyper-allergenic mascara and sometimes highlighting them with a very fine blue or black pencil inside the eye to emphasise their whiteness. When she was going out on an important evening engagement, she occasionally drew a line under the eye, but practice didn't make perfect and it wasn't always a great success. She looked a lot better when she kept it simple.

Inevitably, given the number of times she went to Harvey Nichols, the drawers in her dressing room were bulging with items of make-up, some discarded, others forgotten, some lost, with the ones she was currently using on top. Since she was so fastidious, the room always looked neat and tidy. The same could not always be said for the little kitchen when she was juicing or creating one of her facial treatments.

Diana was keen on face masks and we would amuse ourselves mixing up our own concoctions. One was made from avocado, the white of an egg, lemon juice and honey. She tried it after she had been wearing make-up all day and her face felt dry. At other times she would mash an avocado in the blender and slap the goo on her face. I used to put it on, too, and we would walk around chatting. We used to joke that if anyone had seen us they would have run away at the sight of two women with green faces.

When she was feeling tired after a heavy day, and had an evening engagement later, she would whip up the white of an egg, brush it on her face, and then lie down for forty minutes with a couple of slices of cucumber cut at an angle placed over her eyes. The process was simple enough. Just beat the white until frothy, then apply—and listen to the cracking noise the egg white makes as it dries. As my skin was drier than hers, I was able to use the yolk. By the time we had rinsed it all off again, first with warm, then with cold water, the kitchen looked like the laboratory of a sorcerer's apprentice.

At least some of the mixtures smelt nice and Diana liked light, pleasant scents. She wore Kenzo perfume or something by Penhaligon, which she was particularly fond of. She used their Gardenia in the shower and Bluebell when she had a long soak in the bathtub. One day, after we had been sitting in the bathroom discussing make-up, I walked to the Penhaligon shop and came back with a bottle of their Lily of the Valley. Diana joked, 'Oh good, we can both have a bath at the same time and compare smells!'

Given the choice, Diana would have had less showers and spent more time lounging around in a tub, trying out different bath oils. However, the athletic lifestyle she had embarked on made that impossible.

The need for speed also applied to her hair. She washed it as soon as she came back from the gym to KP, where two girls from Daniel Galvin's salon would be waiting to blowdry it. One would concentrate on one side, while the other worked on the other, which meant that the whole operation was over in a matter of minutes. She could have done it herself but she wasn't very good at grooming her own hair—and besides, it was a luxury she was not prepared to forgo. She justified the extravagance by saying that they made it look much better than she could ever manage.

Her hair was fine and thick and I was amazed that, with all the colour she put on, it wasn't as dry as straw. That, as it happened, was the colour she had always wanted it to be. Her natural colour was dark blonde with highlights put in by Daniel Galvin. It looked good, but she would have much preferred to have been born with the same colouring as Marilyn Monroe's.

Despite all her efforts, however, she was never going to look like Marilyn Monroe. Indeed, there were times when, out of necessity and her secret desires, she couldn't even allow herself to look like Princess Diana.

She had her hair cut by Sam McKnight and it was Sam who cut and styled the wigs she used to disguise herself when she sneaked out of Kensington Palace to meet her lovers.

# 12

# Family Matters

'I hate her,' Diana declared, and, in case I had mishcard what she had just said, repeated it over and over again.

They are just three words, but in uttering them she threw back the curtain to reveal the anguish her own mother had caused her.

Daughters and mothers often fight, I certainly did, but usually put their disagreements behind them. That did not happen to Diana. She carried the resentments she felt towards Frances Shand Kydd with her until the end of her life. It ate away at her self-confidence and influenced everything she did.

It spurred her to devote so much attention to her own children, but also left her mistrustful and wary of people. Her mother lied to her when she walked out, promising to return in a few days. She never did, and Diana was unable to trust anyone wholeheartedly after that, always suspecting she would be let down sooner or later.

I was given a startling insight into the hostility she felt towards the woman who had brought her into this world shortly after Mrs Shand Kydd had given an interview to *Hello!* magazine in November 1995. I was driving back into London when Diana phoned me, asked me where I was, and I said I was on the M4. She was also on the M4, having just dropped Prince Harry back at school, and she invited me to pop into Kensington Palace. Directions have never been my strong point, and she had to talk me all the way to the palace. I arrived two minutes before she did, waited until she came roaring up and then followed her through the gate and up to the house.

She took off her green Wellington boots and we went up to the kitchen where we mixed ourselves a drink of fresh celery and cucumber in the juice extractor and then went into William's and Harry's video games room for a chat. The *Hello!* interview had been playing on her mind for several days. She was upset that her mum had not told her that *Hello!* had phoned and asked for an interview, and furthermore, that she had agreed to give the interview. Diana thought it was selling her out. She was furious and she wanted to get it off her chest.

As we started talking the phone rang and it was her mother on the line. Diana looked at me and said, 'Talk of the devil.'

She was speaking on a large old-fashioned handset and pulled me close so that I could hear too. Her mother was slurring her words and sounded as if she had had a little too much to drink. As her mother talked, I noticed Diana's skin getting redder and redder as she got more and more angry. She was gritting her teeth as she tried to keep control of her temper.

She said, 'Mummy, I am very angry with you.'

Frances replied, 'Why?'

'Because you sold the story to *Hello!*' In the interview Mrs Shand Kydd had referred to her daughter's eating disorders and, without consulting Diana, she had offered the opinion about the loss of her HRH: 'I thought it was absolutely wonderful. At last she was able to be herself, use her own name and find her own identity.' She added, 'I hope and pray she will find contentment. Contentment, I think is more important than happiness. It is a general feeling of well-being, mental and physical.'

Diana regarded these comments as a betrayal of trust. She asked, 'Why are you doing this to me? The rest of the world is cashing in on me. But you're my mother. Why do you have to do it, too?'

Her mother said, 'Darling, I just told my story.'

Diana would not accept her mother's explanation. She was very upset and said, 'You're pissed again and you don't know what you are talking about. I want you to promise me that you'll never do an interview again.'

Her mother went quiet for a few seconds and then said in a deep slurry voice, 'I should have been the star!'

That was the last straw as far as Diana was concerned. She said, 'Mummy, I just can't talk to you,' and hung up.

Her mother had that effect on her almost every time they spoke, and, try as I did, it was very hard to calm her down afterwards. We talked about the problems our mothers had passed down to us, and the guilt we all feel for the rows we had when we were younger, but instead of proving cathartic, it only served to revive the bitter memories Diana had of her childhood.

'She made me feel as if I should never have been born,' she declared.

I tried to reason with Diana, pointing out that she wasn't the problem, that it was her mother who was trying to project her own problems onto her and that they dated back to long before Diana was even born. From what I had just heard, I got the clear impression that Mrs Shand Kydd was a failure who craved the spotlight, and was deeply envious of her daughter's status, both as a royal and as an icon.

In her youth she had been a beautiful debutante, whose photograph had appeared in the newspapers and society magazines, and who had then gone on to make what appeared to be a highly prestigious marriage. 'She had a life once—and now she is trying to deny me one,' Diana said.

It wasn't what her mother said and did in 1995 that was really causing her daughter such distress, however, but what she had done all those years before when she had chosen to leave her husband and run off with her lover. Diana's bitterness extended to Peter Shand Kydd, whom she greatly resented for 'stealing' her mother from her, and she only ever

referred to him as 'my mother's husband', never by name.
The six-year-old Diana must have felt utterly abandoned.
For years afterwards she blamed herself for her mother's departure and thought it was her fault, that she must have done
something terribly wrong. She hadn't, of course, but her
mother's actions stole not only her childhood but robbed her
of a decent adulthood as well.

In those desperately unhappy circumstances, it was only
natural that Diana should become extremely close to her father. Denied the love and comfort of her mother, she told me
how she had turned to him for advice, and although he found
it difficult to show his feelings, he loved her very much. She
was the youngest of his three daughters and his favourite. He
would read her bedtime stories and stay with her until she
fell asleep.

It was patience of a kind that he had not shown his wife,
whose behaviour had exasperated him, but, according to Diana, he never hit her, as Frances had once claimed. 'He
would never have done anything like that,' she said.

Nor was he an alcoholic. She acknowledged that he liked
to drink, but insisted that if anyone had a drinking problem,
it was her mother. Over the years both parents had let drop,
by little hints here or there, what had gone wrong in their
marriage, but Diana didn't believe her mother's version and
said, 'She wanted everything her own way and wanted a
marriage where she could do what she wanted and leave us
with a nanny. When she couldn't get it, she made up these
stories.'

It was Mrs Shand Kydd's account that gained currency,
however, which annoyed Diana, who thought she had spread
the story that she had been abused by her husband to cover
up the fact that she had walked out on her children. 'But if I
come out and tell the truth, it is going to look like mud sling-
ing,' Diana said, 'and I can't do that.'

During her meditation sessions I would tell her to concentrate on the good aspects of people she knew, but she
could not find anything positive to say about her mother. She
described her as selfish woman who wasn't cuddly, never

hugged or kissed her properly, and always thought about herself first. Diana said, 'She should never have been a mother and should never have had children. It was "me, me, me" all the time. She was very selfish and wanted everything to revolve around her.'

When Charles asked her to marry him, Diana flew to Australia to think over the proposal. She was hoping that Frances would be a real mother for once and advise her what she should do. She knew something was amiss in her heart, wasn't sure if she was up to the job, and wanted her mother to tell her, either that it was going to be all right or that she could change her mind and call off the engagement. She never got the reassurance she was hoping for. Instead, her mother promoted the marriage because she wanted the kudos of having the Prince of Wales as a son-in-law.

Lord Spencer was the complete opposite. He was very tolerant of his daughter's weaknesses, even excusing her total lack of understanding about financial matters. When Diana was thirty years old, he was still saying, 'She doesn't understand about money. She has no experience of money—she's too young.' Over the years he had given her 'between half a million and a million pounds' to ensure her independence from the Royal Family, and when life as one of its members became intolerable for her, he was the one she could pour her heart out to. Above all, he wanted her to be happy and always told her to do what she thought was for the best, for herself, for her sons, and the devil take the Royal Family. He had once served as an equerry to the Queen but he had come to regard her as cold and perniciously self-centred. He had told Diana before the wedding that she didn't have to go through with it if she didn't want to, and while he never actually told her to walk out when it went so badly wrong, he did say that he would stand by her if that was what she decided to do.

Her sisters, Sarah and Jane, took a different view. Six and four years older respectively than their famous sister, they had coped better with their mother's departure, and in adulthood had settled into the upper-class lifestyle befitting their

aristocratic background. What the two sisters weren't prepared to do was rock the boat of convention, and when the
Waleses' marriage began to crack apart, they urged her to
put duty to the Royal Family ahead of her own feelings
which drove a wedge between them.

She was upset that she couldn't talk to Jane, whom she
had always regarded as a fun person. They didn't cease all
contact because Jane lived within the KP compound, but at
the age of twenty she had married the Queen's private secretary, Robert (now Lord) Fellowes, sixteen years her senior,
and when Diana's troubles started that put her sister in the
'enemy camp' as far as Diana was concerned. She didn't like
Fellowes. He unquestionably took the stern line with her,
and that made it impossible for her to discuss her feelings
with his wife. She didn't want to get Jane involved. Diana
was being grown up for once, but it did leave a gap.

Her feelings towards Sarah were more ambivalent. She
had been the noisy and naughty one of the family who got expelled from school for drinking and then went to work as an
editorial assistant at *Vogue* magazine, where Jane was also
briefly employed before her marriage. As a girl, Diana had
looked up to Sarah but they had drifted apart as they got older.
Sarah had married farmer Neil McCorquodale, a stalwart of
county society who became the High Sheriff of Lincolnshire.
But as well as suffering from anorexia nervosa when she was
younger, she had also once dated Prince Charles, and Diana
was convinced that she secretly envied her little sister for
making off with the best marital catch. As the daughter of an
earl she bore the title of Lady, but Diana was the daughter-in-
law of the Queen and had become a Princess, and, like their
mother, Sarah rather resented the way the limelight had fallen
on her, only to pass on again. Sarah often seemed to be short
of money, and Diana always lent her some—never expecting
to get it back. She also gave her clothes, but that did not buy
Sarah's support when she decided to leave Charles. Both Jane
and Sarah were of the traditional opinion that she should disregard her own feelings, turn a blind eye to her husband's infidelity, and put the needs of the Royal Family above her own.

Mrs Shand Kydd's attitude was the same. Ostracised since her separation from Earl Spencer in 1967, she saw Diana's marriage to the heir to the throne as her way back into the social fold. After the engagement was officially announced, she reappeared in her daughter's life. She started popping round to Buckingham Palace for afternoon tea, took her daughter shopping, and helped Diana choose her wedding dress. For a while it looked as though the problems of the past might finally have been laid to rest.

The rift was too great, however, and Diana soon became irritated by the return of the woman who had been absent when she had needed her most. The pain wouldn't go away and at one stage even the sight of a picture of her mother was enough to put her daughter's hackles up. Diana said that when someone is injured, you can see the scars, 'but mine are hidden. They are psychological.'

Charles didn't like her either and neither did the boys. William and Harry went to stay with her in Scotland but that, Diana said, was only out of a sense of duty. William, who is an extremely good mimic, used to do a funny but rather cruel imitation of her that involved a lot of slurred words. It was notable that Frances wasn't invited to William's confirmation at Windsor, in March 1997. Instead, she put a notice in the newsletter of Oban Cathedral near her home on the West Coast of Scotland where she worshipped since her conversion to Roman Catholicism. It read, 'For my grandson William on his confirmation day, love Granny Frances.' Asked why she was not at the service, she replied, 'I'm not the person to ask. You should ask the offices of William's parents.'

Mrs Shand Kydd wasn't the only one who found herself uninvited to what should have been a joyous occasion. Diana had spent several afternoons with me visualising what it might be like if all the 'ghastly' people she had cause to dislike turned up at St George's Chapel. 'What would Camilla wear? Something hideous no doubt,' she said.

Camilla Parker Bowles was never on the guest list. However, Tiggy Legge-Bourke was invited, and even helped with

the arrangements. Diana was furious when she discovered
the involvement of Tiggy, whom she so resented, and said,
'If she comes I'll push her face into the font and drown her.'
Tiggy made a tactful retreat and did not attend the ceremony.

Frances's exclusion was on an equally personal basis and
had much to do with her stance in the run up to the Waleses'
divorce. When the marriage crumbled, she had urged Diana
to tolerate Charles's affairs. Diana was shocked by the suggestion and angrily pointed out to her mother, 'You had an
affair—and then you left us. And you made sure there was
another man waiting before you left Dad.' Diana thought that
was disgusting. To her way of thinking, it meant that Frances
had never loved either her husband or her children, because
otherwise she would never have taken a lover, let alone put
him first.

With her own mother expelled to the shadows, Diana had
turned increasingly to her stepmother, Raine. The friendship
had taken a while to mature, however. Her father had married the 46-year-old daughter of the romantic novelist Barbara Cartland in 1976, without first informing his children.
They took an instant dislike to the forceful and dynamic
woman, with an extravagant bouffant of red hair, who
overnight became the chatelaine of their family's ancestral
home. The first they knew about it was when they read about
the wedding in the newspapers.

Four years later, Sarah married Raine's cousin, Neil, but
that did not spare the new countess from the venom of her
stepchildren. They mocked her unwillingness to go to the
front door in case the wind disturbed her lacquered hair,
went around messing up the cushions she had so carefully
plumped, refused to answer her when she spoke and nick-
named her 'Acid Raine'.

Diana, who had only just turned fifteen, was particularly
hostile. Now that her sisters were old enough to leave home,
she had become the centre of her father's attention, and she
hated having her position usurped by this strong-minded in-
terloper. Diana had followed Sarah and Jane to West Heath
School when she was twelve—around the time, she discov-

ered, that her father first became involved with Raine, who was then married to his old Etonian school friend, the Earl of Dartmouth.

Having already lost a mother, she came to believe that Raine was trying to push her out of the way so that she could steal her father, and as a consequence treated her abominably—so much so that at the dining table at Althorp one lunchtime, Lord Spencer had rounded on her for the first time she could ever remember and angrily told her to mind her manners.

To add what they regarded as financial insult to their injured pride, Raine started selling off the heirlooms at Althorp, which Lord Spencer had inherited in 1975 on the death of his father, the seventh earl. Out went six pictures by Van Dyck, a Reynolds, Gainsborough portrait drawings, furniture and family papers from the archives. Diana and her siblings were convinced that they were being deprived of their heritage. 'We went ballistic. We thought she was flogging the family silver,' Diana said. And so she was: amongst the treasures Raine disposed of was a large collection of antique silver and gold ice pails made in 1690 for their ancestor, the first Duke of Marlborough, which were bought by the British Museum for £1 million.

Diana's brother, Charles, was incensed. He mistakenly told his sister that Raine was making copies of the furniture so no one would notice that the original had been sold. Diana believed him, as she did so much else of what he told her. When Diana was in her teens and desperate to find a boyfriend, he told her that she was too fat. She was at a sensitive age and that remark really wounded. Diana didn't blame him specifically for her subsequent eating disorders, but it didn't help.

He was equally discouraging when Diana's marriage to Prince Charles ran into trouble, asking her, 'Have you ever thought that you might be too fat for him?' In this, as in so much else, Charles Althorp was imposing his own opinions on his sister. He did the same to his wife, the model Victoria Lockwood. Because he liked his women to be skinny, she kept herself rake thin, and, like Diana, eventually came to suffer from a severe eating disorder. Diana, who had eventually grown sceptical of her brother and understood the pressure he put his wife under, often telephoned Victoria to try and console her when that marriage started careering off the rails, but to no avail—Charles and Victoria, who had four children, went through a messy divorce in 1997.

In court in South Africa he was portrayed as an arrogant adulterer who treated his wife abominably. It was an estimation that his own father had come to suspect. When it was revealed that Charles had embarked on an extramarital affair within weeks of his marriage, Lord Spencer said, 'He is married to a splendid girl in Victoria but I think he's a little immature.' He went on to say that he hoped he would grow out of it, but admitted that his children 'have gone a little haywire'.

It was a public admission of the feud between father and son which had been fermenting ever since Raine had taken over the running of the family estate—and began selling off its contents. At one stage, relations were so strained that Charles refused to set foot in the Palladian house in Northamptonshire. That prompted Lord Spencer to accuse him of being ungrateful and too 'financially immature' to see the problems that came with owning a house the size of Althorp. He said, 'My son must have known the problems involved. My father left a big debt. We had to pay one and a half million pounds in death duties,' adding, 'Some of the things I have sold have been very dear to me. Selling them was not an easy decision.'

Raine dismissed Charles's objections with the withering comment, 'My stepson thinks Botticelli is a pop group.'

It was the stepson who was born to inherit Althorp, however. In his will Lord Spencer had asked that Raine be given six months' grace at the house. Within an hour of his death from a heart attack in March 1992, the staff were informed that she was no longer welcome. When she came to identify her possessions she was told that she would have to produce receipts. Diana played a leading part in this undignified expulsion. 'I was the one who stuffed Raine's clothes in black plastic bin liners,' she told me.

Her father's death opened a large void in Diana's life, which left her feeling bleak and very alone. She described him to me as 'my safety net—my rock'. He was her real rock, and she started visiting mediums and spiritualists to try and make contact with him from beyond the grave. She often said, 'I can feel him around me.'

However, the support she yearned for came, surprisingly, given all those years of antagonism, from the 'wicked stepmother'.

Their friendship can be dated from when Diana finally broke free from her brother's influence. In the late spring of 1993 she asked the new Earl Spencer for one of the farm houses on the family estate to use as a country retreat following her separation from the Prince of Wales. Their father had promised her he would always have a home there for her if the worst ever came to the worst, and although the promise was only a verbal one, she presumed that her brother would honour it when he inherited Althorp and its 13,000 acres of picturesque farmland. Charles initially appeared willing and offered her the four-bedroom Garden House, which came with its own swimming pool and a small cottage that would have been ideal for her royal protection officers. Diana drove up to inspect the property and went so far as to pick out some colour schemes with her favourite interior designer, the South African-born Dudley Poplack.

Two weeks later, however, Charles decided that he couldn't be bothered with the fuss her presence would have caused. He made it clear to her that he was lord of the manor and he was the boss.

That really hurt Diana. She told me that when he called to discuss his decision she ended the conversation by slamming down the telephone. Afterwards she wrote him a letter which he returned unopened. 'He denied me my heritage,' Diana said, tears welling.

While brother and sister were at each other's throats, Raine had started a romance with Count Jean François de

Chambrun, a minor French aristocrat who was seven years
younger than her and whom she would soon marry. The attraction, she admitted, was physical. 'HRT does wonders for
your sex life,' she later told Diana.

In the throes of early passion, Raine and de Chambrun installed themselves at the Ritz hotel in Paris. Diana had just
been in the city on a shopping trip and as soon as she got
back to London she sent a bouquet of flowers with a note
wishing them well.

Raine responded with a letter of her own which got Diana
very excited. She asked me what she should do and I said,
'Obviously you've got to meet.' Typically, she wanted to invite Raine over straight away but the meeting took a few
days to arrange. It took place at Kensington Palace and Diana was nervous beforehand. She kept asking, 'What if it all
goes wrong?' I told her, 'Then you'll be back to where you
are now, so you won't have lost anything.'

There were a few stilted moments, which was hardly surprising after so many years of animosity, but as they talked
they discovered that they really liked each other. Raine
didn't expect too much too soon. She was far too much of a
diplomat to make that mistake, and instead just let their
friendship develop at its own speed. They talked at great
length about Johnny Spencer, the man they had both loved,
which Diana found very insightful and, as she left, Raine
said, 'If you have any questions don't hesitate to call me.'

Of course, Diana had an endless list of questions. She
wanted to know the answers to so many things and was soon
in almost daily touch with Raine, which is where their relationship really started. They used to speak on the telephone
most mornings and started taking afternoon tea together
once a week, at Raine's apartment in Mayfair or sometimes
at Claridge's hotel.

Underneath the hair and chiffon, Raine was a shrewd ob-
server of life and people. She took the time to listen to Diana's recollections about her childhood and told her, as I did,
that she had to get on with her life and to start looking forward instead of dwelling on the past. By talking it through,

she was able to help her get over a big part of her childhood. She was far better than any therapist and it was a great shame that they did not form that rapport when Diana was a teenager, because if they had, I am sure that Diana would have been spared a lot of her future anguish.

We all need an older woman, and usually our mothers, to whom we can unburden our hearts as we are growing up, but the role of confidante was not one Mrs Shand Kydd had been able or equipped to fulfil. She hadn't been there at the vital times and, when she eventually came back into Diana's life, she brought her own problems with her. A lot of them came out of a bottle. Diana was naturally worried about her, but when she asked Raine what she could do about her mother's drinking, the answer she got was to stop wasting her energy on something that was beyond her control. In Raine's opinion the only person who could stop Frances imbibing was Frances herself.

Diana would have described as callous anyone else who said that, but she took it from Raine because she had come to trust in her stepmother's common sense which was well-seasoned with worldly experience. Raine was especially perceptive about men. She told Diana to do all she could to remain on friendly terms with Prince Charles, for the good of the children but also because it was neither fair nor emotionally honest to dismiss someone with whom, as the Princess admitted, she was still in love. Raine held herself up as her own example and explained that both she and her mother, Barbara Cartland, kept in touch with all their former lovers and husbands, which prompted Diana to observe, 'There must be a very long queue of them.'

Raine was certainly no prude and recommended that Diana took lovers while she was still young and before she settled down again. Diana explained that she found it difficult to go to bed with someone unless she was in love, which started them talking about what kind of man would suit her best. It was Raine's view that she needed a man who would put her on a pedestal 'and spoil you to madness', which is how she thought all women should be treated.

Money was another important consideration. 'She told me to find a man with enough to look after me,' Diana explained to me later.

It was advice that Diana did not always follow, but she welcomed those chats and in the last year of her life would not shift those tea appointments for anything or anyone, even Hasnat Khan.

Raine did not really approve of Diana's relationship with the Pakistan-born doctor but she was far too astute to make an issue of it. Instead she restricted herself to a few carefully chosen remarks about the dangers of becoming too involved with someone from such a different cultural background and so lacking in money.

Mrs Shand Kydd made no attempt to hide her displeasure. As Diana observed, 'she didn't like dark-skinned people' and when she heard about her daughter's affection for Hasnat she telephoned and said, 'Firstly, he's only a surgeon. Secondly he's Pakistani and a Muslim. Thirdly, he's a commoner,' and went on to accuse her daughter of making a fool of herself.

Diana was outraged by her mother's attitude and that, combined with the 'betrayal' of the *Hello!* interview, was the final nail in the coffin of their fractured relationship. She never spoke to Frances again and refused to read any of her letters.

Raine had taken her place. 'She is the mother I never had,' she told me.

# 13
# Charity

The most important thing I did with Diana was to teach her how to heal. It enabled her to bring real comfort to the many hundreds of thousands of seriously ill people she met.

I believe she also helped change the way a great many people saw the world, and at the same time forced the British monarchy to confront its own shortcomings. The Royal Family is still trying to assimilate the lessons she gave them, but one thing is certain: there can be no going back to the old ways. Diana has seen to that.

Until she came along, female members of the British Royal Family were expected to be well-dressed, decorous, demure, gracious and well-mannered. They were not allowed to sully their hands with hard work which, it was believed, undermined the illusion of rank. 'Think of your position' is a cry that has echoed down through the centuries and they were expected to maintain it at all times. Common toil would have lifted the veil of regal mystery. Even ordinary, simple human emotion had to be kept in check. To show pain, joy, grief or sadness was regarded as 'undignified'.

Diana was having none of that. She was a young, modern woman who reacted as her heart dictated, not how custom demanded.

If she was happy she laughed—openly, without embar-rassment, in an embracing manner that charmed and captivated everyone who met her. When she was unhappy, she allowed her feelings to show; and if she saw anyone in physical distress or in need of emotional succour, she did all she could to provide it. There was nothing calculated or premeditated about this. She often said to me, 'Time is in very short supply, so you have to manage it as best you can, and make time for other people, because without them we are not living—we are just existing.'

She applied that attitude to her charity work. The charities she became associated with thought she would be just another figurehead (like the rest of the Royal Family). What they got instead was a patron whose involvement was wholehearted.

Nothing was too lowly or demeaning for her to tackle. She embraced people suffering from leprosy and Aids. She cuddled the wounded and the sick, and, unlike the Queen, she didn't wear gloves. So committed was Diana to her work, that she learned to channel her remarkable gift as a healer to aid the afflicted.

It was while I was teaching her to meditate that I started to train her to channel her energies towards those she was in contact with. She picked it up very quickly and, once she had got the knack, she used to practise on everybody—her sons, William and Harry, her friends, and the people she met through her charitable work. She once worked on me at KP when my back was causing me a lot of trouble, and it really helped ease the pain. It took about fifteen minutes and if she had carried on any longer I would have been asleep on the floor.

When I work I keep my hands a few inches away from the patient. Diana preferred closer contact. She was a tactile person and told me that when she was a child she would always snuggle up to whoever was reading her the bedtime story as she liked the feeling of human contact. On her visits to hospitals and hospices, she would hold the person's hand and look directly into their eyes so they could feel her energy and love flowing forth. She explained, 'Nothing gives me greater joy than to try to help the most vulnerable members of society. It's my one real goal in life—like a destiny.'

Her own past unhappiness gave her an insight into the problems of others. Carl Jung, one of the founding fathers of modern psychotherapy, observed in his book, *The Wounded Healer of the Soul*, 'The doctor is effective only when he himself is affected. Only the wounded physician heals. But when the doctor wears his personality like a coat of armour, he has no effect.'

Experience has certainly left its scars on Diana, but she discovered that they allowed her to empathise with other people's troubles. When, for instance, she visited a refuge for battered women, she came to appreciate that she was not the only one who had suffered in a relationship, and that re-alisation was a turning point.

Her own vulnerability struck a resounding chord, and through no conscious effort on her part she became a focal point for women in troubled relationships. They saw their problems in hers and drew strength from the way she re-fused to be beaten, coming out fighting instead, full of courage and with her chin up. She became a role model to women everywhere and that made her appreciate how she could help others, just by keeping going, and by not bowing to the pressures she was put under. When the opportunity presented itself, Diana knew she could help in a practical, hands-on way.

She didn't tell people she was trying to heal them; she just let it happen. Most of the time I don't think they were even aware of what she was trying to do, but I have no doubt that it was very beneficial. Having seen her do this at Kens-ington Place with her sons and with a couple of the patients, I could see a difference. Diana would transfer some sort of radiance over them.

Lucia Flecha de Lima agreed. She recounted, 'My hus-band had a very serious stroke in Washington and of course I told Princess Diana, who took the first plane from London to be with us.' Lucia and her son had both tried to communi-cate with him as he lay with his eyes closed in his hospital bed, but without success. 'And then Diana said, "May I try?" and I said, "Of course." When Diana said his name, 'He opened his eyes and almost sat up in bed. This is a true story, I'm not exaggerating. I think she had a very special power.'

There are any number of photographs of the Princess, her eyes closed and her mind focused in concentration as she attempted to channel her healing powers towards the sick and wounded. In Bosnia the award-winning British foreign correspondent Christina Lamb saw her holding the hand of a child whose intestines had been ripped open by a landmine. Lamb wrote afterwards how 'the small girl struggled through her pain to ask me if the beautiful lady was an angel'.

Diana had been born with an extraordinary ability, which had only been waiting to be released. By 1996, when she was fully in control of her life for probably the first time, she was able to give a great deal of consolation and encouragement to so many people.

The Princess received scant attention for this at the time. Everyone seemed to concentrate on negative aspects. Instead of seeing how genuinely caring she was, they accused her of doing it for the publicity. That was utterly untrue. I often joined her when she returned from a day's work and she would be so exhausted, she found relief in crying. She was anxious about what she had seen and experienced and was determined to find something she could do to help.

Her late-night visits to hospitals were supposed to be private. They were certainly not undertaken for reasons of self-promotion or to make herself feel better. She knew how frustrating it is to be alone in a hospital, the staff and patients were always surprised and very pleased to see her. She used to make light of it and say, 'I just came round to see if anyone else couldn't sleep!' Although Diana saw the benefits of the formal visits, and she did get excited when money poured in for her charities, she much preferred these unofficial occasions. They allowed her to talk to people and find out more about their illness and how they were feeling about themselves, in a down-to-earth way without a horde of people noting her every word. She wasn't trying to fill a void. It was not a therapy to help other people: it was a commitment born of selflessness.

She was also very inquisitive, and it was because of her desire to know as much as possible about what was going on that she watched several heart bypass operations performed by Sir Magdi Yacoub. On one occasion, in April 1996, she turned up at Harefield Hospital and found Sky TV installed in the operating room. She didn't realise that the television cameras were going to turn up, but she was too seasoned to the ways of the media by then to allow their intrusion to bother her. She told me, 'I didn't care.' Rather than getting upset, she concentrated on what she had read about in books and what was taking place on the operating table. This was a matter of life and death, which always fascinated her. She learned a lot during the procedures, and it was as a result of seeing these operations that she started jogging seriously. 'I was so horrified to see those clogged-up arteries,' she explained to me later. Just as importantly, she hoped that her presence would promote the work of her friend the surgeon, Sir Magdi.

Despite that, she came in for a lot of scathing criticism for allowing herself to be filmed while the operation was taking place. The Queen was 'speechless'. She simply didn't understand why her daughter-in-law would wish to watch something so 'gruesome'. Taking their cue from their sovereign, the diehards at court used this as an opportunity to belittle the Princess. They had been badly shaken by the sympathy Diana had earned during the break-up of her marriage, and in retaliation set out to portray her as unstable with a morbid interest in the suffering of others. Prince Charles's friends also contributed to this by leaking stories to the press which cast the Princess in a bad light.

It was an outrageous thing to do but they were alarmed—by being so caring of others in such a heartfelt and proactive way, she had made the rest of the Royal Family appear distant and insensitive.

In turn, Diana could not understand why the royals were always dispassionate and so unwilling to show what they felt for other people. She was particularly critical of Princess Michael of Kent.

Diana had disliked her from the moment they met, and the fact that they lived next door to each other in Kensington

Palace ensured that the hostility simmered on. Whatever Diana felt about Camilla, it was not as bad as what she thought about Marie-Christine. In her opinion she was 'a waste of space'.

She showed me a Christmas card from Marie-Christine and her husband, the Queen's cousin, Prince Michael. It was a photo of the two of them on a hill with the Princess, who is much taller, standing behind him, which only served to exaggerate the difference in their heights. 'You can see who wears the trousers there!' Diana declared.

She was forever mocking her Australian-educated neighbour whose lofty ideas about her status in life had moved the Queen to observe sarcastically, 'She is so much grander than us.' Marie-Christine's father, Baron Gunther von Reibnitz, had served with Hitler's Panzer divisions during the invasions of Poland and Russia, and had held the rank of Major in the elite SS. A number of Prince Philip's German relations had much closer links with the Nazi party. But despite the fact that von Reibnitz's SS rank had only been an honorary one, and he had not been implicated in any way with the murderous atrocities committed by Hitler's Praetorian Guard, his daughter was stigmatised by association—which is why Diana called her 'SS' or 'the Wehrmacht'. When she went for a walk in the KP garden, Diana would peer out of the window and say, 'The Waffen SS are on the march,' and on one occasion she actually broke into a goose step in front of Marie-Christine.

'I'm just stretching out my legs,' Diana explained as she walked by, kicking up her legs. Marie-Christine responded by referring to Diana as 'That Stupid Girl Next Door'.

A real catfight did in fact occur. Princess Michael kept pedigree Burmese cats. To protect them from the unwanted attentions of stray alley cats, she set traps in the KP gardens which were later taken away by the RSPCA. Diana often used to sneak in through the bushes at dawn and set them free, once leaving in their place a battery-operated toy cat which miaowed like a real one.

Diana was usually quite indifferent to cats, but Marie-Christine's scared her. They were cool, arrogant and haughty with hackles that were quick to rise—a bit like their owner, as Diana pointed out. She used to complain when they came in through her windows, only for Marie-Christine to retort, 'They were here before you were.' One morning, a cat sauntered in through a window in Diana's apartment and came and sat purring on my lap. Diana immediately called for her butler Paul Burrell and ordered him to find a box so that I could take it home with me. I asked her whose it was and when she told me, 'It's SS's,' I replied, 'There's no way I'm taking it home then; it's been microchipped!'

Diana's attitude might have seemed childish and rather mean. There was more than mischief to this feud, however. If any member of staff at Kensington Palace had a grievance, they would go to Diana and she would always do what she could to help. She would record their complaints in the machine she had been given by Sony. Some of the tapes, including the one containing the infamous allegation that a footman had been raped by a member of Prince Charles's staff, were carefully hidden away in her apartment. Others she took and played to her legal advisers, who included Lord Mischon and Anthony Julius, who handled her divorce. What she was too innocent to realise was that every time she consulted one of these solicitors, she was running up a large bill in legal fees, but even when the invoices began dropping through the letter box (and they were very large which irritated her enormously) she carried on consulting them on behalf of the KP staff.

Princess Michael's maid, Julia Dias, came to her for advice. She had contracted breast cancer—and alleged that she had been dismissed shortly afterwards by Marie-Christine, who was a patron of the Breast Cancer Research Society.

Diana had invited Julia over to tea and taped the whole story. She later played it back to me and we sat in tears as we listened to the tape. Diana took the tape to one of her lawyers who contacted Princess Michael to point out that if Julia Dias had indeed been dismissed, the Princess could be taken to an industrial tribunal for unfair dismissal.

Princess Michael vigorously denied the allegation that she had sacked the maid when she became ill, countering that she had helped Julia with her medical bills and maintaining that it was Julia who had wanted to quit and so give up the grace-and-favour apartment that went with the job. Julia, her husband and her son had to leave their home and she died of cancer three years later. Diana kept in touch with her right to the end, which did nothing to improve her relations with the Princess next door.

By this stage she wasn't getting on very well with most of the other women in the Royal Family. Her confidence had grown over the years, and she was no longer the insecure young woman she had once been who had tried so hard to ingratiate herself. Now she was poised and confident enough to judge them as she found them—and she found them wanting. They were too remote, too wrapped up in themselves, too aware of their 'position', too insensitive to the plight of others to meet with the approval of the thoroughly modern Diana.

The exception was the Duchess of Kent. Like Diana, she belonged to an ancient family of English aristocrats, with the added piquancy of numbering amongst her forebears Oliver Cromwell, the prime mover behind the execution of King Charles I in 1649. Like Diana, she had found it extremely difficult to assimilate herself into the Royal Family.

They became close when Diana got engaged to the Prince of Wales, and the former Kate Worsley had guided her through the minefield of arcane protocols. Their friendship endured. 'I understood Diana very well, for obvious reasons,' the Duchess recalled. 'I understood the difficulties as well as the advantages and we kept in touch through thick and thin.'

They were both beautiful and stylish but it was their compassion that drew them together. Diana described her as the next best thing to a saint, and as far as the Princess was concerned she was on a par with Mother Teresa.

Forbidden by tradition from getting what the contemporary world would call a 'proper' job, the Duchess had involved herself in various charities. But very much like Diana, she was unwilling to be merely a name on the letterhead and insisted on doing the real dirty work. 'I have never liked barriers,' Kate explained.

Diana was exactly the same. She found it easier to get on with people who were not her social peers, not because of inverted snobbery, but because she felt that the majority of people she knew, including some of her friends, were self-absorbed and rather empty-headed. Where were they when she wanted them?

She understood that people had other calls on their time, but she was prepared to drop everything if there was a sick child or if a friend called and asked for help. I do the same, which is one reason we got on so well. One day I got a call from a lady saying a baby was going blue at the mouth. I rushed round and did some healing and the baby started vomiting. It saved her life, as it transpired the child was allergic to milk. The Duchess, too, always put herself second, and Diana spoke with awe of the day she accompanied her on her hospital rounds—and how she had put on an apron, rolled up her sleeves, given a patient a bed bath and then emptied the bedpans, not thinking twice about it.

'She was the only member of the Royal Family I ever saw doing anything like that,' Diana told me. 'She was hands on, just like a nurse.'

Diana would have liked to emulate her royal soulmate but confessed that she was worried when she gave a bed bath to an elderly patient in case she hurt him because he had so many bed sores. Kate was more pragmatic and quietly got on with the task.

As a minor royal, the Duchess did not attract the same public interest as Diana, but the independent manner in which she went about her charitable duties did not go unnoticed in royal circles. At first she was quietly dismissed as 'eccentric'. When she converted to Roman Catholicism, a religion forbidden to the Royal Family (her brother-in-law, Prince Michael, had been forced to give up his right to the succession to marry Marie-Christine), eyebrows were raised in disparagement. Then, when she suffered from a bout of ill-health, she was cruelly dubbed 'Mad Kate'.

But never by Diana. She told me, 'Kate is one of the most selfless people I have ever met.' Comparing her to the other female royals, Diana said, 'Her values are humanitarian. Theirs are material.'

Kate Kent was always humble about the work she did with the sick and dying. 'It is a very private time in someone's life if they have a life-threatening illness and I feel it shows a slight lack of respect, and is possibly wrong, if you push your way in,' she said. Where she shared common ground with Diana was in the belief that 'every human being should be treated with respect and dignity'.

Young people were her special concern. Blessed with a beautiful voice (she had sung in York Minster at the age of thirteen) she would sing to the terminally ill youngsters at the hospices she visited. She also made regular calls to a run-down council estate on Humberside to see the work being done to combat the juvenile delinquency that resulted from poverty.

It was an area of interest that absorbed Diana. She loved kids and had children's pictures on the walls of her dressing room and bathroom at KP. Several were by William and Harry. One was a watercolour showing a bright blue house, Mummy in front, matchstick-thin with bright yellow hair and a smiling Daddy standing next to her, a poignant reminder that there were times when Charles and Diana had been happy together. They had been done when the boys were young and she was very proud of them.

It wasn't just her own sons' work she celebrated. Every day she received pictures sent to her by children from all over the world. They were never thrown away but carefully put away for safekeeping, or put into plain or glass and clip frames. The subject matter, so simple yet full of zest for life, was fascinating (to me) and obviously to her too. When I told her I thought they were incredible she replied, 'That's why I've kept them.'

Some of the paintings and drawings were given to her by the kids at the Great Ormond Street Hospital for Sick Children in London. She loved going there and went as often as she could. She dressed carefully and used to wear things that would attract their attention, such as a pendant they could take hold of and play with. She would always crouch down when she was speaking to children or the elderly so she could see them eye to eye. She wanted to get as close as possible in order to break down the invisible barricade that encases royalty. It was an instinctive thing. She could sense that the closer she got to a person, the less likely they were to be intimidated by their preconceptions of what a princess might be. It is hard to be overawed if someone is holding your hand or rubbing her cheek against yours. It breaks down the barriers and makes everything personal; and it allowed Diana to do what she did so well, which was let her healing energy flow into the child she was holding.

Afterwards she would tell me what had happened and about the cases that interested her. She took her concerns home with her and it helped her to discuss it. It was emotionally and physically exhausting for her because she became so personally involved. I would listen, and then, after she had outlined the situation, make a few suggestions. She wasn't prepared to let it be and leave the charity to look after itself. She wanted to take direct action.

If it was a medical problem we would stick our heads together and try and think of the solution. When something really distressed her, she would do her best to try to find the top specialist—and she would usually get them. She had access to some top people. She could phone Sir Magdi Yacoub or Dr Christiaan Barnard and ask them where the medical problem could best be tackled, be it in South Africa or America or the United Kingdom.

Certain causes inspired her in particular and she would give them all her attention. Leprosy was one example. She had been taught at school that it had been eradicated years ago. She said to me, 'When you read all the books you think there is no leprosy left. I thought it had been wiped out. But it isn't; it's still around. There are fifteen million people around the world still suffering from this disease.'

In Indonesia she took hold of what was left of the hand of a leper. You could see the photographers recoil at the thought that she was about to be afflicted with this ailment. But Diana knew better—she had learned that leprosy wasn't contagious at first touch and can be cured by modern medicines. The image which appeared on front pages everywhere made a powerful impression. As the Reverend Tony Lloyd, a director of the Leprosy Mission, observed, 'You have done more for the education of the public about the stigma of leprosy than we have done in a hundred and twenty years.'

AIDS was similar to leprosy in the way it touched on the deepest fears of the imagination. In their ignorance many thought (and still do) that it can be contracted by the merest touch—it is a human response to terrors which are beyond common understanding.

Diana made it her duty to draw back this veil of fear. She explained, 'If I have the power to change the position in society of suffering people I have to do it.'

She had read about the misery of orphans with Aids in the *Wall Street Journal*, and when she visited America in 1989 she insisted on going to the hospital in New York's Harlem where she was photographed holding an infected child. The following day the *New York Times* published a leader attacking the political establishment in Washington, asking why it was that it had taken a British Princess to draw attention to an American problem. Her efforts were having the desired effect, and that encouraged her to keep going. Back in Britain she went to see AIDS victims, making sure that she took a joke, a smile and a friendly touch with her, and it was largely through her efforts that sufferers came to be viewed with greater understanding and considerably more sympathy.

On 11 December 1995, seven days before she received the letter from the Queen urging an early divorce, her endeavours were rewarded with the Humanitarian of the Year Award, which was presented to her by former Secretary of State Henry Kissinger at a benefit dinner at the Hilton Hotel in New York. In her acceptance speech Diana said, 'Just being kind is all the sad world needs.'

It was a great honour but Diana found it embarrassing. She was being more than just humble when she told me, 'I really don't deserve this.' To her way of thinking, doing what she could to help wasn't an achievement in itself—the only achievement came when the situation was corrected.

Failing to get the positive results she was striving for, in July of the following year she announced that she was giving up nearly one hundred of her charities to concentrate on just six: the Royal Marsden Hospital, the Great Ormond Street Hospital for Sick Children, the English National Ballet, the Centrepoint charity for the homeless, the Leprosy Mission and the National Aids Trust.

She thought long and hard before she decided to cut back on her commitments. We talked about it on and off for months after I told her that a lot of charity money never gets to where it is supposed to go. She had no inkling of that and, of course, being Diana, took it to heart. She asked all her charities for a summary of their accounts. When she discovered how much money was going on 'administration', she got very upset. 'Some of these charities are just cashing in on my name,' she complained.

That never lessened her determination to do everything she could to aid those in need. She was forever on the lookout for new projects that might benefit from her involvement. Her attention was caught by child abuse and forced prostitution in Asia. We had both seen a programme about it on television showing how little children were being all but kidnapped and then made to sell themselves for sex.

Diana told me she wanted to do everything she could to eradicate this wicked exploitation taking place in India, Pakistan and, most prevalently, in Thailand. As it turned out, it was one of her final wishes. She didn't have any idea of how exactly she was going to do it, and hadn't got as far as formulating a plan, but she would have found a way, of that I have absolutely no doubt. When Diana put her mind to something, nothing was allowed to stand in her way. As she said, 'Because I have this power I have to use it,' and use it she did—to draw attention to a problem and, in a very practical way, to apply her incredible healing gifts to the victims. In her campaign against landmines, she did exactly that.

# 14

# Fergie

In the enclosed, self-regarding world of the Royal Family the only real friend Diana had was her sister-in-law, Fergie.

They had both been made to feel like outsiders and it was only natural that they should look to each other for support. When they were together they could gossip, exchange secrets, bitch about their royal relations, create mischief and hatch little plots. They came to depend on one another.

Fergie was heavily criticised for her flamboyant style and the way she dressed, but Diana was always supportive. She admired her long wavy red hair, was forever remarking on what a 'good-looking' woman she was, and she dismissed Fergie's critics with the remark, 'They don't know her.'

They really were like sisters, despite their dissimilar characters. From what Diana told me, and from what I observed at first hand, they approached life in very different ways. Fergie had an easy-going attitude towards sex which Diana could never emulate.

It was the Duchess of York who gave Diana advice on how to try and put some excitement into her marriage, and it was the Duchess who seemed able to enjoy a fling without worrying too much about what it meant or where it was going to lead.

The Princess was always looking for long-term commitment. For her, love affairs were emotional commitments and that led to relationships she would have been wiser to have avoided. Fergie, on the other hand, was spontaneous and physical, and Diana told me how she envied Fergie for being able to have sex just for the sake of it, without first having to convince herself that she was in love with the man.

Diana liked Fergie's rebellious spirit, of her 'to hell with what the world thinks' attitude, and the way she could do things without feeling the least bit guilty afterwards. The Duchess would learn the hard way that the opinion of others does count, but while they were still part of what they called 'the firm', she was the one who followed her instincts in a way that Diana never could. If Diana was *Majesty* magazine, Fergie was very much the *Cosmopolitan* woman with a racy line in conversation spiced with ribald humour and explicit detail.

Those contrasts made for a lot of fun and they enjoyed each other's company. But theirs was a love-hate relationship and there was a lot of jealousy involved, especially on Fergie's side. She was resentful of Diana's looks, her slim figure, her popularity and the way that men found her more alluring.

Fergie took a shine to John Kennedy Jr, but it was Diana who got him. She also took a fancy to the film actor Kevin Costner, and threw herself at him when they met, but again it was Diana who came out ahead. Costner repelled Fergie's advances and instead telephoned the Princess and offered her a part in *Bodyguard II*. Diana turned it down but that did not placate the Duchess. She felt that she was playing second fiddle to the Princess, and that was certainly true from the point of view of the public, the Royal Family and handsome and famous men like Costner. In private it was a different matter, and Fergie made up for lost ground by being the forceful and dominating one when they were together, and, when the opportunity presented itself, of having a light-hearted dig at the Princess.

That sometimes led to rows, and for the last six months of her life Diana refused to speak to Fergie. I know it deeply upset the Duchess, who said, 'I wish so much that I had seen her and got back to what we had for all those years.'

These quarrels were quite normal as far as Diana was concerned. She had disagreements with everyone at one time or other, including Rosa Monckton, whom she once wrongly suspected of spying on her for the Government when she was campaigning for a ban on landmines. Her friendship with her old flatmate Carolyn Bartholomew also had its ups and downs. But these tiffs always blew over. After a period of not speaking, she would suddenly telephone again and start talking as if nothing had happened, and I am sure, given a little more time, she would have patched things up with Fergie. As the Duchess so plaintively pointed out, they had known each other before they wed their Princes, and their friendship had helped sustain them during the difficult times.

Throughout their marriages, and especially towards the end, the two had been natural allies against Prince Philip. He was rude about them both in the letters he wrote to Diana which I saw. He had a vicious temper and a sharp tongue, and once suggested that Diana and Sarah should both be in a 'loony bin'—an astonishingly insensitive remark, given that when he was a youngster his own mother, Princess Alice, had been quietly committed to a private sanatorium for two years.

We talked a lot about his attitude towards them, and the impression Diana had was that Philip thought Fergie was a tart—and that Diana wasn't much better. With a father-in-law like that to contend with, you need all the friends you can find.

They were also united in their dislike of the Queen Mother, whose snobbery and offhand manner alienated them both. 'She isn't interested in anyone who isn't important,' Diana explained. As a second son, Prince Harry hardly ever got a look-in, and Fergie had never figured highly in the royal pecking order. Nor did Diana, once her divorce from Charles came through. To the Queen Mother's way of thinking, it was the monarchy that counted, not the feelings of the individuals who made up the living, feeling part of the institution which is supposed to exemplify the British family.

She could be imperious and the girls hated that side of her. They took their revenge by ringing her late at night on her private line in her bedchamber, and then hanging up before collapsing with laughter. It was silly and inconsiderate, but they thought it was funny. It was their way of getting their own back on a woman who had made their lives so miserable. At one stage they even made an agreement to go for a divorce at the same time.

Diana never really wanted a divorce from Charles and quickly backed out of the deal. Fergie was upset with Diana for not keeping to the pact, but it hadn't ever been anything more than a silly wistful fantasy. Diana was astute enough to sense that in any battle of wills, it was the Royal Family that was bound to come out ahead, and after Fergie left Prince Andrew she was ruthlessly ostracised.

According to Diana, the manner of her going was strange. A silly rumour was doing the rounds at the time alleging that Prince Andrew had been getting up to something with a footman. Diana had always liked Andrew and thought that the Yorks' marriage would survive. She was very taken aback, therefore, when she heard this calumny. Diana kept the tapes in the top drawer of her desk in a sliding partition, like a tray, on the left-hand side. There were quite a few there and she played me a tape she made with George Smith, a member of the Waleses' household who later said he had been twice raped by a member of Prince Charles's staff. Smith spoke pretty incoherently and quietly and his words sounded slurred. Diana got upset about that story, but there was not much detail as to what happened. He also gossiped about what was going on in the other royal households, which Diana found very funny. She then went on to tape him again and the stories changed slightly, but when she took it to her lawyers there was no case there. Any rape case needs the police. Diana liked trying to make things better for anyone who felt they had been done an injustice and she had been taping members of her staff for some time if they felt they had a grievance. She then gave them the benefit of her advice, having first spoken to her lawyers.

Fergie adamantly denied that anything of that nature involving her husband had happened, but the idea alone was
enough to disturb Diana who felt that this would undermine
Fergie's femininity and strip away her womanhood.

She was right to have worried. Underneath her frothy, exuberant exterior, Fergie was vulnerable. She wasn't as emotionally insecure as Diana, and took the rejection of the
Royal Family far better than the Princess ever could, but she
was distressed by the divorce terms that were imposed on
her. Diana thought that Fergie got a bad deal. She was allowed to work afterwards, which Diana wasn't. This was just
as well because if she hadn't been able to go out and make
her own living, she would have run out of funds even
quicker than she did.

According to Diana, most of her settlement was locked
away in trusts and the only cash she got was £250,000 and
she let that run through her fingers like sand. Diana wasn't at
all surprised when Fergie ran up huge debts (at one point
they topped £4 million) because she was always incredibly
generous. Diana used to say that if Fergie hadn't given so
much away, she would never have got herself into that financial mess.

At Christmas, Diana's limit for presents for her godchildren was £50 per head, as she had so many to get. Fergie
cast financial prudence to the wind and just went mad and
bought the most extravagant gifts imaginable. One year, for
instance, she bought Prince William a night-sight for his
rifle—at a cost of £4000. It was the same with her charities
which she supported out of her own pocket. When friends
and even ordinary people she hardly knew were in trouble,
she would always do what she could to tide them over, regardless of the extra strain that put on her already over-
stretched bank account. It was not something she was ever
given credit for, because this was something she did without
fuss or fanfare.

Diana respected her for that and told me that she wanted
Fergie to do well and marry a rich man, or, preferably, make
lots of money of her own and become a millionairess, so

that she could 'stick one in the eye', as she put it, of the Royal Family—Prince Philip and the Queen Mother, in particular. She felt so sorry for Fergie and thought it was disgraceful that the Royal Family had watched the mother of two of the Queen's granddaughters sink under a mountain of debt without offering to bail her out. 'They're being vindictive,' Diana said.

Fergie had to take a large share of the responsibility for her downfall. As Diana's father, Lord Spencer observed, 'She's not a real princess, she's a slap-them-on-the-bottom princess.' Always impetuous, she continued to embroil herself in situations without first considering the consequences, and her affair with her so-called 'financial adviser' John Bryan was the final straw as far as her royal relations were concerned. She was staying at Balmoral when the photographs of her lying topless on a sunbed in the south of France having her toes sucked by Bryan appeared in the newspapers. The Queen and Prince Philip were in residence and the guests included Charles, Anne, Andrew, Edward, Princess Margaret and her daughter, Lady Sarah Armstrong-Jones.

While the rest of the family were perusing the papers, Fergie retreated to the sanctuary of Diana's bedroom. She recalled, 'She couldn't say anything, she was just there for me—and she was great.'

That isn't quite how Diana saw it. As she told me later, she regarded the toe-sucking incident as 'very tacky—how could she allow herself to get caught like that?' Diana was never judgemental about Fergie's taste for often unsuitable men, but being photographed entwined half-naked with one, in full view of a camera, offended Diana's inherent sense of propriety.

Fergie stayed at Balmoral for another three days, swallowing Valium and enduring the harsh stares, disdainful silences and the Queen's anger. Yet even in the midst of a scandal Diana was unable to hold the high ground for very long. Diana had once remarked to the pursuing pack of photographers who followed her everywhere, 'You won't need me now you've got Fergie.'

Not true. Diana was the star, Fergie the stand-in, and on the Sunday she left the castle it was Diana who was again dominating the front pages, this time with the publication of the 'Squidgygate' tape. But she was the mother of a future king and that gave her a protective shield that Fergie never enjoyed. Diana told me that the atmosphere inside the castle was colder than the weather outside, but it was Fergie who continued to bear the brunt of regal disapproval. Princess Margaret put the Royal Family's feelings in a letter which said, 'You have done more to bring shame on the family than could have ever been imagined. Not once have you hung your head in embarrassment even for a minute after those disgraceful photographs. Clearly you have never considered the damage you are causing us all. How dare you discredit us like this.'

Such sanctimonious hypocrisy infuriated Fergie. As she left the castle she recalled, 'I looked at the assembled company and thought to myself, "There but for the grace of God go the lot of you."'

There was a lot of truth in that. The Queen's behaviour had always been beyond reproach, but that certainly wasn't true of other members of her family, as Diana often recounted. Princess Margaret, for all her moralising, had indulged herself with a succession of lovers, including the comedian Peter Sellers, Robin Douglas-Home and 'toy boy' Roddy Llewellyn. Prince Charles had a mistress. Prince Edward's sex life had been the subject of endless gossip, and Diana was always telling me about the rumours of Prince Philip's extramarital affairs.

'He's had lots of lovers,' she giggled, and hinted that he might even have another family squirrelled away somewhere. A rumour had been doing the rounds of London society, on and off, for the best part of sixty years but Diana never produced a shred of evidence to back up her allegation. However, just talking about it was an indication of quite how bitter relations between the Princess and her father-in-law had become.

Even by those standards, Fergie's fall from grace had

been spectacular, and Diana wasn't going to let her forget it. She had not voiced her disapproval to Fergie during that dreadful week at Balmoral but afterwards she was forever teasing her about that embarrassing toe-sucking episode. Fergie, who was feeling hounded and insecure, didn't like it, and she found it even more hurtful when Diana made references to her weight.

When they went away on holiday together in the south of France, where they stayed in the villa belonging to Fergie's former lover, the motor racing entrepreneur Paddy McNally, the two of them used to binge eat together. The difference was that Diana had managed to bring her eating disorders under control and was able to rein back, while Fergie carried on gorging with the inevitable consequence that she became ever larger. She still thought that Fergie was attractive, but wondered why it was that such a naturally good-looking woman could allow herself to become so overweight.

'Is it an emotional thing?' she asked me. She had done her analysis and concluded that overweight women were suffering from the pain of past relationships. It was, indeed, down to emotions. Diana knew Fergie was a mixed-up girl who had never come to terms with her mother leaving home—or with her father's interest in young women, which came to light when he was discovered visiting a massage parlour. It eventually cost him his job as the Prince of Wales's polo manager, and highly embarrassed Fergie. Diana felt for her. On top of that, she was still nursing the unhappy memory of being cast aside by McNally. Diana said that Fergie was using her weight 'as a buffer so that men will not find her attractive. She is trying to protect herself from being hurt in the future.'

As a way of helping her control her weight, Diana had put her onto colonic irrigations which she had at the Hale Clinic when she was pregnant with Princess Eugenie, who was born in 1990. She was very disapproving, however, of Fergie's fondness for slimming pills. She could always tell when Fergie was taking them because her personality changed. Diana loved her when she was her normal bouncy, cheerful self, and said that when she was on the pills 'it was like talking to a completely different person'.

She urged her to follow a natural diet instead, and was pleased when Fergie started following her advice. But she was highly critical when Fergie put her daughters on diets as well. Diana had spent a lot of time reading up on how to eat properly and got very annoyed with her sister-in-law for making Beatrice and Eugenie diet, as she reckoned that would make them grow up with a complex—and quite possibly fat, as well. Diana said it wasn't fair of Fergie to impose her problems on her young daughters, and warned her to be careful and to try to understand what she was doing to the girls. She gave her some good practical advice.

Fergie didn't listen, and from what the girls told Diana (and she in turn told me), she could be a very demanding mother. They didn't like being made to dress identically as they grew older because, as they pointed out, they weren't the same, but the Duchess had her own fixed ideas and there was nothing either they or Diana could do to change them. Those differences of opinion did not affect their friendship, however, and the two sets of children got on really well together—so much so that one of Diana's Christmas cards was a picture taken by Fergie of William, Harry, Beatrice and Eugenie because, as Diana explained, 'They are the future.'

However, Diana was not prepared to tolerate the references Fergie made to her in her autobiography, *My Story*. The paragraph that claimed, 'When I lived in Clapham, Diana helped me by giving me all her shoes (and, less happily, her verrucas)—we wore the same size,' made Diana furious. She swore to me, 'I've never had verrucas,' and went on to state that their feet were not the same size, that hers were bigger, and that she had only ever given Fergie one pair of shoes which she hadn't worn because they were too small for her.

An already volatile situation was made worse by Fergie's willingness to talk about the Princess when she went on American television to promote her book. I was listening in at Diana's invitation when Fergie returned to London for a few days during her publicity tour, and I heard her say, 'This is your book you're promoting, it's your life, it's everything to do with you and it's great that you're doing it. But please don't talk about me on TV. I've asked you before and I'm asking you again—don't.'

But Fergie did, Paul Burrell told the Princess what had been said, and Diana flew off the handle. 'I'm never speaking to her again,' she declared. She refused to take her calls, got rid of the mobile telephone with the number that Fergie had used to call her up, and thereby cut all contact with her sister-in-law. As far as I am aware, she only spoke to Fergie once after that.

The Duchess kept trying to make contact and said, 'We often used to have silly rows like any sisters—but after six months we'd make it up.'

There was to be no rapprochement this time. Six months later Diana was dead.

# 15

# Courageous Work

Diana would have seen the campaign to get landmines banned as her greatest legacy.

Tens of thousands of innocent men, women and children are maimed and killed every year by these monstrous, indiscriminate weapons, and her courageous attempts to have them banned put their eradication on the international agenda.

If anyone ever doubted her heartfelt concern for the welfare of others, this cause must surely have dispelled it. It needed someone of her fame and celebrity to bring the matter to the world's attention, and her work required an immense amount of personal bravery. She faced physical peril and endured public ridicule. It also resulted in Diana being issued with a very sinister threat.

I was with Diana in her sitting room at KP when she beckoned me over and held her large old-fashioned black telephone away from her ear so that I could hear. I heard a voice telling her she should stop meddling with things she didn't understand or know anything about, and spent several minutes trying to tell her to drop her campaign. Diana didn't say much, she just listened, and I clearly heard the warning: 'You never know when an accident is going to happen.' She went very pale.

The moment she put the phone down we started talking about what he had said. I tried to be reassuring which was not easy—she was clearly very worried. She told me that she wasn't going to be put off, but after that call she felt that it was vital to take precautions. She gave me and her friend Elsa Bowker a copy of the Profiting Out of Misery dossier. I took it home and hid it at the head of my bed under the mattress protector.

Ever since we had first met, Diana had expressed fears about her safety. She was convinced that she was being followed, that her apartment was bugged, and that the British Secret Service, the SIS, was out to get her. There were moments when she truly believed that her life was in peril.

The incident involving her car brakes fuelled her concern. It happened in 1995, after she had dismissed her royal bodyguards and was driving unaccompanied through London in her Audi. As she approached a set of traffic lights which had just turned to red, she put her foot on the brake but nothing happened and the car kept coasting forward. When it eventually came to a halt she leapt out, abandoned it where it was, and went straight back to Kensington Palace in a taxi, whose driver refused to accept his fare and asked for her autograph instead. She rang me and said, 'Someone's tampered with my brakes,' and this was followed by that note expressing her fears for her life. In the conversations we had afterwards she told me that she was certain that she would die young—and that her death would not be through 'natural causes'.

Afterwards she wrote in a letter which Paul Burrell somehow managed to get hold of, 'My husband is planning an "accident" in my car, brake failure and serious head injury in order to make the path clear for Charles to marry.'

She wrote to her friends Lady Annabel Goldsmith, Lucia Flecha de Lima and Elsa Bowker. She also wrote to me. In the letter I received she warned, 'The brakes on my car have been tampered with. If something does happen to me it will be MI5 or MI6.'

I took that with a large pinch of salt. At the time, because of the arguments over the divorce and the rows over the future of William and Harry, she was taking a lot of sleeping pills and they can make you forgetful and delusional. I told

her to get the car checked, which she did, and she discovered
that the failure had been due to normal wear and tear. I told
her, 'Don't be ridiculous—no one wishes you harm.'

When I listened in to her conversation with its apparent
warning, however, I was not sure any more. The conversation frightened Diana and it certainly scared me.

But she never wavered. She was totally committed to the
cause. 'It doesn't matter what happens to me,' she told me,
over and over again. 'We must do something. We cannot allow this slaughter to continue.'

I was one of the people who encouraged Diana's involvement in the landmines crisis. It all started in the summer
1996 when Bosnia was enmeshed in a ferocious, genocidal
civil war. I had been following the crisis on television and in
the newspapers, and had noted the efforts the humanitarian
agencies were making to try and alleviate the suffering of
the people caught in the crossfire between the warring factions. When I received a telephone call from my friend Morris Power, the head of the Red Cross in Tuzla, a small town
north-east of Sarajevo, I told him how pleased I was that so
much money was coming through.

He used to carry people on his back to safety during the
fighting and was considered a hero there. Looking after
those he had helped to save was proving extremely difficult,
however. He replied that there was no sign of any of that
money where he was, and he went on to tell me how disappointed he was that things were not being handled properly.
Food and support were not getting through, and in fact, over-
all, very little was being done. I immediately offered to
come over and do what I could to help. He said, 'Don't be so
stupid—civilians aren't allowed.'

I met up with Diana that evening at a friend's house in
Hampstead, and while we were sitting on her balcony, en-
joying the summer warmth and sipping Perrier water, I
asked if she could do me a favour. She replied, 'Anything
you want.' When I told her I wanted her to get me over to
Bosnia, she was very taken aback.

'How?' she asked. She was about to resign from most of

her charities but I reminded her that she was still President of the British Red Cross. 'Oh,' she exclaimed with a giggle, 'I forgot!'

I then told her what Morris had said, and at the end of the evening we went our separate ways—Diana back to Kensington, me to my home in Hendon which she described as 'the back of beyond'. I went to bed and thought no more about it but early the next morning I got a call from Diana who declared, 'You're going to Bosnia—expect a phone call.'

It came from Mike Whitlam, the head of the British Red Cross. I told him what I had heard and said that I wanted to get out there as soon as possible. I made it clear that I was not asking the Red Cross to pay anything, only to do what they could to smooth my way so I could join Morris. He had promised to pick me up from the airport in Zagreb, across the border in Croatia. Mike agreed to help, and it was under the patronage of the Red Cross that I was able to go.

I travelled out on the same flight as Paul Boateng, the Minister for Home Affairs in Tony Blair's government, who was on a fact-finding mission, and we had a brief but friendly chat in the airport. My reception in Zagreb was a lot less hospitable. Morris had booked me into a decent hotel where I had been promised a top-grade room. Croatia had been very pro-Hitler's Germany during the Second World War, however, and when they saw the Star of David earrings I was wearing I was shown into what can only be described as a tiny cubby hole. We complained to the front desk. I became very angry (I couldn't help myself) and called them 'Nazis'. The manager was called and I was moved to a decent room.

It had all been very unpleasant and I was glad to get out of there, even if we did leave at 5.30 the following morning, which was the unearthly hour that Morris called to collect me and drive me across the frontier into Bosnia. The borderlands were a real eye opener. It was rugged, mountainous country where virtually everything was bombed out and there was almost no one to be seen. We passed a crashed plane that had just been left where it fell and I had to keep reminding myself that this was part of modern Europe.

We stopped off at a bombed-out house where we found
an old and frail couple lying on wooden planks on the floor.
They had no beds or blankets but they struggled up to greet
us and make a cup of the coffee Morris had brought for
them. I don't like coffee but I couldn't refuse what two people who had almost nothing were prepared to share. I started
crying as Morris explained that this was one of the houses
which were meant to have been fixed up after the bombing,
but nothing had happened. It was an example of what wasn't
being done and I was stunned. Here were people who had
slipped through the safety net and almost nothing was being
done, or could be done, given the problems of getting aid to
where it was needed.

From there we drove to Tuzla where I was able to take a
shower under a dribble of water. What I couldn't get was
fresh water to drink and I had to make do with cans of soft
drink, which I loathe but which always seem to be widely
available in war zones. Why was it, I wondered, that Pepsi
and Coke can get through but food and medical supplies
can't? I made friends with the housekeeper in the house
where we were staying and, despite the fact that we shared
no common language and had to communicate by signs and
facial expressions, she told me that, because the shops didn't
have any food, people were having to make do with what
they could grow themselves. We talked about the difficulties
with some UN and NGO workers we joined for a frugal dinner in a local café that evening and I heard some real horror
stories, which had me in tears again.

Over the next few days I went out and saw for myself
what was happening in that war-ravaged country. There were
any number of things that truly shocked me. I met many
more old people who had lost everything they possessed and
in the village of Zenica there was a young woman who had
lost even more.

She had been captured by Serb soldiers when she was
sixteen years old and held for two years. During that time
she had been repeatedly gang-raped and fallen pregnant with
a child that had been forcibly aborted. She was eventually

rescued, but by then she was completely crushed. She had blanked the world out and no one could communicate with her. She was in a permanent daze. I put my arms around her and looked into her eyes. She looked back, but she didn't see. She had lost the ability to connect with other people.

In another village I saw a man lying on the floor coughing blood. I was told that the Red Cross doctor had said he had asthma but I said that was the wrong diagnosis; that it wasn't asthma, it was cancer because I had seen it before. I offered to take him to hospital and promised to pay for his treatment, but cutting through the red tape was extremely difficult. I had a row with Morris and said I was not leaving until I could take him to hospital. He became so angry with me that he picked me up and carried me out to the car.

I wasn't going to be pushed around like that. I said I wasn't leaving until I had done something to help and, with tears streaming down my face, I started screaming and shouting so loudly that he caved in. He rang the Red Cross in Switzerland and told them about the man and that I was going to pay.

It was a despicable situation and I had to wait three days before Morris's Red Cross driver arrived at 6 a.m. and we went to pick him up. I went to the market on the way and bought him a pair of socks and some vests. But we did get him to the hospital and the X-rays confirmed what I had known from my experience with members of my own family: that he was suffering from cancer. He was riddled with it and the director of the hospital said that he had no more than three months to live. My heart felt as if it had sunk into my stomach and the tears welled up in my eyes. He wouldn't accept any money from me, but said, 'At least you will have allowed the man to die in dignity.'

I helped take him to the ward where he was given morphine to ease his pain, while I went out and bought him some pyjamas and slippers and a dressing gown. It wasn't much, but it was something.

On the following day I saw my first landmine. We were driving in the direction of Sarajevo when Morris pointed out what he called 'the wings' in the road. He stopped and said,

'Open your door very slowly—and don't get out of the car whatever you do.' It looked like a garden sprinkler, no more than three inches in diameter and shaped like a propeller.

I said, 'Oh those wings, what is it?' He replied, 'It's a landmine.'

Further along the road, there were two little children walking through the rubble and wreckage beside the road, holding hands and seemingly unaware of the dangers all around them. They looked so innocent and I took a photograph which I called 'the picture of hope'. I was looking for anything that would give me a straw of optimism to grab hold of in the hell that was Bosnia. I went to villages where there were a lot of landmine victims and their injuries were horrendous. While I was there, I transferred most of my savings over to Morris in Bosnia so Morris and I could buy clothes and food for the people he was trying to help. I had to. It never occurred to me that Diana might want to help.

I was there for ten days and called her the moment I touched down in London. She asked me to come straight to Kensington Palace. I refused. It was late and I was exhausted and wanted a night's sleep. The next morning, however, she was on the phone very early, urging me to come round and to bring my photographs and notes with me. I stopped off to get my films developed and then went on to KP.

Diana knew what I had witnessed because she had called me in Bosnia and I told her. Looking at the photographs and hearing my descriptions provided a more vivid account. Diana and I shared an empathy which enabled her to imagine things that had happened to me as though she was there and she was with me in the house with the old couple, with the cancer patient, with the raped girl and out there amongst the landmines. We both ended up in tears that morning.

I told her, 'Landmines aren't killing the military—they are killing children, animals and the elderly.'

She said, 'Can I help? Do you think I could make a difference?'

I replied, 'If you can't, nobody else can.'

It was around the time that she was cutting back on her

charities, whittling them down from a hundred and eighteen to just six. The difference was that, from now on, she was determined to put her energy and effort into causes where she thought she could do some real good, and the landmine problem had clearly moved her. She called me back to KP the following day and asked, 'Do you know how many landmines there are in the world?' I didn't. No one did precisely. There were more than thirty million landmines of different types held in stockpiles and many times more scattered over eighty countries. Diana had looked up the facts and figures and discovered that almost ten thousand people and animals were being killed, and many thousands injured, by these weapons every year. The fact that this included animals, the elephants of Angola, and children in particular, really upset her. She held up a sheaf of papers documenting this terrible toll and declared, 'I am going to do it.'

I was very moved. I said, 'Brilliant. You are the only one who can because no one else has the guts to do it. I can't see anyone else with your celebrity status going off and being able to cope with the horrors. You have to do it.'

She told me that the worst country for landmines was Cambodia, so that was where she wanted to go. She was very determined, but under the conditions of the divorce she had to seek official permission for a trip like that and the Government rejected it out of hand because of the dangers of kidnapping. I agreed, because it certainly wouldn't have looked good or helped anyone if she had been abducted.

It was then that she decided on Angola, which had been devastated by twenty years of warfare and littered with more than twelve million landmines. She had a lot of other things on her mind just then. Her divorce was near its finalisation, she had become involved with Hasnat Khan and his family, there was the visit to Australia to open the Victor Chang Institute, plus two trips to the United States, but once she had decided on something she could be very single-minded. I had got her involved in July and by the following January she was on her way.

When the Government had reluctantly given their con-

sent, I told her, 'You must go there to highlight the plight of
the people. You can't go as a fashion icon. Wear jeans and
T-shirts.' She agreed, but, being Diana, that meant something stylish. She went on a shopping expedition and came
back with Armani jeans, chinos and polo shirts from Ralph
Lauren and sneakers from Todd's. Although she did also
take one well-worn dress with her.

Once there, she rang me whenever she could from the
Governor's residence. (I can still remember the telephone
number as I called her too.) She always announced herself
by saying, 'Angola calling Hendon.'

This was no safari, though. She found the sight of the mu-
tilated children she met in the hospitals very hard to deal
with. She felt their distress in a way few others do. Adding to
her anguish was the fact that she wasn't getting on with the
reporters and photographers accompanying her, who she felt
were being too intrusive. She said that all they wanted was
close-up pictures of her with maimed and disfigured children in excruciating pain, and angrily demanded, 'How can
they have so little heart?'

I pointed out that if she wasn't there, they wouldn't be either. She needed the media to promote the landmine cause.
She recognised that and used herself as the focus to raise
money to buy the prosthetics, the artificial limbs that the
kids—or anyone else who had had the misfortune to step on
one of those concealed weapons—desperately needed.

On the day she walked through a field of mines, she rang
me up beforehand and said, 'Can you please pray for me?
They've cleared as many of them as possible, but I have
been warned that something might have been missed.'

The Halo Trust had suggested she do it as a way of sending a clear message to the world, and they were right, because it was the one picture everyone will remember. She
agreed, which was very brave of her, because her safety
couldn't be guaranteed. As she took her first step, she said to
herself, 'I must be mad.'

The Red Cross's Mike Whitlam was just as uneasy. A
Halo Trust worker had recently lost his leg in an area that

had been swept for explosives, and he admitted that, 'even though we were walking an area that was cleared and going to look at a live mine, which *she* blew up, I was just a little bit worried that, you know, they might have missed one. I did feel a hell of a lot of responsibility for that trip, because everyone was saying, it's down to me.'

But Diana kept walking. She called to tell me, 'My heart was in my mouth every step of the way, my jaw was clenched tight, and I have never been so sure-footed because I knew that the slightest bit of pressure could have set one off, so any one of my steps could have been my last. But it was just something I had to do.'

Even when faced with such danger, however, she never lost her sense of humour and could be quite light-hearted. She also made the effort to look smart. Burrell had done her hair for her the morning she walked through the minefield. And why not? She knew what the photographers expected of her and looking good didn't mean she didn't care. Quite the opposite. So moved was she by the experience and the sight of all those injuries that she wrote out a cheque for £250,000, drawn against her divorce settlement, and donated it to help treat the landmine victims. She didn't discuss this with Charles until afterwards, and I never found out what he thought about her trip, but I do know that William and Harry were thrilled. They thought they had the bravest mum in the world and I agreed with them.

Having done her bit, she could have left it there, but Diana wanted to do more. She was upset that so many of the prostheses didn't fit, and she thought it was wrong that, after suffering so much, they should have to wear uncomfortable artificial limbs. She was deeply moved by the plight of Sandra Txijica, who had lost a leg. She couldn't understand what had happened to her. She was only thirteen years old, and all she wanted was to be able to walk and wear pretty dresses. It was only through Diana's efforts that she got the new limb she needed.

She was so humbled by her experiences in Angola that she had no real idea of the impact she had made. Rather, she kept saying, 'I can't do enough to get rid of those land-mines.' She had seen the damage they caused, the memory often reduced her to tears and she was determined to keep the momentum going.

In August, she insisted on visiting Tuzla where she stayed with the Bosnian mother of Morris's ex-girlfriend, Sandra. The house, built in a strange Dutch-German style, was on a hill overlooking the small waterway that ran through the town. I had dined there several times and I had recommended it to Diana because it was as safe as anywhere in Bosnia while the fighting was raging.

She flew there in a private jet belonging to George Soros, the billionaire currency dealer, accompanied by Burrell and Bill Deedes, and was shown around by Jerry White and Ken Rutherford, two members of the Landmines Survivors Network who had both lost limbs in explosions. Her tour took her along the same route I had followed almost a year earlier, and, although she was only there for three days, she still managed to meet most of the same people. She also went round the hospital where her sense of humour did much for the morale of the patients. There was nothing snooty about her.

She used to tease Bill Deedes, the 83-year-old former editor of the *Daily Telegraph* who had become a distinguished and much-loved columnist, by sidling up to him and saying, 'Would you like a gin and tonic?' Lord Deedes, a great drinking companion of Margaret Thatcher's husband, Denis, was noted for his fondness for a tipple, but all she ever handed him was a small bottle of Evian water. That was Diana all over.

Diana liked playing practical jokes and hearing dirty jokes, and her laughter was infectious, which was why she was able to make even the wounded smile. When it came to her charity work she had extraordinary self-control, and never allowed anyone to see how distressed she was. That was the remarkable thing about Diana: she could ignore horrendous injuries, the sight of which made others recoil, and treat the victims in such an ordinary, light-hearted way. They mattered to her as people and she really cared for their welfare. Diplomatic niceties and royal protocols did not concern her. She had the ability to speak over the heads of governments to those directly affected, in an emotional and forthright manner, and it won her the respect and admiration of millions.

But if that was a rare gift, it was also one that certain people with vested interests took grave exception to. For Diana was a woman with a mission, which made her a very dangerous opponent.

She did a lot of research on landmines, asking questions of people on the ground, checking with those in authority whom she had met as Princess of Wales, cross-examining anyone she met who knew something about the subject. She said, 'If you see someone with a gun you know you have an enemy, but the landmines are something you can't see,' and she compiled a dossier which she claimed would prove that the British Government and many high-ranking public figures were profiting from their proliferation, in countries like Angola and Bosnia. The names and companies were well-known. It was explosive. And top of her list of culprits behind this squalid trade was the Secret Intelligence Service, the SIS, which she believed was behind the sale of so many of the British-made landmines that were causing so much misery to so many people.

'I'm going to go public with this and I'm going to name names,' she declared. She intended to call her report 'Profiting Out of Misery'.

The British defence industry is the world's second largest after the United States, accounting for twenty-five per cent of all arms sales, employing 345,000 workers and generating an annual turnover of £17 billion. In challenging this vast Government-backed commercial conglomerate, Diana was taking on some extremely powerful people and they rounded on her when she returned from Angola.

Peter Viggers, the Conservative MP for Gosport and a member of the House of Commons Defence Select Committee, condemned her call for a ban as 'ill-informed' and compared her to 'Brigitte Bardot and cats. It doesn't actually add much to the sum of human knowledge. It doesn't help simply to point at the amputees and say how terrible it is.'

Ministers echoed Viggers's lambast by calling her 'ignorant' and describing her as a 'loose cannon'.

The worst assault came from Nicholas Soames, the Minister of State for the Armed Forces. Diana had never liked her husband's friend and said he talked as if he had 'a penis stuck in his mouth'. The antipathy was mutual. After the *Panorama* interview he had gone on television to claim that the Princess was in 'the advanced stages of paranoia'. The landmines issue reopened these old wounds.

Diana flew back from Bosnia on 11 August. Two weeks and six days later she was dead.

Two days later I took the big brown envelope she had given me containing the Profiting Out of Misery dossier and put it into a big pan, covered it with oils and set fire to it. I used tongs and a long carving knife to make sure that it was all properly burned. It was not something I wanted to hang on to for a moment longer.

# 16
# Diana's Court

Diana was exuberant about everything she did, and that extended to her friendships.

She didn't so much walk into a room as explode, scattering smiles and jokes and good humour in a way that embraced everyone. When she saw someone she knew, her face would light up, her arms would fly out in welcome and more often than not she would wrap them in a warm hug, while new acquaintances were made to feel like old friends.

Very few are blessed with that kind of star quality, and we were all captivated by her charisma. It was almost as if she was skipping on air, and even those who had been critical of her in the past came away enchanted after spending only a few moments with her.

Whenever we met, she always made me feel as if she was truly grateful for my time, and she exuded interest in everything I was doing. Most of us try and hide our insecurities behind a mask. Diana never bothered with that sort of psychological subterfuge. She was refreshingly open and interested in everyone around her in an unaffected and outgoing way that shone through in her photographs, which I am sure is why she enjoyed such enormous popularity.

She wasn't a paragon of virtue. She was much too human to exist on a pedestal. She had her moods and only wanted to hear her opinions confirmed rather than the more unpalatable truth. She could be capricious, found it impossible to keep a secret, and had a tendency to fall out with people over the most trivial of matters. She was also inclined to tell little lies. Nothing big, just silly little things. She once told me that she wasn't eating red meat when I knew that she was—because I'd seen her do so.

But if these were faults, they were rather minor compared to the flaws in some of her royal relations. She didn't need the props of privilege to sustain her. Quite the contrary. The staged set-pieces that are part of the royal performance either bored or irritated her: it was when she was out mixing with ordinary people, especially those in need of comfort and attention, that she was at her expansive best.

No person can operate in a vacuum, of course, and Diana needed the support and encouragement from her confidantes. She was surrounded by people, but there were not many she could really talk to. She had a lot of acquaintances, but few real friends; too few. With friendship comes a certain amount of intimacy, of sharing your feelings and innermost thoughts, and there were not many people she could confide in. Because she was the Princess of Wales, and many people were too dazzled by her status to see the whole person.

Try as she might, she could not switch the Princess role on and off like a light switch. Marriage to Prince Charles had removed her from ordinary life in a way that she had not foreseen, and it was a long struggle to rediscover the simple pleasures of giving and sharing confidences. Prince Philip summed up the attitude of the Royal Family when he said, 'It is much safer to unburden yourself to a member of family than just a friend. You see, you're never quite sure. A small indiscretion can lead to all sorts of difficulties.'

As Diana observed to me, 'They don't have friendships—they have allies. They are a tribe and their instinct is tribal.'

That was savagely illustrated by Princess Margaret, who initially had been very supportive of Diana when she married into the Royal Family, only to turn against her when she refused to submit to their arcane customs. They rowed over butler Harold Brown, whom Margaret employed after Diana had let him go. When Diana suggested that Brown leave the grace-and-favour apartment at Kensington Palace that had gone with his job, Margaret had rounded on her and reminded her that it wasn't hers to give or take. In a steely voice, she told Diana, 'Just remember who owns the flat—and who owns yours, too.'

Shortly after the *Panorama* interview, Margaret wrote Diana a stinging letter of rebuke, accusing her of letting everyone down and being 'incapable of making even the smallest sacrifice'. That really upset Diana. She thought she would always be able to count on 'Margo'. I told Diana that she was naive to think that Margaret, who was royal through and through and very superficial with it, would support her against the family. I was right, because their friendship never recovered, and Margaret started referring to Diana as 'that silly girl'. Diana came to the conclusion the Royal Family had no idea how to treat friends, even if indeed they had any, which she reckoned they didn't.

'They take you in until something goes wrong. Then it's "them and us",' Diana decided.

The only people they mixed with on anything approaching equal terms were their own relations or a few grand aristocrats, but they were not privy to what the senior members of the Royal Family were thinking. The Queen Mother veiled herself in regal majesty, Prince Philip's irascibility repels conversation, the Queen is discreet to the point of being tongue-tied in case anything that might possibly pass for an opinion might pass her lips, while Charles is so 'anally retentive', as Diana put it, that even his own wife never really knew what was on his mind.

Diana was so much more forthcoming. She liked to discuss matters in a frank and honest manner, and those people she did feel comfortable with shared in the minutiae of her life and were rewarded with her trust. We were a mixed bag, which included, as well as me, journalists and several dynamic older ladies. We were selected, not for reasons of class or background, but because Diana genuinely liked us and we became her private court.

Her women friends tended to be older than her because she had seen and experienced a lot more than friends of her own age, which rather set her apart from her own generation. She loved to chat and gossip about trivia, but not for long. She needed to talk about more meaningful things and found that she was able to relate much better to those who would listen and give the understanding that only comes from personal experience.

Fergie and Lady Cosima Somerset had been the exceptions to that general rule but all courts have their intrigues and scandals and they fell from favour.

The Duchess of York was ostracised after breaching the unspoken code of confidentiality, but the estrangement from Cosima was more complex. For a while she was a regular caller at Kensington Palace and had accompanied Diana on her visit to the cricketer Imran Khan's cancer hospital in Lahore, Pakistan. When it came to matters of the heart, however, the twice divorced 'Cosi', born in the same year as Diana, proved too self-indulgent for the Princess's sense of propriety.

Officially, she was the daughter of the Marquis of Londonderry. She was actually the daughter of Robin Douglas-Home, the nightclub pianist and nephew of the former Prime Minister, Sir Alec Douglas-Home. He had once enjoyed an adulterous affair with Princess Margaret. Then, in 1967, he had formed a liaison with Lord Londonderry's wife, Nicolette, which led to the birth of Cosima.

At the age of twenty-one Cosima had married Cosmo Fry, heir to a chocolate fortune, only to part almost the moment the honeymoon was over. She later wed the Duke of Beaufort's youngest son, Lord John, by whom she had a son and a daughter.

Diana met her at the Richmond home of her putative aunt, Lord Londonderry's sister Lady Annabel Goldsmith, and the two soon became friends. 'Our mutual interests included the spiritual and the psychic,' Cosima said.

It was not an easy relationship, however. Cosima was overloaded with her own problems stemming from the upheavals in her family background. As well as dallying with Douglas-Home, her mother also had an affair with the 1960s R&B singer, Georgie Fame, and had borne him a son while she was still married. When Lord Londonderry found out, the marriage came to an end, the boy was disinherited, and, although she married Fame, Nico ended up taking her own life. The following year, in 1968, Robin Douglas-Home, whose mother was Diana's great-aunt, also committed suicide. When these family skeletons eventually came tumbling out of the closet, Cosima went through a long period of public soul-searching.

'In all the darkest moments somehow she sensed my need for comfort without my having to ask,' she recalled of Diana.

Despite that empathy, there was only so much time Diana was able to devote to the troubled woman, given that she was in the middle of her own divorce. She started calling Cosima the 'Prozac Queen'. When the telephone rang at KP one day, Diana asked me to answer it, which I did, pretending to be a new member of staff. I then put my hand over the mouthpiece and said, 'It's Cosi.' Diana told me to tell her she was out.

What really undid their friendship was Diana's discovery that Cosima, in a manner reminiscent of Nico, was having an affair with Lady Annabel's husband, the buccaneering financier Sir James Goldsmith. Cosima wrote later of the 'generous and unconditional friendship' Diana gave to her, but the Princess did not excuse her for what she regarded as a gross act of betrayal. Despite the fact that they were not actually blood relations, Annabel had always treated her 'niece' with kindness and consideration. She was Cosima's godmother and regarded her almost as a daughter, and it was Annabel who, when Cosima was eleven and at the request of Nicolette who couldn't face doing it herself, shouldered the responsibility of telling her who her real father was. For Cosima to go behind her back and into the bed of her husband was, in Diana's opinion, disloyalty of the worst kind. Diana was really very shocked by Cosima's behaviour.

Part of the blame must lie with Sir James, a notorious womaniser who once remarked, 'When I marry the role of

my mistress falls vacant,' and blatantly lived with a mistress
on his frequent visits to Paris. Diana met him many times at
lunch at Ormeley Lodge, Annabel's house on Ham Common
on the outskirts of London, where he would expect everyone
to sit and listen while he dominated the conversation. He
was forceful, immensely rich and, when it came to women,
very insistent. He was also very charming when he chose to
be, but in Diana's eyes that was no excuse for Cosima's conduct and she cut her out of her life. She may have been a
'soul sister', as Cosima kept insisting, but Annabel was a
friend and that counted for a great deal more.

Annabel and Diana had first met when Diana was a little
girl, and they met up often when she became the Princess of
Wales. 'Laughter,' Annabel said, 'was an essential ingredient
in our relationship.' She became a regular guest at Ormeley
for Sunday lunches, which Annabel described as 'chaotic.
Everyone helps themselves and lunch is eaten so fast that
Diana eventually started to time us. "Right," she would say,
"today was an all-time record—fifteen minutes." Laughter
would ring round the table and everyone would speak at
once. No ceremony here, and Diana loved it.'

Diana always took a bunch for flowers with her—and her
gift of putting people at their ease. As Annabel recalled,
'Few people realised just how funny she could be. Fellow
lunch guests who were meeting Diana for the first time were
often overwhelmed by her naturalness and quick wit.'

After lunch Diana would go for a walk in Annabel's
beautiful garden and talk. She trusted Annabel totally and
got on well with Annabel's children, including Jemima who
was thirteen years her junior. She thoroughly enjoyed being
in such a close family atmosphere, and if she had William
and Harry with her she would take them too. She was always
full of beans after a visit to Ham Common. Annabel wasn't
in the business of handing out advice, but she was a very
good listener and Diana appreciated having someone she
could talk to who was wise and worldly enough to understand her problems.

The same was true of Elsa Bowker, who had been born in

Egypt to a French mother and a Lebanese father and had later married a British diplomat. She was very wise and assumed a grandmotherly role in her life, while Lucia Flecha de Lima, the wife of the Brazilian ambassador to London was, Diana said, 'the mother I would have liked to have had'.

Another woman whom she turned to was Rosa Monckton. They were introduced by Lucia, whose daughter, Beatrice, worked for Tiffany's in London where Rosa was managing director.

Diana felt that Rosa had been dealt a bad hand in life, losing one baby and then giving birth to another, Domenica, who suffers from Down's Syndrome. Those problems naturally drew Diana to her. She called Domenica, who became her goddaughter, 'a little gift', explaining, 'We can learn about love from her as Down's Syndrome kids are completely uninhibited about giving affection.' (In a gesture of compassion) Diana allowed Rosa to bury her still-born child in her garden at Kensington Palace.

Rosa recalled, 'Diana was by my side and a constant support, day and night, throughout those intensely difficult and private moments.'

Despite their closeness, their friendship was a strange one because the Monckton family were very much part of the Establishment Diana had come to fear. Rosa's grandfather had advised the Duke of Windsor during the abdication crisis of 1936. Her brother Anthony is a senior officer in the British Secret Intelligence Service and her husband Dominic Lawson is editor of the *Sunday Telegraph*.

Due to Diana's concern about the Establishment and the Intelligence Services, she was understandably wary of Rosa at times.

Unlike Diana, who was willing to drop everything for a friend in need, she was one of those people who put their own commitments first. Diana could not be a hundred per cent relaxed with her, as she felt there was always a part of Rosa that had something more pressing to do. But Diana did not allow that to disrupt their relationship.

She often sought Rosa's counsel, and often consulted

Elsa or Lucia, although she rarely paid any heed to what they said. 'She frequently asked me for advice but rarely took it,' Rosa said. The historian and journalist Paul Johnson found her equally obdurate. He recalled, 'She used to have me over to lunch to ask my advice. I'd give her good advice, and she'd say: "I entirely agree. Paul, you're so right." Then she'd go and do the opposite.'

She didn't always take my advice, either. She listened to my advice and there were times when she said, 'You are one hundred per cent right'—and then go off and do precisely the opposite. I said, 'You can take my advice or you can leave it. If you don't want to take it it's up to you, but when things go wrong, don't come back and have me say, "I told you so".' She said she wouldn't—but she often did. She was impulsive and sometimes petty but that was just her way. It was also understandable. Throughout her marriage she was forever being told what to do, and how to behave, and had reached the point when she said to herself, 'No more—I'm going to do it my way.' She didn't always get it right but after being held in check for so long, I believe she was entitled to make her own mistakes. I admired her for the way she faced up to the challenge—and after so many years locked in the royal cocoon it was a challenge—to break free and discover what she could do for herself.

When it came to the practicalities of her work, however, Diana was always willing to accept professional advice, and the person who helped her put her thoughts into words was Richard Kay, the tall, curly-haired royal correspondent of the *Daily Mail* who always looked pale and harassed. Diana thought that he looked like a cadaverous Richard Gere.

When I first met Diana she was already friends with Richard, who had become close to her on her visit to Nepal 1993. We met him at KP on a Saturday night in 1996. I was there with a therapist called Ursula and Diana announced that she wanted us to meet someone who turned out to be Richard. Shortly after the introductions were made, Ursula went to use the lavatory just off Diana's bedroom—and pressed the panic button instead of the light switch. A few seconds later half a dozen policemen came bursting into the apartment. One of the police officers saw Richard and asked, 'Ricardo, what are you doing here? Your name isn't on the list.'

There is a police sentry box by the main gates into Kensington Palace where you are required to stop and give your name to the officers on duty. It transpired that Richard passed it most afternoons but used different names in order not to attract too much attention to himself. He didn't want his name being entered into the log every day. But while the policemen were in on the ruse, the policemen who came rushing in weren't, which was why they were so surprised to find him there.

Richard stayed for dinner, while Ursula and I prepared a pasta dinner. Diana watched in fascination as she had no idea how to cook anything, apart from toasted sandwiches, baked potatoes and tea. (Later she was extremely proud of herself for being able to microwave an instant meal.) He used to visit often, and passed on the latest Fleet Street gossip about the Royal Family. There was always a lot of friendly banter between them, and she used to tease him all the time, which he didn't like.

She could also be very offhand. On his birthday one year, we all went to lunch and Diana gave him a present which wasn't in the least bit personal (a tie or a diary), which had obviously come out of the stock of gifts she used to keep. Richard commented on that and she was embarrassed enough to look a little sheepish. They were like brother and sister—or an old married couple.

Their disagreements were usually over something he had written about her or, just as often, something she thought he should have written or done. For instance, when he confessed that he had gone against her instructions and not voted against the monarchy in the debate broadcast on the BBC in January 1997, she got very annoyed. She had continually pressed the redial button on her telephone to register yet another vote calling for the abolition of the monarchy and felt that he had let her down by not doing the same.

In turn, he was very possessive about her and when her acupuncturist Dr Lily gave an interview to another newspaper he went crazy, saying it was a betrayal of Diana. What he really meant was that she had let him down by speaking to someone other than him. He had no real right to complain, however, because Diana gave him a lot of exclusives.

The popular conception is that Diana was hounded unmercifully by the press, and so she was on many occasions. In Italy, she once got stuck in a crowd, which she never liked, and found herself surrounded by a mob of paparazzi. She said it was the most frightening moment of her life. She told me, 'It's like mental rape,' and it got to a point where a camera flash felt like a physical attack.

At the same time, however, Diana was not averse to using the press to get across her own version of events, and Richard was the reporter she employed. If something was written that she didn't like, she would get hold of Richard at once and give him her response. She used to call him at all hours of the day or night and he became her mouthpiece. When, for example, another newspaper wrote about Diana's extravagant expenditure, Richard countered with a story about how she had pulled a drowning tramp out of the pond in London's Regent's Park.

As well as writing favourably about her, he also helped her prepare her speeches. She used to tell him the gist of what she wanted to say and he would go home, write it and then deliver it back to KP. He was very good, as he understood her. The speeches weren't too long and had just the right amount of the emotive factor. He made a valuable contribution for which he took no credit. It didn't always spare him from Diana's displeasure, however. She could be demanding and was quick to take umbrage if he didn't do exactly what she wanted. Even a small slip-up could set her off.

When on one occasion the opening paragraph of a story he had written didn't meet with her approval, she stopped speaking to him and slammed the phone down when he called. He rang me in a panic, so after I had read the offending piece I called Diana and told her that there really was nothing wrong with the article, which taken as a whole was very favourable.

It didn't do any good. Richard came over to see me and told me how distressed he was: she had screamed at him and refused to take his calls. I gave him some healing and Diana happened to phone while he was there. I said, 'Guess who's here?' She replied, 'It's Richard—and I don't want to speak to him.'

When he had gone, I called her back and told her she was being ridiculous and that she really should apologise for upsetting her friend in such a way. She went very quiet, because the one thing Diana didn't do was apologise. But she took the hint, and after leaving him to stew for a couple of days called him as if nothing had happened. He was very relieved. At that time, she really was his whole life and their relationship continued right to the end. Richard was the last person Diana spoke to before she died.

She was always rather circumspect about what she told him, however. Diana kept her friends in compartments, to the extent of having different mobile telephones, each with a different number which she would give out to different people. It was her way of separating her life into different parts and she never told Richard about Hasnat Kahn, terrified it might leak out. When he found out about it, as he inevitably did, Richard was very upset.

She was equally guarded with Paul Burrell. She had been quite fond of him though, and used to pull his leg when the opportunity arose. We were once watching a documentary on television about the Royal Family and when Paul flashed on the screen in his full footman's livery, Diana turned to him and said, 'Lovely calves, Paul.' He liked the attention and went out of his way to court it. More than once, however, she decided she couldn't trust him and started to freeze him out.

Burrell went to the United States most years to see friends and buy original Disney cartoons from the various films which he liked to collect. When he flew off in September 1996, however, he went with a different purpose in mind.

He was going to be interviewed for the job of butler to the actor and director Mel Gibson. He hadn't told Diana but she knew what he was up to—and didn't care. She just heaved a sigh of relief that he wasn't around, because he had been irritating her for months. He was always hovering around, bowing and scraping, listening to what she was saying and then giving her his opinions, rather like Iago in *Othello*. After a while she stopped talking to him altogether and started sending him his instructions by handwritten note.

Matters became even more strained when Diana discovered him rifling through the personal papers in her desk. She was furious. She went absolutely ballistic. Her detective, Ken Wharfe, heard the row, came into the room—and was greeted by the sight of Burrell on his hands and knees, kissing her foot and pleading with her for forgiveness.

Wharfe asked, 'What is going on?' When she told him what had happened, he told her, 'Get rid of him now, ma'am.'

The next day Burrell arrived with his wife, Maria, to beg to keep his job. It was only when he came back with his children, who were weeping, that she relented, but relations between the Princess and her butler never fully recovered.

What amazed me was Burrell's inability to learn from experience. Some time later I stepped in to stop Diana from firing him, which she fully intended to do after she had again caught him reading through her correspondence.

She was seething. I reminded her that of all the people around her, he was the one who would have done anything for Diana, the one she could always rely on. She could have trusted him with her life. He was in love with her, not in the sexual sense but in an obsessive way, and I am convinced that if she had dismissed him he would have considered taking his own life. She agreed to keep him on, but relations between them remained tense.

One Sunday afternoon when I arrived at KP, Diana asked me to help her check her china which she kept in a special room. She had just noticed that plates and tureens had gone missing, and she decided to make a proper inventory. I went into the cupboard, which was like a walk-in wardrobe but with shelves, and saw to my amazement there were dozens of dinner services, not with eight or twelve plates each, but up to six times as many. I stood on a chair and called out what was there and she ticked it off against the list. She was furious when she realised how much had disappeared. 'It looks as if someone is collecting their own dinner service,' she said.

According to Diana, this kind of pilfering went on all the time at the various palaces. She told me about a footman who created a miniature royal palace in his flat, complete with Buckingham Palace towels in his bathroom, Buckingham Palace sheets on his bed, King George V's hairbrushes on his dressing table, a plate from every one of the Queen's dinner services hanging on his walls, and George V's crested ciphered glasses on the dining table. His treasure trove was discovered and he received a letter from the royal household saying, 'We understand that you have some items that belong to Her Majesty in your possession and if you would like to parcel them all up and have them delivered to the side door of Buckingham Palace nothing more will be said about it.'

The footman who stole Queen Mary's wedding ring was not treated so leniently. He was sent to prison. She didn't suspect Paul of being responsible for the disappearing china, but, as the butler, it was his duty to ensure that this kind of thing did not happen. However, the suggestion that Burrell had more of Diana's property in his possession than could logically be explained would eventually land him in court. I was able to help him because I was the only person who actually saw Diana give things to Paul.

I was at KP on the day Diana was having a clear-out. She was standing near Charles's old study which had been converted into William's and Harry's video games room, looking at a gigantic black bin liner. I said, 'Don't tell me you are collecting the rubbish.' She said, 'No, I'd just forgotten how much junk we had accumulated.' She summoned Paul, opened the bag and showed him what she was giving him. It was the usual collection of cast-offs—William's and Harry's clothes which would have been suitable for his sons, Alexander and Nicholas; Game Boys, Nintendo and CDs she didn't want. There were also some dresses for Paul's wife Maria which would have to have had six inches taken off the hem if they were ever going to fit, and numerous designer shoes (they shared the same shoe size) and handbags. There was no mahogany box, and Hewitt's signet ring certainly wasn't there, but at least I had seen her give him something.

Paul's lawyer, Andrew Shaw, learned what I had witnessed and I gave him a statement. The police also contacted me and asked me to give a statement to them. I took advice from Shaw who said that what the police were trying to do was to get everyone to give them statements in order to negate anything they might have said previously, which I found very annoying. But I did tell them that, knowing Paul as I did, he had probably got himself into such a state that if he had taken some other things, he would have done so in the belief that he was looking after them for her.

When Paul called to thank me for coming forward he became very confused. He talked about Diana being naked in front of him and kept repeating, 'Diana is with me.' I had to be very firm with him. I said, 'Diana *never* walked naked before you. And she is *not* with you. You were just like this when your mother died. Don't you remember how you kept telling us that you could hear her talking to you? You were with your mother more than anyone else at the time.'

Then he started asking if I remembered certain incidents, because he was no longer sure when something was factual or not. He was obsessed about the letters in which Diana talked about her fears for her life, but they weren't written to him. And the story about Diana slipping out of KP, naked except for a fur coat, to go and meet Hasnat was pure fantasy.

What really happened was that Diana and I were talking over tea in the afternoon before they were due to meet. She said, 'Wouldn't it be funny if I just turned up in a fur coat, lots of jewellery—and nothing underneath.' I laughingly warned, 'But imagine what would happen if you were stopped by the police!'

Burrell just happened to come in and put the tea tray down as we joked about this. He overheard what we were saying and got the wrong end of the stick. Diana didn't even have a fur coat. She didn't like them and had given away the only one she ever possessed, which had been a gift. It was unkind to suggest that the Princess he professed to adore would ever have been so wanton as to drive out into the night without any clothes on but everything was getting mixed up in his mind. He was clearly under a great deal of stress and told me that he was taking antidepressants.

I must admit that I was getting rather hassled myself. To prepare me for the Burrell trial Jeremy Britten from the BBC showed me around the Old Bailey. We went into the Number One court and he told me where I would be standing, where the journalists sat, and where Paul would be. I also went into the Criminal Court Witness Service where the witnesses wait. It was very intimidating, but I was prepared to go through with it. I do not like to see miscarriages of justice, whether it was him or Charles in the dock.

Shaw was planning to use me as surprise witness because my evidence would certainly have raised doubt about the prosecution's case in the minds of the jurors. They kept me hanging around for days, waiting to be called, but in the end I never got my day in court. The case collapsed dramatically when the Queen suddenly recalled that Burrell had told her he was holding some of Diana's goods for 'safekeeping'.

Her intervention was probably just as well because Paul had accumulated information that would have been very damaging to the Royal Family.

After Diana died he had seen Mrs Shand Kydd, complete with a bottle of wine, sorting through her papers and consigning many of them (she confessed to between fifty and a hundred in court) to the shredder in order to protect her daughter's reputation. I know that Diana kept a personal diary with a clasp and lock in which she recorded her thoughts and feelings. That has never been found. Neither have those infamous tape recordings, nor those highly confidential documents which Diana showed to me and which I am sure are still in existence, but which have yet to see the light of day.

For instance, what became of the Prince Philip letters? I can only speculate where they went, but if Burrell, who knew a lot of Diana's secrets, had been made to take the stand, I believe he would have revealed a lot more than the Royal Family would have been able to cope with.

To be around Diana was to enjoy the company of someone who had always been full of verve and enthusiasm. I was terribly sad that everything ended in this squalid way, with servants and family fighting over the titbits of her memory. It wasn't what Diana would have wished, and she would have been horrified by the pain it caused William and Harry.

# 17

# The Last Summer

From what I observed, the member of the Fayed family who really worshipped Diana was not Dodi but his father Mohamed.

He would do absolutely anything for her. He showered her with gifts, kept telephoning to ask how she was, and, when the opportunity presented itself, put all the trappings of his wealth at her disposal—and all this long before his son started escorting her.

I asked her one day, 'Hasn't it occurred to you that he might really fancy you?' She giggled and said, 'He's old enough to be my father, and his language is very naughty, isn't it?' she said. 'He probably has everything bugged, even the bars of soap. But he makes me laugh,' and when he offered her things, she accepted them without always questioning the motives behind it.

It was Dodi, of course, with whom she had a relationship, although I am absolutely convinced that, while they have slept in the same bed, they never actually made love. He had too many problems—and Diana wasn't cut out to play the role of a sexual Florence Nightingale. What she wanted to do was make Hasnat Khan jealous and she thought that the playboy Dodi was just the man to do so.

They got together on holiday in St Tropez in the south of France where she had been invited by Mohamed. By that time she already knew a lot about the Fayeds, and Mohamed in particular, who had been a friend of her father, Earl Spencer. The two men could not have been more different. Lord Spencer was an aristocrat of the old school, while Mohamed was an outspoken and often vulgar Egyptian who had worked his way through the alleyways of Middle Eastern commerce with the help of his arms-dealer brother-in-law Adnan Khashoggi to become the very rich owner of Harrods, the world's most prestigious department store. The disparity in backgrounds didn't seem to bother Lord Spencer, who liked shopping at Harrods and enjoyed Mohamed's generosity and robust sense of humour.

It didn't perturb Diana, either. She was well aware that he was an anti-Establishment figure, and that people were only nice to him because of what he could do for them, but she took him for what he was—bluff, over-the-top, and just a little dangerous. She had been wise enough not to take up his offer to bring William and Harry to visit the Duke of Windsor's old home in the Bois de Boulogne in Paris which he owned. 'My instincts told me not to put my head over the parapet with that one,' she explained. But she also told me that he had been very good to her after her father died, and that counted for a lot.

Dodi was a very different character. He was much weaker than his father. He also had a well-publicised cocaine problem, which made him difficult to deal with at times. But he was extremely attentive, and Diana liked that. Prince Charles had regarded her as a petulant child, Hewitt had used her as a sexual play thing, Oliver Hoare saw her as a trophy, and Hasnat Kahn did not have the courage to commit himself. Dodi treated her like a princess.

He flattered her, indulged her every whim, and made himself totally available for her, all of which was a pleasant change from what she had experienced before. The others had wanted a little piece of her but were not prepared to give her their undivided attention in return. Dodi was. He also knew how to treat women. Every woman likes romance and that is exactly what Dodi gave her. When he said, 'Let's go for dinner,' he would whisk her off by private jet to Paris, take her to the Ritz where he would hide a Cartier bangle under the napkin for her to find. It was heavy wooing of a kind that is very hard to resist, and Diana was charmed. He also happened to be good-looking and well-mannered, with boats and cars and all the other toys of the rich with which to amuse her.

I cautioned her not to get too taken in by Mohamed's superficial charm. So did Rosa Monckton who said, 'I strongly advised her not to go on holiday with the Fayeds.' Diana wasn't listening. She had planned to go on holiday with American fashion designer Lana Marks, but she had backed out because of a family bereavement. It wasn't that easy for her to find a holiday destination at the drop of a hat. She couldn't just phone a friend and say, 'Let's go off somewhere.'

That summer she had toyed with accepting an invitation from Gulu Lalvani, the Indian electronics magnate, to join him at his beach house in Thailand.

The American billionaire Teddy Forstmann was also urging her to come to his mansion in the Hamptons on Long Island. They had been introduced to the aerospace tycoon in 1994 by the banker Lord [Jacob] Rothschild at a dinner at Spencer House, Diana's family's London home overlooking Green Park. 'I was flattered she had read up on me,' he recalled, and afterwards she asked him to escort her to a party at Annabel's, the Mayfair nightclub named after Annabel Goldsmith. They became friends, and when Diana was on a holiday with Lucia Flecha de Lima in Martha's Vineyard they became tennis partners. On several occasions he put his Gulf Stream 5 jet at her disposal. After he refused her request for £21 million to help finance a hospital, however, a friendship that had never been more than platonic quickly cooled.

In the end she decided to go to the Fayed villa in St Tropez because it offered sunshine, a yacht (Mohamed went out and bought one specially for her visit) and the bodyguards who she believed were skilled enough to protect her privacy. The family atmosphere that she had always craved also appealed. 'It makes me feel safe and secure,' she explained.

She reminded me of Jackie Onassis. For as well as having extravagant fun, she was rebelling against all those constrictions that had been part and parcel of her life. Diana was ignoring the world at large in much the same way that President Kennedy's widow did when she married the Greek shipping millionaire, Aristotle Onassis. Although it had caused an enormous furore at the time, she went ahead with it anyway. She didn't like being dictated to. Nor did Diana. She got little bees in her bonnet and if she felt it was right for her she couldn't be talked out of it. She called it 'my instincts', and they took her to the south of France and then on to Paris.

The trouble was that it all suddenly spun out of her control. Mohamed set his heart on marrying her to his son, and Dodi, forever in his father's thrall, meekly went along with that and dumped Kelly Fisher, an American model he was engaged to. It would have been an enormous coup if he had become the father-in-law to the mother of the future King. But this was most definitely not what Diana wanted.

It had nothing to do with him being a Muslim or the fact that he was foreign. Hasnat Khan was both and she would willingly have given up everything for him if he had plucked up the courage to ask. But she had fancied Hasnat. She was attracted to a lot of other men. She thought that David Hasselhoff of *Baywatch* was 'very hunky'. She thought that John Travolta had 'magnetism', and we had a long discussion one evening about David Duchovny, who played Agent Fox Mulder in the *X-Files*. She asked me, 'Do you think I could ever get a man as good-looking as him?' She thought he was absolutely gorgeous. So did I, to which she said, 'Simone, I can't believe we like the same type of men.' I replied, 'No we don't, because I would never have gone for Charles.'

For all his good points, Dodi wasn't in quite the same category as Duchovny. She didn't really fancy Dodi. To put it bluntly, he simply wasn't her type.

She had met him at polo matches at Windsor in the late 1980s, and again in 1991 at the première of Steven Spielberg's *Hook*, which he had helped finance, but he had left little impact on her. Diana was very open about her relationships and we were always discussing whom she had met and whom she fancied, yet she never once mentioned him afterwards.

Frances Shand Kydd had observed that Dodi was hairy from the neck down and Diana had never liked that. She once asked me, 'What do you think of men with hairy backs?' I said, 'They look like gorillas.' We were just having a joke (Diana went on to say that she didn't like bald men either). Even so, I thought it was a very odd question, which led me later to believe that her relationship with Dodi was not as intimate as everyone assumed.

She was not the kind of woman who jumped into bed with every man she met. She wasn't like that. She had to get to know and respect them and, most importantly, fall in love with them first. The differences between her and Dodi were simply too great for them ever to have found the common ground which could have developed into something more. He was a late sleeper; she was always up early. He was lazy; she was active and always on the go. He was frivolous; she was a thinker. He also had a weakness for cocaine, which does not enhance sexual performance.

Diana knew all about the drug. She had seen the effect it had, and she was well aware of the problems of having a relationship with someone taking drugs. We had discussed it at great length and talked about the difficulties that arise when drug-induced energies seep through your aura and start mucking up your life. It's damaging and she wouldn't have wanted that.

It was not that she didn't like the man Prince Philip scathingly referred to as 'an oily bed hopper', because it was very obvious that she did like Dodi (but just because you are with someone it doesn't mean you have to have sex with them). When I came back from Bosnia Diana asked me where I had slept and I told her that I had shared a bed with

Morris Power of the Red Cross. We were just friends, nothing more, and it wasn't a problem for me (although it might have been for him as I talked so much and he really needed his sleep). Diana understood completely. She said, 'I thought I was the only one who had relationships like that.'

If she really had been having an affair, she would have told someone because she could never keep something like that quiet. She was someone who liked to talk about her experiences with her women friends. On this occasion, however, she never said anything, most probably because there was nothing to say.

What kept them together for those few short weeks in 1997, apart from the pleasure they took in each other's company, was Diana's determination to wean him off drugs. He became her mission of the moment. She was the therapist and he was the patient in their relationship. That was hardly a reason to get married, however.

There were also her sons' wishes to take into consideration. How would they have taken it? Not very well, I suspect. They had enjoyed frolicking on the French Riviera on that first holiday, but they were both very British in their outlook and were really at their happiest following traditional country pursuits. The jet-set lifestyle was all very well for a few days, but not as a way of life.

Mohamed would doubtless have moved heaven and earth to give her what she wanted, if she had agreed to become his son's wife. He would have bought her houses, and laid on planes, and financed her charity work, but Diana was well aware how much more effective she would be as the Princess of Wales working independently, rather than plain Mrs Dodi Fayed working as an employee of her father-in-law. She was also far too savvy to commit herself to wed again so soon after the trauma of her first marriage. As she pointed out, 'Having been married to a man who was controlled by his mother, why would I marry a man who was controlled by his father?'

She had her fantasies, as we all do, but she was quite realistic when it came to planning for the future. She had spent enough time with Mohamed and his family to appreciate that the security arrangements he insisted on were more suffocating than anything she had experienced as a member of the Royal Family and what Diana really wanted at that stage was her independence.

'I don't want to be bought—I have everything I want,' she explained to Rosa Monckton.

She also wanted a break from the prying eyes that followed her everywhere in Europe. She had become sick to the eyeballs of the paparazzi who were making her life a misery. She told me, 'It's like living in a goldfish bowl with all these people coming to look at you and you're just there swimming around in circles with no escape.'

Hiding behind a blanket of security was not the answer, however. She had got rid of her own Royal Protection officers for that very reason, and she had no desire to incarcerate herself in another gilded prison.

She seriously considered moving to the United States. The reasons she gave to me were that she wouldn't be bound by any restrictions and would have a lot more space for herself. She found out the privacy laws and discovered that she could have security guards who wouldn't encroach on her. They would live in the grounds of her house but they would not follow her around everywhere, as the Scotland Yard policemen had done and Mohamed's bodyguards now did.

Hasnat had initially been involved in the scheme, but when he backed out of her life, Diana went ahead anyway. She got quite excited about the prospect of settling in America. She liked the true democracy, the freedom of speech and the space America offered, and she pointed out that it was so much cheaper to live there than in Britain.

She employed a discreet estate agency to help her and they sent her the brochures for some wonderful houses, mostly in California. When I went over to KP one day, she had them piled on her desk. We spread them out over the floor of her sitting room. Some of them were big, even by the standards of Kensington Palace, with their own gyms, tennis courts and swimming pools, and the large office space

she required for her charity work. A couple even had their
own private beaches. There were a few which were gaudy
and not to her taste, which was very feminine, but most of
them were magnificent.

'The boys will love it there,' she said, and with daily
flights out of Los Angeles, she could have easily popped
back to London for half-terms and they could have flown
over to be with her for part of their holidays.

The house that particularly caught her eye was one in
Malibu that had once been owned by Julie Andrews and her
husband, film director Blake Edwards. Built in the style of a
Mexican hacienda, it lay in its own five-acre estate with its
own private access to the beach, which meant that it was all
but impossible for anyone else to get to. On the hill above
the house was a glassed-in gym with views over the Pacific
Ocean. When Mohamed learned of Diana's interest in the
house, some time between her first and second visit to
France, he went and bought it, ostensibly for Dodi but in fact
as a possible wedding present for the couple.

That was bound to annoy Diana. She wanted her own nest
and often told me, 'If I get a house I want it to be mine and
mine alone.' She didn't want to live in someone else's house,
as she had done since she moved out of her bachelor girl flat
in Colherne Court in London's Earls Court into the palaces
belonging to her mother-in-law. She said, 'I want a property
in my name now.'

This was no idle pipe dream. She really wanted to uproot
herself and start again. Given the time, I am sure she would
have done so. She had had enough of Britain. The Royal
Family were putting obstacles in her way and she had good
reason to feel that the government of Tony Blair had let her
down badly.

In opposition Blair had made it is business to get to know
Diana. He had invited her to his home in Islington and she
thought him magnetic and attractive in his own way, but it
was his wife, Cherie, who most intrigued her. Diana made
some funny remarks about her disproportionate face and her
strange mouth, but added, 'You don't look at that—you look

at where she had got to in a man's world. You have to give her the kudos of getting there.'

She was fascinated by powerful women, and the fact that Cherie was a successful barrister interested her. It was an example, she said, of what women could achieve if they put their mind to it. She had somewhat mixed feelings about her as the Prime Minister's wife, however. She was convinced that Cherie wore the trousers in the marriage and was slightly wary of her.

They had several lunches together, and Diana got on well with his children. She took her boys with her on one occasion and they kicked a football around in the back garden with Euan, who was the same age as Harry. After one of their meetings she asked her astrologer Debbie Frank to do Tony's and Cherie's birth charts, as she wanted to know how good he would be for the country—and for her.

But if the signs were good the relationship never developed, and whatever rapport they had quickly dissipated. As the fast-rising star of the Labour Party and later its leader, he made her all sorts of promises about what her future role would be. She was very hopeful, because he was the one who had approached her and promised her a job as a roving ambassador if he won the election. It was exactly the role she wanted and which she would have been so good at. She also met Blair's strategist, Peter Mandelson, and the new Foreign Secretary Robin Cook, who was impressed by her charm and dedication. Everyone appeared to be very excited about getting Diana 'on side', as they called it. She told me, 'At long last I can be put to good use.'

When he came to power, however, Blair reneged on his pledge. He could have spoken to the Queen about it as soon as he was elected, which is precisely what he said he would do. When Diana said she was going to do something, she did it. Tony Blair didn't. She rang him on several occasions and raised the matter when she went to see him at Chequers, his prime ministerial country house, taking William and Harry with her. She called me from there to say how beautiful it was, and how the food was delicious and what a good time she was having. But whenever she mentioned the post he had promised, all he did was prevaricate. After yet another fruitless telephone call to Blair, she said to me, 'I'm just being brushed aside. It's not going to happen.'

She was insulted that he didn't take her seriously, and she felt very let down. The Labour Party was always talking about caring for others, and no one would have been better at that than Diana. Her profile was a worldwide one, she commanded the respect of people everywhere she went, and as a roving ambassador bringing attention to the plight of others, she would have done wonders for Britain's international reputation.

It was what she really wanted to do—not for her own satisfaction but because she genuinely cared about other people. Despite the way Tony Blair treated her, it was what she was utterly determined to do, even if it meant carrying on her work under her own steam. Dodi Fayed was merely an interlude and she would quickly have become bored with him.

But fates intervened and at twenty-three minutes past midnight on 31 August 1997, she was killed in a car crash in Paris with Dodi at her side.

According to investigative film-maker David Cohen who made the Channel 5 documentary, *Diana: The Night She Died*, a handbag containing cocaine was found in the back of the wreckage of the Mercedes. The handbag and its contents mysteriously disappeared.

Diana had been given the drug once, and vowed to me that she would never try it again. She is the only person in that car who would have been carrying a handbag, but if she really did have some cocaine in her possession it could only be because she had confiscated it from Dodi.

Helping others was her calling in life—right to the very end.

# 18

# The End

On the night of 31 August 1997 I had gone to bed early for a
change and was fast asleep when a friend called me to say
that Diana had been involved in a car accident.

It was long past midnight but I leapt out of bed, ran to put
my contact lenses in and then turned on the television.

The first reports said that she had broken a leg, but I had
a terrible sense of doom. It felt like a rock in the pit of my
stomach accompanied by a prickly sensation that spread
from head to toe.

I had had that same experience the morning my father
died. I had driven over to my parents' house and I told my
father that I knew there would be a death in the house before
the day was out. My mother happened to be very ill with
cancer, but Dad, who everyone thought was as strong as an
ox and had just been given the all clear after a full medical
check-up, was having none of that and told me not to be so
ridiculous.

At four o'clock that afternoon, however, he suffered a
heart attack and was rushed to hospital. I went with him. As
I waited by the bedside, my long dead grandparents came in
spirit. They seemed to be standing in front of a large, dif-
fused but very bright light. They were waiting for him and at
about midnight he passed on, walked out of his body and
went to meet them.

I saw them disappear into the light. When I looked down on the bed, my father's physical body was still there. He looked amazingly serene and peaceful. I told Diana what I had seen and she said that she had felt something very similar when her own father died. She had come to accept death as part of the life cycle and that, while death may be the end of the physical, it is not the end of the spiritual body.

Even with that thought to sustain me, however, I was reduced to a state of shock when my premonition was confirmed and the newscaster announced that the Princess of Wales had died of her injuries. Diana had often told me that she would never 'make old bones', and was certain that she would 'die young in unnatural circumstances'.

It was disturbing when that prediction came true, and for the whole of the following week I was in a state of suspended animation. I felt as if I was living in a surreal world where life was going on around me, but I was not part of it. Diana had been my confidante, someone I could share my thoughts and fears with, and I had loved her as a friend. Fairytales are supposed to have a happy ending. This one had ended in tragedy.

What made the grief even harder to bear was that Diana and I had not spoken during the weeks before. We had had our tiffs before but this one was very petty. I had been to heal a mutual acquaintance and had telephoned Kensington Palace afterwards. Diana wasn't there and I spoke to Paul Burrell, just to leave a message asking Diana to call me back. He told me that I sounded tired. I said, 'No more than usual,' but then I made the mistake of telling him whom I had been treating.

Diana called the moment she got home. She was in a fury and asked why I had gossiped with Burrell. I told her I hadn't, that Burrell was exaggerating and that all I had told him was whom I had been healing. She retorted, 'You shouldn't have been speaking to him at all—he's not a friend, he's a member of staff.'

We spoke several times on the telephone in the following days, but the row carried on. After her death, it was Burrell who went through her address book and selected who amongst her friends would and wouldn't be invited to the funeral. But I was honestly relieved not to be asked because I knew it would be a media circus.

Instead, I stayed at home and watched it on television with another of the Princess's friends and cried when Elton John sang *Candle in the Wind*. He had originally written the song in homage to Marilyn Monroe, who, like Diana, died young, leaving her image frozen in the beauty of her youth. It was a fitting tribute but Diana would not have appreciated the comparison. She admired Marilyn's sense of humour and very much wished that she had been blessed with the same womanly figure, but it was Jackie Onassis whom she really related to.

On that miserable day, however, it was impossible not to be moved and we lit a candle of our own in her memory. We then went to the Hendon Way to see the cortège drive by. We each took a bunch of flowers and somehow were pushed forward by the crowd and touched the car as it passed.

It was a poignant moment clouded with regrets at the way everyone seemed to be trying to claim a piece of her memory, without regard for her personal wishes.

Diana had seen much death in her humanitarian work and she was not afraid of it. But she was very clear about what she wanted to happen when she died.

She told me she would like to be buried in the Spencer family plot in the local church. Instead, the lady who loved the world was committed to the ground in the loneliness of an island in the middle of a lake.

She would have liked to have a hospital or hospice built in her name. It would have been the most fitting memorial, as it would have embraced her humanitarian nature. Her friends involved with the project knew very well what her wishes were, but they let her down in death as they had in life and went ahead and constructed a memorial fountain in Kensington Gardens. Diana would have been horrified that over £3 million was wasted on a project that doesn't help anyone (and was so badly designed that it was closed to the public for much of the time).

Tony Blair tried to hijack the national anguish for his own political ends.

The treatment of her godchildren was just as contemptible. She talked about them frequently, loved them all as her own, and wanted to make sure each and every one of them would have an independent start in life. Her wishes were clearly written in her will but they were dismissed by her own family.

Perhaps that was inevitable. It was her membership of the Royal Family that had defined her, and no matter how hard she tried to take charge of her own destiny, she was never able to break free from an institution that was there before she came onto the stage and will still be there long after she departed.

As immutable as it may seem, however, not even the Royal Family can escape her legacy. The outpouring of public mourning is testimony to the effect she had on the British people, and the Royal Family had to bow to public pressure and pay tribute to this often confused, sometimes difficult, occasionally irascible but always openhearted woman. We are a much more caring nation than we used to be. We have discarded our stiff upper lips and learned to show our feelings. I consider that to be in large part thanks to Diana. And that is how she would have wished to be remembered: as the woman who cared for others and made others do the same.

# Update
## 2007

In the ten years since Diana died, hardly a day has passed when I have not thought of her. Sometimes, between my sleeping and waking, she has come to me in the form of a dream, or I have felt her presence and seen her sitting on the end of my bed. She often wakes me up early in the morning, which is not my best time, and there she is standing by the side of my bed. She will sit down and we have a chat and then I go back to sleep. As she never wore an overpowering perfume, there is nothing to linger after she has gone, but she smells very fresh and looks slightly younger than when I knew her.

To many people, this may sound crazy, but I have either been blessed or cursed with the ability to see things others can't. I have noticed that people who seek me out for readings will often ask me about threatening events in the future and seem less interested in the happy things that might lie ahead.

In November 1996, Diana and I were sitting in her lounge having tea when I had a vision of a car accident. Diana was concerned about it and remembered how right I'd been in regard to Prince William's accident when he'd badly hurt his leg. She thought for a moment, took another sip of chamomile tea, and exclaimed that she needed to protect Charles. I told her I couldn't see who was in the big blue car, but that there were four people. She then expressed her fears for her boys, but again I stressed that I couldn't see who was in the car, that all I saw was a terrible accident. A small flash of light, from what I could only describe as a micro-mini explosive device, had gone off beneath the rear wheel axle of the vehicle, which made it impossible to steer. After the initial shock and concern, Diana changed the subject, and we finished our tea.

Having been interviewed by the police myself in 2004, I was anxious to read the report on Diana's death, code-named Operation Paget, that took former Metropolitan Police Commissioner Lord Stevens three years and £3.69 million to produce. It was finally released in December 2006 and ran over 800 pages, only to conclude that her death was a tragic accident exacerbated by the fact that the driver of their Mercedes, Ritz Hotel security officer Henri Paul, was two times over the British blood alcohol limit and travelling at twice the speed limit.

William and Harry had hoped the results of Operation Paget would finally end the frenzied speculation that followed their mother's death, but as I suspected, it was not to be. Mohamed Fayed had no intention of letting go; he condemned the Operation Paget inquiry as "garbage" and a "cover-up" and vowed that even if it cost him his last penny, he would expose the truth. I don't think he will ever accept the findings. His lawyers have already managed to delay the inquest until October 2007, and Fayed is still claiming that Prince Philip was behind an Establishment plot to kill the couple to prevent the prospect of the future king having a Muslim stepfather.

This doesn't make sense, as Operation Paget confirmed through a rare interview with the Muslim surgeon Hasnat Khan that he had an intimate relationship with the Princess for two years and she had even at one time thought it possible they could marry. The report concluded that although Hasnat Khan was a Muslim, his relationship with Diana was accepted by those who knew about it and he was not perceived as a threat to the British Establishment.

Fayed also claimed that the Princess was pregnant by his son, that they had chosen an engagement ring together and were about to announce this news to the world.

Lord Stevens concluded that Dodi may well have picked out a ring at jeweller Repossi's Paris shop, but it was not one chosen by the Princess and she had not spoken of an engagement to friends, who pointed out that she had only known Dodi for a few short weeks.

Neither was Diana pregnant. There were claims that she was unlawfully embalmed in Paris to cover up the early stages of pregnancy, but embalming was customary practice, and in Diana's case was done to make her body more presentable for her family to see. Because she had suffered massive blood loss by the time she reached the hospital and had received large amounts of transfused blood, it was impossible to test for pregnancy from her hormone samples. In July 2006, however, detectives checking the Mercedes found a considerable amount of pre-transfusion blood in the footwell near where she had been sitting. Tests of the dried blood carried out by a renowned expert in London confirmed that the blood was hers and carried no traces whatsoever of the pregnancy hormone.

I knew Diana was definitely not pregnant at the time she died—not only from the coroner's report, but also from the statements of her friends and doctors, including our mutual friend, Dr. Lily, who saw Diana just before she went away on that fateful holiday with Dodi Fayed. Although Fayed claims in the report that Diana had told him she was between two and four weeks pregnant, he should have realized that Diana couldn't keep a secret and would have told her closest friends. She was also taking birth control pills, as she had done for years, and according to Rosa Monckton, with whom she had just shared another holiday, she was still menstruating.

As I have discussed, there was a period after her car brakes failed in 1995 when Diana became somewhat para-

noid about her safety. The report confirms that she even
spoke to her lawyer, Lord Mishcon, about fears she was to
be "put aside"—and not just herself, she confided, but her rival Camilla Parker Bowles.

Prince Charles, she told Mishcon, wanted them both out
of the way to clear his path to marry another. That "other"
woman was not named in the report, but I know, as we spoke
about it many times, that it was Tiggy Legge-Bourke. The
Princess had a fixation about the royal nanny. Although entirely unfounded, she was convinced that Tiggy had become
pregnant with Charles's child and had an abortion, and was
also afraid that Tiggy was trying to take the boys away from
her.

In the report both Hasnat Khan and I confirm that Diana
was convinced her brakes had been tempered with. Certainly Diana felt extremely vulnerable at the time. It is difficult to imagine what it was like for one girl alone, fending
off the criticism, hostility and disdain of the entire British
Establishment, including the Royal Family and some members of the government.

These fears prompted her to pen the undated, unsigned
note, allegedly found by her butler, Paul Burrell, in which
she wrote that she feared dying or being injured in a car
crash orchestrated by her husband. The letter was written in
1995, when she was at her most vulnerable, not a year later
as he claimed. As I have said, I had a similar letter from her,
stressing her doubts for her safety, but it never once suggested that Prince Charles might be the one responsible. The
inquiry report, with statements from many people, agrees
and categorically states that the Prince had nothing to do
with her untimely death, which backs up my statements that
Diana and Charles were good friends in the ten months or so
before the car crash in France. I believe that even now Prince
Charles is still haunted by the death of Diana.

Still, the Stevens report leaves a number of questions
unanswered. There was a huge mix-up with the blood samples of the driver, Henri Paul, and others, some of which
showed extremely high levels of carbon monoxide. He

clearly wouldn't have been able to drive with that amount of the gas circulating in his body. This mix-up demonstrates a lack of professionalism in the initial investigation.

I also find it puzzling that, although it is not mentioned in the report, the underpass where the car had crashed was not cordoned off, but once the car had been towed away and its occupants were en route to hospital, a big street-cleaning truck came along to sweep the road with chlorine.

As for the claims that British security services had staged the car accident, Lord Stevens believed not. According to the report, the only official person who knew Diana was in France was Brigadier Charles Ritchie, military attaché, who had seen the crowds outside the Ritz.

The report also says, "The NSA [National Security Agency of the United States] declared that it held 39 documents in which reference was made to the Princess of Wales," but accepted the NSA's assertion that "none of the material held was relevant to the events surrounding the crash." Still, I find it very surprising that at least one U.S. secret service had the Ritz Hotel under some sort of surveillance, and knew Diana was there on August 31, 1997, but the British MI5 and MI6 didn't know anything.

After reading through the report on Operation Paget and seeing some major questions left unanswered, I feel that instead of taking the results as gospel, we have to keep an open mind. To date, I do not believe it has been definitively proved that the car crash in Paris was an "accident."

Forty-five years have passed since the death of Marilyn Monroe, and the truth is only now coming out about her death. Like Marilyn, Diana has also become a legend, and maybe in another forty-five years, the truth of the tragedy that ended her life will be revealed.

Diana's genuine compassion for the great mass of ordinary people made her ask a great deal from herself. It was impossible for her to show care to every suffering person in the world, but she stretched herself as far as a person could.

Diana was an icon to the world. She was a mother to her sons and she was a friend to me.

# Index